JAMES MONTGOMERY: ABOLITIONIST WARRIOR

Colonel James Montgomery in Kansas in 1862, not long before he resigned from the Army. He would receive a new military commission in January 1863, and serve with distinction through the next two years. (Collection of Kansas Historical Society)

JAMES MONTGOMERY: ABOLITIONIST WARRIOR

ROBERT C. CONNER

CASEMATE
Philadelphia & Oxford

Also by Robert C. Conner:

NONFICTION
General Gordon Granger: The Savior of Chickamauga and the Man Behind "Juneteenth"
FICTION
The Last Circle of Ulysses Grant

Published in the United States of America and Great Britain in 2022 by
CASEMATE PUBLISHERS
1950 Lawrence Road, Havertown, PA 19083, USA
and
The Old Music Hall, 106–108 Cowley Road, Oxford OX4 1JE, UK

Hardback Edition: ISBN 978-1-63624-142-5
Digital Edition: ISBN 978-1-63624-143-2

A CIP record for this book is available from the British Library

Printed and bound in the United Kingdom by TJ Books.
Typeset in India by Lapiz Digital Services, Chennai.

For a complete list of Casemate titles, please contact:

CASEMATE PUBLISHERS (US)
Telephone (610) 853-9131
Fax (610) 853-9146
Email: casemate@casematepublishers.com
www.casematepublishers.com

CASEMATE PUBLISHERS (UK)
Telephone (01865) 241249
Email: casemate-uk@casematepublishers.co.uk
www.casematepublishers.co.uk

Cover: Contemporary hand-colorized photograph of James Montgomery as colonel of the 2nd South Carolina Volunteer Infantry Regiment. (New Hampshire Historical Society)

For Charlie Goodding, old friend from Missouri; and Kansas-rooted Willa Arber.

Contents

Preface and Acknowledgments

I traveled widely in James Montgomery's footsteps while researching this book, from Ohio to Kansas, and to Civil War sites ranging from Beaufort and Combahee Ferry, South Carolina, to Darien, Georgia, Palatka and Olustee, Florida, and Kansas City, Missouri. I here record my gratitude for help received along the way from dedicated local historians including Mary Throop, genealogist at the Ashtabula County [Ohio] District Library, Daniel L. Smith from the Battle of Westport Visitor Center in Kansas City, Ola May Earnest, director of the Linn County Historical Museum in Kansas, and Lauren Gray, head of reference at the Kansas Historical Society in Topeka.

Thanks also to my local research librarian, Roberta Ambrosino of the Round Lake Library in upstate New York, and Tena Swisher, Montgomery's great-great-granddaughter.

Many others, mostly volunteers, who staffed and preserved the various museums and historical sites which I visited also deserve thanks—although the United Daughters of the Confederacy, who in the early 20th century approved the inscriptions on monuments to memorialize the battle of Olustee, were not striving for objectivity in their reporting and analysis.

I also acknowledge here, and elsewhere in this book, Tom L. Holman's unpublished (though available online) 1973 doctoral dissertation on Montgomery, which in addition to its own merits pointed me to other valuable sources.

Thanks to the Library of Congress, for its extraordinary and easily accessible collection of high-quality images in the public domain, which provided most of the illustrations.

As for standard sources, any Civil War historian will rely on the multi-volume *The War of the Rebellion: A Compilation of the Official Records of the Union and Confederate Armies*, published by the U.S. government between 1880 and 1901. This time, I accessed it online through the Cornell University Library. I have found genealogical web sites such as Find-a-Grave and its parent, Ancestry, Clan Montgomery and others useful. And, as with my two previous books about the Civil War era, I somewhat guiltily acknowledge frequent use of the online Wikipedia encyclopedia, while not relying on it as a cited source.

This time, as previously, many thanks are due to the book's first editor, my wife Barbara. I also thank Casemate Publisher Ruth Sheppard, President David Farnsworth, Megan Yates, and other members of their team.

Finally, this book quotes many contemporary sources which use language in ways that would not be acceptable today. While I have written around and avoided using the most offensive terms, I have not sought to disguise facts such as most Black soldiers in the Civil War being organized into regiments designated "United States Colored Troops."

Introduction: From Guerrilla Outlaw to American Soldier

For the first part of his career, to the extent he attracted public notice, James Montgomery was often viewed as more of an abolitionist ruffian—or perhaps a murderer—than the "warrior" described in the title of this book. But, like most Americans of the Civil War era, he was profoundly changed by its history. His military achievements mounted through the war despite controversies he stirred up along the way. In 1863, he advanced to brigade command in South Carolina, and then the next year performed well both at the Union defeat in Olustee, Florida, and at the victory of Westport, Missouri. By the end of 1864, he could take his place among the thousands of other American soldiers who had proven themselves brave and capable combat commanders. In so doing, Montgomery continued to contribute to the abolition of slavery, a goal he now shared with a greatly increased number of Americans.

It is not certain he was a lifelong abolitionist. Although born and bred in what eventually became the anti-slavery hotbed of Ashtabula County, Ohio, Montgomery spent many years in slave states, mostly Kentucky, where he married twice and began to raise a large family. At the least, like two more famous border-state men who rose from humble origins, Abraham Lincoln and Ulysses S. Grant, he was never comfortable with slavery, always at some level morally opposed to it. Although all three men were supporters of abolition by the last year of the war, Montgomery's identification with the cause came much earlier than Lincoln's or Grant's.

While it took the Civil War to turn most northerners into abolitionists, with Montgomery it was the prewar conflict in Kansas. Like John Brown,

Montgomery first rose to prominence when he played a leading role on the free-state side in the irregular guerrilla conflict of "Bleeding Kansas," in the mid to late 1850s. There first, as later in the whole country, slavery proved to be too much for American democracy to handle, short of military intervention. In the Civil War, which the prewar conflict in Kansas had helped bring about, Montgomery's U.S. Army service would begin and end in the general vicinity of home—although his most important military role came in the Deep South in the middle of the war.

While most northerners, especially in the Army, were dubious at the start of the war about abolishing slavery, or employing Blacks as soldiers, Montgomery was not. According to a 20th-century historian, Montgomery, along with colleagues such as Thomas Wentworth Higginson, "because of their personal abolitionist convictions could no more ignore the opportunity of striking hard blows against slavery than they could have stopped breathing by an act of will." They were among "the radicals who led the way," breaking the path for "the moderate and the cautious who joined the movement after it had taken on respectability and even a degree of popularity."[1]

Montgomery moved at the beginning of 1863 to the Department of the South, campaigning in Florida and in forays off the Sea Islands of the South Carolina and Georgia coast. These included the famous Combahee River raid in South Carolina with Harriet Tubman, and the controversial burning of Darien, Georgia, over the objections of Colonel Robert Shaw. (The latter incident led to the unsympathetic depiction of Montgomery in the 1987 movie *Glory*. While in some ways a good film, its negative portrayal of Montgomery is a plot device which cannot be relied upon for historical accuracy—as will be discussed later in this book.)

After Shaw's death in action at Fort Wagner, South Carolina, Montgomery commanded a brigade in the siege of the fort and beyond. He continued in brigade command the next year at the battle of Olustee in northern Florida. Almost all his troops in the South were African-Americans, which has involved his historical reputation in more controversy. Nor were his prior activities, including the prewar defiance of federal authority, necessarily forgiven. At any rate, being neither a regular officer nor a volunteer with influential political connections, and as a man mostly associated with Blacks and abolition, Montgomery was not a prime candidate for promotion. He was left a colonel and in the Department of the South, from where much of the U.S. contingent had been withdrawn and sent north to the war's main front in Virginia. In declining health, and not having seen his family for almost two years, it is hardly surprising that he resigned his commission and went home. But then the war, in the person of Confederate Major General Sterling Price and his fall 1864 offensive across Missouri, came to him. Montgomery once more took the field with U.S. forces, commanding a regiment of Kansas militia and doing good service, especially at the battle of Westport.

Now 50, he settled back down with his large family (including one new daughter born in 1865) in fertile eastern Kansas, his health somewhat damaged by wartime service. It was back to family, farming, and the preacher's circuit, the practices of peace in an old-fashioned landscape. Yet his obscure home countryside along with the whole country had been transformed by what Lincoln, who did not live to see much of it, called "a new birth of freedom." While that birth was not fully accomplished for another hundred years, Montgomery could still take comfort in his modest but not insignificant role in bringing it about.

Anyone who studies the Civil War era will be aware of the wealth of largely untold yet fascinating personal histories of those who lived through and helped shape it. The majority of the most important abolitionists, such as Brown, William Lloyd Garrison, Frederick Douglass, Charles Sumner, Thaddeus Stevens, and Harriet Beecher Stowe, did not actually fight in the great war which they had helped bring about. Some of those who did, including Tubman and Shaw, fought alongside Montgomery. But Montgomery saw more of the war than either Tubman or Shaw, and most of his fighting was done alongside ordinary soldiers—many of them African-Americans. He also saw more of the war than most of his pro-slavery opponents in Kansas and Missouri, such as former U.S. Senator and pro-slavery militia leader David Atchison, who became a Confederate major general in 1861 but in early 1862 resigned his commission and moved to Texas, where he avoided military activity. As a colonel through most of the Civil War, Montgomery had a more interesting and productive career than many generals.

His professional conflicts with colleagues including Shaw (not long before the latter's heroic death), his sometimes ruthless methods of fighting enemies and harsh discipline meted out to his own Black troops, are among the elements of controversy in his career. While such disputes were not unusual in that contentious time, it cannot be denied that Montgomery's willingness to resort to violence in peacetime and defy lawful authority, and his occasional executions of both deserters and prisoners, raise serious questions both of morality and *realpolitik*. There is an evergreen argument about ends and means in warfare, in particular regarding the purported justification of inflicting death and suffering on civilians and prisoners. To what extent Montgomery did such things needs to be assessed, but not necessarily defended, even though others on both sides did as much and more along the lines of hard warfare, including many more senior military and political leaders. By the end of the Civil War, there were few innocents. Yet civilians on both sides would be treated far worse and killed in enormously greater numbers just 80 years later, during World War II.

Montgomery came to share Brown's view that a civil war to free the slaves was both inevitable and justified, and that the prewar fighting in Kansas, Missouri, and Virginia was a necessary preparation for it. Arguably, they were both vindicated by events. But if their form of lawless violence helped win Kansas freedom when pitted against equally unscrupulous opponents, it also can be argued that similar tactics by their ideological foes, before, during, and especially after the Civil War, would eventually defeat Reconstruction and undo the civil rights of most African-Americans. Montgomery himself had to learn, through the discipline of military life, to abide by the rules of civilized warfare.

Black civil rights in the South would not be restored until the mid-20th century. That later victory was the result of a very different kind of struggle, led by nonviolent African-Americans such as A. Philip Randolph, Rosa Parks, and Martin Luther King Jr. But in Montgomery's era, as events were to prove, there was no peaceful way to abolish slavery in the United States.

Montgomery is a bridge between the abolitionist movement and the soldiers who turned its dream into reality. This book will be the first published biography. It is a story worth telling.

CHAPTER I

Westward Bound

The Montgomery family was originally from Scotland and then Ireland and included other notable soldiers in its ranks.

The American general Richard Montgomery, killed in late 1775 at the battle of Quebec, was a distant cousin with more upscale Irish roots—or at least that's what contemporary writers, and probably James Montgomery, believed.[1] An equally famous Montgomery and possible ancestor, Gabriel, was captain of the Scots Guard in 16th-century France, who after killing King Henry II while jousting (apparently by accident), became a Protestant ally of England and fought against the French monarchy.

The Montgomery name seems to date from the Norman conquest of England in 1066, being originally Montgomerie.[2] While most of the Scotch-Irish Montgomerys in the northern part of Ireland were Presbyterian, the Anglican Church of Ireland branch would include Bernard Montgomery, who in World War II became the greatest British general since the Duke of Wellington. When commanding ground forces under the American Supreme Commander Dwight Eisenhower during the 1944 Allied invasion of Normandy, he was promoted to field marshal by the British government—almost nine centuries after the Norman invasion in the other direction, in which Vicomte Montgomerie d'Exmes may have participated. Whether or not James and Bernard Montgomery were in any way related, they shared a certain single-minded orneriness, often paying scant respect to military superiors. One dubious old claim is that James Montgomery was the namesake and great-grandson of "a

Scotch Highland chieftain who came to America by way of Ireland"—which does not seem to be accurate.[3]

It is true that Presbyterian Scots, like the Montgomerys, were encouraged by 17th-century British governments—and associated Irish aristocrats such as Hugh, the first Viscount Montgomery—to settle in Ulster, in the northern part of Ireland. While the object was to dilute Roman Catholic power and resistance to British rule, most of the immigrants were not members of a ruling class in either their old or new countries and were often fleeing poverty in Scotland. In Ireland, some of their descendants remained to clash with Catholics in "The Troubles," which have extended into the 21st century. But the Irish ruling class in the 17th and 18th centuries was confined to mostly English-descended adherents of the established Anglican church, the Church of Ireland (in American terminology, Episcopalians). Many of the Scots-turned-Irish Presbyterian Protestants, such as most of the Montgomerys, looked west across the Atlantic, as did their Catholic neighbors. The British colonies in America seemed a place where they might build themselves a future free from rising land rents and associated poverty, and be able to exercise more religious and political independence.

According to W. J. Montgomery's family history, John and Isabella Montgomery lived in rural Aghadowey, in what is today Northern Ireland, in the 17th century. Their son William Montgomery was born in 1675 and grew up to marry Mary Aiken. The second of William's and Mary's six children was James Montgomery, born in Ireland in 1702, and the actual great-grandfather and namesake of the subject of this book. William, Mary, and their family emigrated to America through the port of Boston on September 1, 1718, moving first to Maine and then settling in Hopkinton, Massachusetts, 30-odd miles southwest of the city. The party of emigrants included other friends and family, and was led by the Rev. James McGregor, minister of the Presbyterian Aghadowey Church.[4]

This James Montgomery in 1731 married Mary Henry in Hopkinton, the same town east of Worcester where his father died two years later. By 1738, the James Montgomery family had moved another 80-plus miles west to Blandford (in some records spelled Blanford), Massachusetts, where his son Robert Montgomery was born in either 1738 or 1741, and where James died in 1779. Robert was the only boy among four children. The move to Blandford was at least in part motivated by a doctrinal dispute within the Hopkinton Presbyterian Church, which adopted a platform offensive to "Scotch Presbyterians" like James Montgomery.

Robert Montgomery was the son, father, and grandfather of men named James Montgomery, his grandson being the subject of this book. Robert Montgomery married Mary White—who was born in Connecticut in 1741—in 1764. Their son James Montgomery was born in Blandford. Robert and Mary Montgomery had 12 children who lived past infancy, including Thomas, born in 1767. James was the fifth child.

Robert Montgomery was on the Patriot (American) side during the Revolutionary War against Britain. After serving as a local peace officer or "tythingman" in Blandford, he enlisted in the First Regiment of the Ulster County, NY, militia, under the "land bounty rights" program. This helps explain—along with a family connection—why after the war the Montgomerys moved west to Harpersfield, in the northern part of Delaware County in south-central New York. Robert had likely earned land there as a result of his time in the regiment, which was from 1779 to 1782. It is unclear if he saw active service.

By the 1790 U.S. Census, the Montgomerys were established at Harpersfield, New York.[5] Robert is listed as head of a family of 13, which apparently included James. The town was named after its founder Alexander Harper, a Revolutionary War colonel on the Patriot side and kinsman to the Montgomerys. He was the son of Robert Montgomery's aunt, Abigail Montgomery Harper.

James Montgomery's first wife, Maria or Mamre Gaylord, died young. Their son Levi was born in 1796, the same year James married his second wife, who was yet another Mary, Mary Baldwin, though nicknamed Polly, which must have helped differentiate her from kinfolk. They were the parents of Col. James Montgomery, the subject of this book.

Mary "Polly" Baldwin was the daughter of Isaac Baldwin, 1730–1791, who was the son of John and Mary Adams Baldwin. The family was well established in a rural area between Hartford and New London, Connecticut, and Providence, Rhode Island. Polly's mother, Patience Rathburn Baldwin (1734–1823), was from Exeter, Rhode Island.

These New England roots add an English branch to the Scotch-Irish Montgomery heritage of James Montgomery the younger.

Polly was the 11th of 13 children of Isaac and Patience Baldwin, and the only one not born in Connecticut. Her father Isaac, like Robert Montgomery, apparently served on the Patriot side in the American Revolution. He was a private in the 4th Regiment, Ulster County NY Militia, serving in the Wyoming Valley of northeastern Pennsylvania.

Although Polly presumably grew up at first with her siblings in Connecticut, she was born in 1772 in Catskill, Greene County, New York. At some point the Baldwin family moved, like the Montgomerys, west to New York state. The Baldwins settled in the Elmira area of Chemung County in New York's Southern Tier, where Isaac and Patience died in 1791 and 1823, respectively.

Polly Baldwin married James Montgomery in Schoharie, NY, in 1796. These were all rural areas, and the Montgomerys were farming folk like most American colonists. James the elder and his son James also found other occupations, but farming was a default trade which they would fall back on throughout their lives.

Americans were famously restless and ready to move west with the frontier, and the Montgomerys, like millions of others, continued to follow that pattern. From Harpersfield, NY, numerous members of the family, including Robert and his first cousin Col. Alexander Harper, moved in 1798 to the Western Reserve south of Lake Erie. The Western Reserve land had been opened to settlement by the 1795 Treaty of Greenville, which ended the Northwest Indian War.

Harper died and was buried there the same year, reportedly the first White man in the Western Reserve to have a marked grave, and the place was named after him with the same name as the town he had founded in New York from which they had all come—Harpersfield. It would become part of Ashtabula County in the state of Ohio.

The family members coming from Harpersfield, NY, to the undeveloped Ohio frontier included James and Polly Montgomery, his brother Thomas Montgomery and family, their brothers Levi and John Montgomery, and their parents, Robert and Mary Montgomery—along with Col. Alexander Harper and family, and probably others.

The original family journey to Buffalo from central New York, before they embarked on Lake Erie, was not easy, according to an 1880 account in the *Ashtabula Sentinel*.[6] "Their team was two yoke of oxen and wagon and one or more horses, carrying with them what farming tools they could," plus two or three cows, traveling mostly through wooded wilderness. "Some of the way they cut their own roads, but they persevered, and after some three weeks of hard toil they reached a place called Black Rock, below Buffalo." There they sold one yoke of oxen and bought a boat, on which the oldest men, plus women and children traveled on Lake Erie, while the younger men drove their cattle south-westward along the lake's southern shore, in front of shale bluffs. They all slept on the beach at night, where "The wolves howled some, but the fire kept them off."

James and Polly Montgomery first settled in Conneaut on the shore of Lake Erie. Conneaut is in the northeastern corner of Ashtabula County, which is itself in the northeastern corner of Ohio.

An 1878 *History of Ashtabula County, Ohio* by Platt R. Spencer mentions the couple, saying they journeyed from Buffalo, NY:

> in open boats, the intervening country being but a trackless forest. The parents and their four children disembarked at night, sleeping on the beach beneath their sheltering boats. Arrived at Conneaut, a building was constructed from the barks of trees, until a more substantial one of logs could be made.
>
> … The husband followed the business of boating between Conneaut and Erie [Pennsylvania], thus supplying the infant colony with provisions. … He served for a time in the War of 1812, and later served for two successive terms in the legislature at Chillocothe, then the seat of government for the state.
>
> James Montgomery moved to Austinburg in 1813, and here soon after was born his son of Kansas celebrity—the famed "guerrilla chieftain," the "fighting preacher."[7]

That, of course, was James the younger, the subject of this book.

The Town of Austinburg, also in Ashtabula County, is east of Harpersfield and about 10 miles south of Ashtabula City. Other Montgomery relatives owned farmland in Harpersfield, and the James Montgomery family moved to Mechanicsville, in the western part of Austinburg, close to the Harpersfield line.

Conneaut harbor, Ohio, in 1901, a century after Montgomery's father operated businesses there. Photo by Naef & Joslin. (Library of Congress)

While still in Conneaut, in addition to his boating business, James Montgomery the elder ran a hotel-cum-tavern and built a grist mill.[8] He apparently moved inland to Austinburg in order to farm and be closer to family, and possibly to avoid potential British raiders on Lake Erie in the War of 1812. He also engaged in other pursuits there, including land speculation and politics, serving in various town and county posts, and being elected twice to the state legislature. He was not, however, representing Ashtabula County in the legislature, but two sparsely populated counties to its immediate south and southwest, Trumbull and Geauga.[9]

The family by this time—at least Robert and Mary, and their son James and his wife Polly—had moved on from the Presbyterian denomination to Congregational. Their politics tended to be Federalist, which was generally the party of northern, pro-business, pro-British, and anti-slavery politicians such as Alexander Hamilton, as opposed to the pro-French, libertarian, Democratic-Republican party led by the Virginia slaveholders Thomas Jefferson and James Madison.[10] Many churches, too, in the North had, since the 18th century, been moving in an anti-slavery direction, under the influence of preachers and theologians such as Jonathan Edwards the Younger.

Ohio was admitted to the Union as a free state in 1803. While Ashtabula County would become a center of abolitionism, and a key base of support for John Brown, at this time most of Ohio was settled around the Ohio River on the state's southeastern and southern borders with the slave states of Virginia and Kentucky. That section of the state was generally more Democratic and less opposed to slavery. Even in later years, it was the Ohioan Clement Vallandigham, who would lead the

Copperhead Democrats. The ruthless Confederate guerrilla William C. Quantrill also came from Ohio.

On the other side of the Ohio ledger, though, would eventually be most of the state's population. That included the anti-slavery politicians Joshua Giddings, Ben Wade, and Salmon P. Chase; the Union generals Ulysses S. Grant, William T. Sherman, Philip Sheridan, and William Rosecrans (plus Union soldiers and future presidents Rutherford B. Hayes, James Garfield, Benjamin Harrison, and William McKinley); academic institutions such as Lane Theological Seminary and Oberlin Collegiate Institute; along with anti-slavery immigrant communities in cities, including the German-Americans of Cincinnati. James Montgomery the younger would become part of this majority of Ohioans and Americans. But he would be ahead of most of them in the timing and vehemence of his abolitionist convictions, and in his willingness to take direct and sometimes violent action.

He was born in either the town of Harpersfield or Austinburg, Ashtabula County, Ohio, on December 22, probably in 1814 (or possibly 1813), either at the home of one of his Montgomery relatives in Harpersfield or at his parents' home.[11] The James and Polly Montgomery family lived in rural Mechanicsville, in the town of Austinburg, in-between the hamlets of Austinburg to the northeast and Harpersfield to the west, on a bend of the Grand River. It was, by this time, a typically large frontier family. There was James the elder's eldest son Levi, from his first marriage, and seven surviving children of James and Polly who were older than James the younger: Davis, Lewis, Mary, Nancy, Laughton, Julia, and Hannah, who was born in 1808. A younger brother, Hugh, would come along in 1820.

James Montgomery was christened in March 1815 at the Congregational Church in Austinburg. The congregation had first met in Robert Montgomery's home, and a later generation in 1876 built the Congregational Church which still stands and functions in the hamlet of Austinburg.

Austinburg and neighboring Harpersfield remain rural towns of gently rolling farmland—much of which was cleared by the Montgomerys and other early settlers. Austinburg, according to a contemporary source, had a population of 771 in the 1830 U.S. Census, with a Presbyterian church, "a store, two flour mills, one oil mill, one woolen manufactory, two fulling mills, two carding machines."[12] Harpersfield had a larger population of 1,145, and was "divided into farms of 100 acres each … Here are one store, two flouring mills, two saw mills, one fulling mill, and two forges, where considerable quantities of bar iron are made."[13]

The Grand River provided a trading route for the products of the local farms and mills, transported by boat or (in winter) sled. As more settlers arrived in the area, and "the young James Montgomery approached manhood," his father sold off some of his land in one-acre lots and moved the family about 12 miles east to the no less rural and remote town of Denmark, still in the same county. "The Montgomery family accumulated several hundred acres of land in Ashtabula County and their business centered around cattle, grain and land speculation."[14] In 1825, when James was about 10, his mother Polly Baldwin Montgomery died.

Both James the elder and younger would become part-time "itinerant ministers in the Western Reserve, sometimes in company with Reverend Joseph Badger, preaching to both Whites and Indians."[15] The Western Reserve included not just Ashtabula County but large areas to its west and south. This was a bold thing to do for the young Montgomery in a still partly wild and unsettled territory, and it set a pattern for his later life, both secular and religious. While his denominational affiliations would vary, Protestant Christianity remained a vital force for him, providing a key motivation for the abolitionist and soldierly endeavors which are the primary focus of this book, as well as for everything else he did.

Badger had founded the first Congregational church in Austinburg with James the younger's grandfather Robert Montgomery. His uncle, Thomas Montgomery, and family also were members.[16]

The Grand River Institute (today the Grand River Academy) was founded in 1831 in Austinburg by Congregational leaders to educate would-be ministers, and it is possible that the teenage Montgomery was among its first students. He would later embrace other forms of Protestantism beyond the Presbyterian and Congregationalist denominations.

If not at Grand River, he must have acquired some education at one or more of the local academies which were being opened in the area around this time. This "academic education"[17]may have included attendance at Ohio University in Athens, in the southeastern part of the state, in 1832 and 1833.[18] Histories of Kansas published in 1868 and 1883 both refer to Montgomery's "excellent academical education."[19]

James the elder died in 1834. In 1837, when he was about 22, James Montgomery moved south and west to Kentucky, not far south of Cincinnati, Ohio. There he "taught school and entered the ministry of the 'Campbellite' church,"[20] which was sometimes simply called the Christian church or the Church of Christ.[21]

Later in his life, when he had acquired the reputation of a fearsome commander in guerrilla warfare, people making Montgomery's acquaintance were often surprised to discover that he was in fact well-spoken and informed, abstemious, educated—an often mild-mannered and civilized man. He embarked on his teaching and preaching careers at a time which the biographer of a younger contemporary, Frederick Law Olmsted, describes as

> the beginning of the second phase of what one historian has called "the refinement of America." During the nineteenth century gentility spread from the upper to the middle class. Gentility meant self-improvement. People collected books. They formed scientific societies. They attended reading clubs, literary circles, and musical evenings. ... They built more elaborate houses, new civic buildings, and beautiful churches. They established libraries, teaching academies and athenaeums.[22]

No doubt these constructive activities were being done more in Olmsted's Connecticut than in northern Kentucky, but they happened there, too, and the young Montgomery was a participant.

This was also a time of religious revival. While Thomas and his son Alexander Campbell had both preached in the Western Reserve, and likely converted Montgomery to their form of religion, the term "Campbellite" was more likely used by critics than adherents of the new Christian practice. Both Campbells were born and brought up in the north of Ireland; the father, raised an Anglican, became a Presbyterian. They shared the Scotch-Irish roots of the Montgomerys and emigrated to the United States in 1807 and 1809. In America, they were connected to the Baptists, but also with those Christians who eschewed denominational labels. They—and Montgomery—were part of the evangelical upsurge of the Second Great Awakening, and from the 1830s their movement was identified as the Disciples of Christ.

According to Holman,

> Montgomery became a minister in the new sect … He followed the movement to one of its strongest centers, the area around Lexington, Kentucky. Preaching the new faith that stressed democratic simplicity and harmony rather than abstruse theology produced converts but not an income adequate to the needs of daily existence. Being well educated, Montgomery established himself as a school teacher.[23]

Another historian calls

> the Campbellite faith … a rather obscure offshoot from Presbyterianism that placed heavy emphasis on personal salvation and gave a great deal of leeway to preachers in their interpretation of the Bible. Whether this fit Montgomery's already headstrong personality or whether it helped mold that personality into the often stubborn man Montgomery became is difficult to say … but the Campbellite faith's general individualism fit him well.[24]

He would ply the trades of teaching and preaching in Kentucky for a crucial period of his life, when he married, became a father, was widowed, and remarried. It is also likely that he did small-scale farming to provide food for the family, and hunted game, especially after he moved to the more remote Appalachian area of Morgan County, where he also was involved in lumbering. Most rural American men engaged in such pursuits, and their familiarity with firearms would, for many including Montgomery, prove useful in the turbulent era to come. Many Civil War soldiers, on both sides, shared his Scotch-Irish roots and stubbornly independent nature.

Montgomery prospered enough to purchase some wooded land, "then built and operated a sawmill on the Licking River until several floods washed out his operation."[25] His first wife died young, leaving two surviving children, James and Nancy. He soon remarried to Elizabeth "Clarinda" Evans, who was almost 12 years younger than he and would survive him by more than 30 years. They would raise James and Nancy, who had been born in Kentucky in 1842 and 1844 from James' first marriage, along with seven children of their own: Evan, Mary (Jane), John, Julia, Hugh, Lewis, and Nellie. James and Clarinda were married in 1844 or 1845 in the Morgan County seat of West Liberty, where she was from. Born in 1826, she would have been about 18 years old to his 30. They remained residents of that rural county in the foothills of the Cumberland Mountains, about 70 miles east of Lexington, in the 1850 census. By that time, the county had 40 one-school districts. The economy was based on agriculture, including cattle, tobacco, and timber production.

Kentucky was a slave state, and many White Morgan County residents would incline to the Confederate side during the Civil War, by which time Montgomery was long gone. He, of course was unsympathetic to slavery even in his long Kentucky residence, although—or perhaps in part because—his first teaching ventures there included acting as a tutor to the children of planters in the prosperous Licking Valley near Cincinnati.[26]

Many years later Montgomery met Robert Gould Shaw, when both were colonels in the Civil War. The latter reported in a letter to his mother that Montgomery "looked like a schoolmaster, & he says he did teach school in Kentucky for many years, and learnt more about managing men there, than at any other time."[27]

When Montgomery first moved to Kentucky, a generation before the Civil War, it was still possible to debate the issue of slavery in slave states. Thomas Jefferson, a lifelong slave owner in Virginia (which unlike Kentucky would join the Confederacy), was in his younger days a strong critic of the peculiar institution. While Jefferson obviously found a way to live with slavery, he did abolish the international slave trade to the United States during his second term as president. But contrary to the expectations of the Founding Fathers, slavery was not in subsequent generations dying a natural death. In part because of the invention of the cotton gin in the late 18th century, the purported end of the slave trade (it was illegally revived before the Civil War) did not endanger the underlying institution, which was proving economically viable. By 1820, when Montgomery was five, Jefferson regarded the increasingly tense debates about the issue as a sign—like a "fire bell in the night"—of the grave threat it posed to the American experiment.

A generation later, the threat was still growing as the slave system, and the political and economic power structure behind it, grew more entrenched. Montgomery had become "a strong supporter of Cassius Clay and his radical abolitionist paper in Lexington."[28] Cassius Marcellus Clay was a White man born in 1810 in Kentucky into a wealthy slave-holding family. (His famous namesake, the 20th-century boxer from Kentucky who changed his name to Muhammad Ali, was originally named after his own father, who was named after the 19th-century abolitionist.)

While influenced at Yale by the abolitionist William Lloyd Garrison, Clay was then less radical than Garrison, becoming a more gradualist emancipationist on the slavery issue. These views did not prevent his election to three terms in the Kentucky legislature. After freeing his own slaves in 1844, Clay the next year founded an anti-slavery paper in Lexington, which was destroyed by a mob in 1846. That was a sign of the increasing polarization of American politics, and the growing difficulty of reaching a peaceful political settlement of the slavery issue. Not that northern cities were immune from pro-slavery or, later, effectively pro-Confederate mobs. They created numerous disturbances in major cities from Philadelphia to Boston, culminating in the New York City draft riots of 1863.

Clay went on to publish his abolitionist paper in Cincinnati, while continuing to edit it from Lexington. In the 1850s he helped found the Republican Party, and in the next decade served in the Lincoln and Johnson administrations as ambassador to Russia, before returning to Kentucky.

A novel by Harriet Beecher Stowe, *Uncle Tom's Cabin,* was published in the early 1850s, at first in 1851 in installments in an abolitionist periodical, and then in book form the next year. It swiftly became a worldwide popular sensation. The book's plot is anchored in Kentucky, where Montgomery had lived since 1837, and the state where "perhaps the mildest form of the system of slavery is to be seen."[29] That sometime mildness is shown as incapable of protecting the African-American protagonists from the system's worst excesses. The novel was almost certainly read by Montgomery, whose views were moving closer to Stowe's and her fellow northern abolitionists. While Stowe spent most of her life in New England, she gathered the material for her most famous novel while living in Cincinnati, across the Ohio River from Kentucky. A few years later, her clergyman brother would be shipping rifles—"Beecher's Bibles"—to Kansas.

The change in the political climate, in Kentucky and across the country, made any slave state a less comfortable home for Montgomery, who was becoming less willing to compromise his anti-slavery opinions. His economic losses due to flooding were an additional motivation to sell up and move west again, in search of opportunity and freedom. In 1852, the family traveled by boat on the Licking, Ohio and Mississippi rivers, to Missouri—another slave state, to be sure, but one in which they did not intend to remain.[30] Some of them may have traveled in a homemade canoe. Montgomery in Missouri scrambled to make a living doing farm work and other jobs such as teaching.[31] Their first new home was Pike County, in the eastern part of the state west of the Mississippi River.

But before long they moved west across the state to Jackson County—probably again by river, this time mostly the Missouri. Then they moved a little south to Bates County. Both those locations were on the border with what would soon become Kansas Territory, when it would be opened for settlement.

And when it was, in 1854, the settlement of Kansas would be dominated by conflict around the slavery issue, as would American history for the next decade and more, along with the personal destiny of James Montgomery.

CHAPTER 2

Bleeding Kansas and John Brown

The Kansas-Nebraska Act was signed into law by President Franklin Pierce on May 30, 1854. Its main sponsor was Illinois Senator Stephen Douglas, a Democrat, and its main provisos included the creation of Kansas Territory (which extended well into modern-day Colorado) and Nebraska Territory to its north (also extending far to the west and north of the state's present-day boundaries).

More important, the new law allowed voters (meaning adult White males) of the western territories to decide for themselves whether future states to be created out of them should permit or prohibit slavery. This had the effect of overturning the geographic Missouri compromise line of 1820, which was mostly kept in place by its successor law of 1850, the preceding two major efforts by the federal government to peaceably resolve the issue of slavery. The 1850 law also had produced the Fugitive Slave Act, which was detested by all anti-slavery people and remained in effect. The Fugitive Slave Law which compelled northern states to act as slave catchers convinced many abolitionists that the federal government was profoundly corrupt on this issue, and that no peaceful or law-abiding advocacy for their cause was likely to succeed.

Under the old Missouri compromise line, still in effect in the central part of the country until 1854, Kansas would have been designated a free state. Its repeal was seen by abolitionist and other anti-slavery politicians, including moderates like Abraham Lincoln, as the latest outrage perpetrated by the "slave power" which had such a grip on the federal government. But the new Kansas-Nebraska Act meant that the fate of Kansas was up for debate—and more direct action—by both sides of the slavery issue.

Many Democrats, including Douglas, Pierce, and the future president James Buchanan, along with the mayors of major cities like New York, were northerners. But the party's base was the slave-holding South. Most Democrats expected that residents of Missouri, a slave state, would move west across the border into Kansas, and turn that territory slave, too. In fact, in 1854, that appeared the most likely outcome to most independent observers, with Kansas becoming a slave state and Nebraska (to its north) a free one. Both sides, supporters and opponents of slavery, saw this struggle for the geographic heartland of the continent as crucial for the long-term success of their cause. In that judgment, both sides were correct.

Anti-slavery New Englanders were not reconciled to Kansas becoming a slave state and determined to do what they could to prevent it by organizing expeditions of like-minded settlers. Meanwhile many residents of the Midwest, including from Montgomery's home state of Ohio, were moving to Kansas. While some may have been opponents of slavery whose primary motivation was ideological, the settlers also hoped for economic advancement and their own personal freedom, like most Americans who lit out for the frontier. Many, including Montgomery, had both motivations to move.

Abolitionists were able to establish emigrant aid societies across the North designed to help similarly minded settlers move to Kansas. This spurred an opposite ideological impetus from the pro-slavery side, especially encouraging settlement from Missouri into southeastern Kansas.

Twenty-first-century historian Nicole Etcheson wrote:

> In May 1854, fewer than 800 white settlers lived in Kansas Territory. In the nine months after the territory was opened, that number would increase tenfold until, by the first territorial census, there were over 8,000 white settlers with 192 slaves in Kansas.[1]

The great majority of those new settlers came to eastern Kansas, because the vast Territory to the west became increasingly arid until reaching the Rocky Mountains.

In 1854 the 39-year-old Montgomery moved his family to Linn County, Kansas, which borders Missouri and is about 80 miles south of Kansas City. Most of the county's initial settlers, like those to their immediate south in southeastern Kansas, were pro-slavery, some coming with their slaves from Georgia. This had an important effect on Montgomery's subsequent career. He "soon became the recognized leader of the minority there" and remained a leader of anti-slavery residents even as they became a majority by the start of the Civil War in 1861.[2] Linn County became a focus of conflict because it was in-between the solidly pro-slavery counties to its south and the rest of the Territory to the north and west, which over the course of the 1850s came to have a strong free-state majority. Since the southeast was the part of the state most favorable to slavery, and its supporters were often prepared to resort to violence to uphold their position, free-state settlers felt the need to respond in kind, and their armed struggle would continue off and on even while the rest of Kansas Territory was pacified under a free-state majority.

Linn County was good farming land. Montgomery bought for 11 dollars—five dollars down—a claim from a pro-slavery Missouri man who had decided not to settle there. It is unclear whether that decision was related to any threat made against him, or any foresight about the coming civil conflict in Kansas and the United States. Montgomery did not yet have a permanent title. He and other squatters would eventually have to pay $1.25 an acre to the U.S. government, once its surveys were completed.

After buying the claim, Montgomery went back to Westport landing, near Kansas City, to finish a barn he was building for a doctor there. With his $300 in earnings, he bought supplies for the coming winter and cows and calves for the new farm in Linn County.[3] This land was about five miles west of Sugar Mound—today's Mound City—which, like Linn County's Sugar Creek, was named for the prevalent sugar maple trees, many of which would be cleared by the incoming farmers. The property would remain Montgomery's home—when he was home—for the rest of his life. The first, recent White settlement had been mostly by pro-slavery men, some of whom tried to intimidate free-state settlers into leaving the area and the Territory. Montgomery would not go.

War, according to Carl von Clausewitz, is "a continuation of political commerce, a carrying out of the same by other means."[4] Several decades of political turmoil over slavery in the United States led to violent conflict in Kansas and neighboring Missouri from the mid-1850s until the actual outbreak of the American Civil War in 1861. And in Kansas, the violent conflict was directly precipitated by a political one. While there are reasonable moral objections that can be raised against the violent actors on both sides in Kansas and Missouri, including Montgomery before and during the Civil War, there is no doubt that the initial injection of fraud into the election process in Kansas Territory came from the pro-slavery side, especially in 1855.

According to the former Kansas senator and 1996 U.S. presidential candidate Bob Dole:

> … in Kansas's first territorial election, there was no question of voter fraud. Thousands of Missourians, having no intention of living in Kansas, crossed the border and voted to elect members of the territorial legislature who would do their bidding. This was the first step in their efforts toward making Kansas a slave state.[5]

These incursions often involved armed intimidation of election authorities by Missourian "border ruffians," some of them drunk. Montgomery, unlike some of his free-state allies, was not a drinking man.

Atchison, a former U.S. senator from Missouri, was a key player, and a slavery-supporting town which was named after him had been established in northeastern Kansas.

> Missourians, at the behest of Senator Atchison and pro-slavery leader Benjamin Franklin Stringfellow, had flocked across the border and voted for pro-slavery candidates to the territorial legislature. Many used violence and intimidation to prevent free-staters from succeeding. Governor Reeder nullified the first vote of March 30, 1855, as the number of ballots cast far outnumbered the number of eligible voters. The May 22, 1855 election was also skewed by Missourians, organized by Atchison and Stringfellow … Governor Anthony Reeder [first governor of Kansas Territory] went to Washington to try to convince President Franklin Pierce not to accept the results of the second election. … Reeder was fired by President Pierce in August 1855.[6]

The pro-slavery side's use of violence and intimidation to fix elections would have a profound effect on American politics far beyond Kansas. Men who disagreed about race relations and what to do about slavery, such as Lincoln and Douglas—who ran against each other for an Illinois U.S. Senate seat in 1858—could at least agree that White voters must not be denied their democratic rights. That logic would eventually lead Douglas to support the Union in the Civil War. Meanwhile, those on the spot in Kansas had to decide how to respond.

On February 20, 1855, Montgomery spoke in favor of the free-state (or free-soil) side at a convention in Sugar Mound. He also spoke at a subsequent meeting held for the purpose of nominating candidates for the scheduled March 30 election to the Territorial Legislature.[7] His arguments drew attention and put him in the forefront of free-state politics in that area. But the pro-slavery side won Linn County's two delegates at the election. According to Cutler's 1883 history of Kansas, the decisive margin came from "illegal" votes cast at the Keokuk precinct, whereas at Sugar Mound, the other precinct, all the votes were legal.

The argumentation over this and subsequent elections extended well beyond Linn County, and for the next several years the pro-slavery and free-state sides disputed the legitimacy of the Territory's votes and institutions. Meanwhile, governors appointed by U.S. Presidents Pierce and Buchanan (both northern Democrats anxious to appease the pro-slavery southern base of their party), with the support of the U.S. Army, attempted to enforce what the U.S. government regarded as law. The new territorial laws—regarded as illegitimate by free-staters—included prohibitions against anti-slavery speech.

Intimidation and death threats finally turned into armed clashes toward the end of 1855 around Lawrence, west of Kansas City. Lawrence was the nerve center of the free-state side. Montgomery was not involved, and Linn County was quiet at this time.

The violence escalated dramatically in 1856. Missouri Border Ruffians led by Atchison invaded Kansas to disrupt and rig elections, and in May undertook the "sack of Lawrence", which included the destruction of two free-state newspaper presses. This was immediately followed on

May 24–25 by the Pottawatomie massacre, where John Brown led family members and others to murder five pro-slavery men in cold blood.

One of the effects of the massacre was to further stir up pro-slavery fighters, who killed one of Brown's sons. Brown's band went on to fight two more equally matched defensive skirmishes over the next few months, at Black Jack and Osawatomie (between Lawrence and Linn County). The result was he became famous or infamous across the United States. He soon left Kansas, and at that point had not yet met Montgomery. Upon his return in 1858, the two men would become allies, though not always in agreement about tactics.

In the summer of 1856, when three separate parties of pro-slavery raiders marauded in eastern Kansas, Montgomery became the leader of resistance to the one moving north from the town of Fort Scott in southeastern Kansas, which had been attacking and burning out free-state

John Brown in the 1850s. (1899 photomechanical print reproduction of photograph. Library of Congress)

settlers in Linn County. On August 25 (or possibly the 26th), armed free-soil men led by Montgomery surprised the pro-slavery group of about 150 men led by George Washington Clarke at Middle Creek, about nine miles west of Osawatomie. They wounded two of the Border Ruffians and drove off the rest, who left most of their baggage and horses behind.[8]

Montgomery's free-soil advocacy was not confined to paramilitary action. He was increasingly involved in politics, as well. Some of his like-minded friends had been intimidated into pulling up stakes and leaving their claims, fearful of threatened violence. Montgomery was in Lecompton, the territorial capital northwest of Lawrence, conferring with the new governor, John Geary, about potential threats to Linn County, when the county was invaded in October by a strong pro-slavery force (Holman says 400 men) from Missouri.[9]

The raiders burned several houses and a store in Sugar Mound, and sought out the Montgomery farm a few miles west, intending to capture or kill him, and in his absence destroyed the cabin there. Returning to his burned-out home the next day, it was readily apparent to Montgomery that more than politics, or the uncertain prospect of help from Lecompton, would be required to protect his family and friends—many of whom had by now fled—and the free-soil cause in Kansas. This attack on and destruction of their home must have been a traumatic event for the whole family. He built a stronger, more formidable home base on his property, on the north side of Sugar Creek. It was "a new site on the side of a hill … providing a wide range of vision and this home would be known as Fort Montgomery. It would give shelter to the Montgomerys and many others" over the next years of border warfare.[10]

The Kansas historian John N. Holloway, who stayed with and interviewed Montgomery after the Civil War, described him as:

> the principal actor in the Territorial history of southeastern Kansas … a humane man, nothing fierce or savage in his character; a devout Christian … Although a resident of a slave state for a number of years, he has always been bitterly opposed to slavery extension … He is about six feet high, slim and nimble as a deer, with intelligent features, high forehead, large nose and a most piercing and penetrating eye; a tenacious memory, sound logic, talks fluently with an agreeable voice, and in the best selected and arranged words.[11]

Other sources, however, put Montgomery's height as two or three inches short of six feet. It may have been the way he carried himself that left the impression of greater height.

Another 19th-century Kansas historian, Charles Tuttle, described Montgomery's character as "intrepid, and yet considerate; a felicitous combination of sound judgment and mercy."[12]

Now this civilized, Christian man committed himself to irregular, not legally authorized, pseudo-military action, in the unorthodox yet effective manner which quickly brought him to prominence.

At first on his own, and soon joined by a few free-soil comrades, Montgomery retaliated against the Missourian invaders. According to Tuttle's possibly exaggerated account:

> He availed himself at once of his knowledge of the country to attack the marauders wherever he could find an advantage ... Every design succeeded, and the invaders were soon in deadly terror of a clump of brush, an angle in the rocks, or any cover that might conceal their foe.[13]

According to Holloway, Montgomery:

> skirted Little and Big Sugar Creeks and the Osage, firing from the cover of brush or rocks, wherever he could get sight of the enemy. So swift, concealed and lucky were his movements, that he spread confusion and terror among the pro-slavery men.[14]

But neither historian at this stage mentions casualties, and in fact these are likely much fewer than implied, as in much of the discussion of "Bleeding Kansas." Montgomery, like the pro-slavery marauders against whom he was retaliating, was at this time seeking to scare off enemies rather than kill them, and his sniping was aimed at that end.

One not implausible estimate is that there were only 56 political killings in the Territory between 1854 and 1861. While 1856—with 38 killings according to his account—was much the bloodiest year, the great majority of those deaths were well north of Linn County and did not involve Montgomery.[15] Other estimates are a little higher, and the numbers may not include people killed in Missouri by Kansas jayhawkers including Montgomery. He at first regarded these Missouri incursions as primarily defensive measures to protect free-state Kansas, although liberating slaves became another key motivation.

But the pre-war killing over slavery in the Kansas Territory and Missouri, which seemed so appalling to most Americans at the time, would soon be far exceeded by the casualties there and elsewhere of the actual Civil War. Most of the prewar violence did not involve killing. Montgomery said his men had to "subsist on the enemy. Therefore we feed ourselves at pro-slavery larders and our horses at pro-slavery corn cribs."[16] If, however, these depredations encouraged pro-slavery settlers to pull up stakes and leave Kansas, Montgomery probably viewed it as a collateral benefit.

While the Democratic federal administrations of Presidents Pierce and Buchanan, and the Territorial governors they appointed, were inclined to recognize the pro-slavery winners of disputed local elections in Kansas, the free-state settlers like Montgomery, who had seen for themselves the intimidation, fraud, and destruction perpetrated by the Missouri-based Border Ruffians, were not. This meant they could potentially come into conflict with federal militia and troops, though these were not usually confrontations sought out by Montgomery. Similar disputes extended to the most local level, for example with free-state residents intimidated into leaving, then returning to their claims and finding pro-slavery settlers ensconced there.

Meanwhile, Montgomery scouted out the Missouri area where the raiders on Linn County had come from and embarked on a retaliatory expedition with six comrades. There they "captured and destroyed a quantity of arms, procured fresh horses and returned … none the poorer for their expedition."[17] Both sides increasingly felt themselves justified in taking the possessions of their enemies, in recompense for economic losses they had suffered, and on occasion took cash for their troubles.[18] On the other hand, Montgomery the warrior Christian "prohibited profanity or pilfering, and gave away to needy Free State men the horses he seized, once no longer needed by his men."[19]

Leading another raid of 10 men into Missouri the winter of 1856–57, Montgomery sought to liberate slaves, and while returning home on his own, was confronted by federal militia. He declined to surrender and made his escape.[20] It should be noted that while the threat of violence was a crucial factor, at this time there are still no reports of people being killed as a result of Montgomery's actions. But even as free-soil settlers were beginning to prevail in most of the Territory, largely as a result of vigorous but nonviolent politics, the situation for them in southeastern Kansas, closest to the slave power which dominated the southern United States (plus Missouri), remained precarious. Montgomery saw himself as upholding "law and order," including the ability of free-state families like his own to live in peace and work the soil.[21]

Many such families had fled because of threats or violent acts by the pro-slavery Border Ruffians. "During the winter of '56 and '57 the pro-slavery men held the claims and appropriated to their own use the stock that the free-state men had left. They kept up their military organization and committed some depredations the ensuing spring."[22] During 1857, new anti-slavery immigrants coming into the Territory, plus the return of some on both sides who had been driven out, set up new conflicts and disputes between settlers over who had the right to claim stock and land.

Fort Scott, a town and former Army post about 25 miles south of Sugar Mound near the Missouri line, was the home of many pro-slavery residents. Clarke had set out from there in August on the raid turned back by Montgomery. Some people held slaves there, as the U.S. Supreme Court's Dred Scott decision of March 6, 1857, held they had a right to do. That broadly anti-Black legal ruling outraged every anti-slavery person, from Lincoln to Montgomery, confirming the latter in his belief in the necessity of direct action.[23] A federal judge in Fort Scott, Joseph Williams, appointed by the new President Buchanan, was regarded by free-state settlers as prejudiced toward the side of their pro-slavery opponents. Settlers on both sides near the Kansas-Missouri border were becoming increasingly agitated and unwilling to compromise as a result of recent events there and in Washington, DC.

There was a revolving door succession of federally appointed governors, with one, the future Union general John Geary, succeeding in pacifying most of the Territory outside the greater southeast (where Sugar Mound and Fort Scott were located). Through most of Kansas the free-state settlers were increasingly confident of ultimate victory. While they still sometimes used the tactic of boycotting polls, their long-term goal was to win elections at them and control the Territorial government.

But "the Border Ruffians of the worst character had congregated at Fort Scott," where they would "drink, gamble and carouse; occasionally sally out, rob, insult, and plunder the free state settlers."[24] The latter were unsatisfied with the proceedings of Judge Williams' federal court, seeing federal appointees as inclined to favor pro-slavery policies and settlers. They set up a rival "Squatter Court" to dispense their own brand of justice, for example arresting three men who had stolen and butchered hogs, requiring them to make restitution. Federal authorities led by a U.S. marshal objected to this assertion of sovereignty, but were rebuffed by Montgomery and free state forces in an encounter in which one man was wounded on the federal side. Mostly at this time Montgomery operated by implicitly threatening violence but not actually carrying it out, especially against federal authorities.

He was also cooperating with "General" James (Jim) Lane, a Mexican War combat veteran, whose "Free State Army" or Kansas Militia operated under the authority of a free state convention held in July 1857 in Topeka. The free state irregulars, including Lane's and Montgomery's men, also were known as jayhawkers. Lane explained that "the Irish Jayhawk with a shrill cry announces his presence to his victim, so must you notify the pro-slavery hell-hounds to clear out or vengeance will overtake them. Jayhawkers remember: 'Vengeance is mine, sayeth the Lord, but we are his agents.'"

Disputed elections produced rival sources of authority, with Montgomery being elected in August as senator of a purported free-state provisional government. He did not take possession of the office because the anti-slavery politician, Charles Robinson, helped negotiate a compromise under which the free-staters continued to advance toward their overall goal.[25] New settlers were in the process of creating an anti-slavery majority, although the southeastern part of Kansas would lag behind the rest of the Territory. This accounts for Montgomery's increased prominence over the next few years, as the leader of anti-slavery

Jim Lane, Montgomery's superior officer in "bleeding Kansas" and in the first part of the Civil War. (From Brady's National Photographic Portrait Galleries. Library of Congress)

forces in (or near) what was the last stronghold of the pro-slavery side, while the rest of the Territory became more peaceful.

In September 1857, "For the Protection of the Ballot-Box," Lane and the adjutant general of the "Kansas Volunteers" commissioned Montgomery as captain of the "Little Sugar Creek Company."[26] This job was in connection with the territorial election to be held the next month—which the free-state side won. Lane would remain prominent in Kansas and U.S. political and military life, his career often intersecting with Montgomery's, until his suicide in 1866.

Lane had a compromised position on racial equality, as did a substantial portion of free-state supporters. He was a former Douglas Democrat who had supported popular sovereignty to determine the slavery issue. But Lane was alienated from the Democratic Party by the electoral fraud of pro-slavery forces. Many other popular sovereignty advocates, and eventually even Douglas himself, moved in more or less the same direction. But that didn't mean they had enlightened views on racial issues.

While opposing the introduction of slavery, Lane also wanted to ban free Blacks from settling in Kansas. Robinson opposed this restriction.[27] Montgomery would be working closely with both men over the next few years, especially when the Civil War came in 1861. It is very likely that he was in accord with Robinson's views about Blacks at this time and probably well before. He would, soon enough, demonstrate through direct action his adherence to Black liberation. In Kansas, partly because of the leadership of radicals like Montgomery and Brown, the focus of the free-state movement moved beyond protecting the democratic rights of White settlers, to accomplishing the liberation of Black slaves. As time and the Civil War went on, pretty much everyone in the U.S. anti-slavery movement, including Lane, would adopt this position.

The progress being made by free-staters across most of the Territory was seemingly jeopardized by developments in Washington. While the territorial political factions had produced rival constitutions in mutually disputed and boycotted elections, it was the pro-slavery Lecompton constitution which was accepted by President Buchanan—but not by the new anti-slavery Republican Party. Nor did Buchanan's fellow Democrat Douglas, author of the Kansas-Nebraska Act, support Lecompton, because he acknowledged the electoral fraudulence from which it had sprung.

Kansas free-staters had boycotted the referendum on Lecompton, primarily because they regarded the wording of the question as supporting slavery in one form or another no matter how people voted. On the subsequent January 4, 1858, vote for representatives under the auspices of the Lecompton constitution, free-staters were divided about whether to participate. Most favored a continuation of the boycott, holding to the validity of the October 5, 1857, election which had produced a free state legislative majority. A free state convention, whose leaders included Lane and Robinson, was held on December 2, 1857. It passed a resolution describing the scheduled January 4 election as "a crime and a misdemeanor against the peace of this Territory, and the will of the majority."[28]

Montgomery of course favored the radical, non-participating side, as he told his fellow free-staters at the polling place in Sugar Mound on January 4, 1858. The radicals opposed participating in what they regarded as a corrupted process and constitution.[29] Montgomery also may have suspected that the ballot box was stuffed with illegal pro-slavery votes.[30] Many of his allies were understandably confused, but when he read them an analysis in the anti-slavery Lawrence *Republican*, they demanded the return of their ballots, which they had already cast. When this request was refused, Montgomery made a speech denouncing what he called the fraud of the vote and smashed the ballot box on the floor, scattering and grinding up the ballots and thus invalidating the election there. Not all the free-staters approved of this procedure; nor did federal authorities. It would be one of the actions resulting in criminal proceedings started against Montgomery in subsequent months.

Yet the course of events would sway most of the moderate free-staters behind Montgomery. According to one contemporary, writing a few decades later:

> They all, without exception so far as I have ever been able to hear, learned to look upon James Montgomery as the one always-safe leader in their troubles, and to do full honor to his exalted memory. They respected and loved him more as they understood him better. Time may not have wholly justified his violence on that January day at Sugar Mound, but both time and circumstance have proven his act to have been prompted by the very highest and purest consideration for the cause whose battles he was fighting and for the people in whose behalf he was playing so dangerous but disinterested a part. He had nothing of the demagogue about him. He cared no more for popularity or popular applause than he did for the whims of his opponents. Devoutly religious, opposition to the extension of human slavery was to him the cause of God; and, when once his judgement was formed, he drove straight to the conclusion that his highest and holiest duty was to consummate that judgment. Yet he was always considerate towards others.[31]

Armed confrontations in the area between free-staters and pro-slavery forces continued through the winter, with one of the former complaining that:

> Bourbon County Banditti have been committing more robberies upon the settlers in that region … They are allowed to do because the pro-slaveryites think they will drive away all Free state men by so doing. Such being the case there is no

> law to punish the thieves. They even attempted to hang one man because he would not go away. The man is here at the Mound now. Captain Montgomery was here this evening telling about the affair ...[32]

Montgomery, according to the letter writer Joseph Trego, planned a retaliatory expedition with his militia company to Fort Scott, but this February event did not amount to much as the purported robbers could not be found, according to another free-state sympathizer.[33] Fort Scott, in addition to its military role, is the county seat of Bourbon County, Kansas, which is immediately south of Linn County.

Montgomery separated himself from some of his putative jayhawker allies whom he regarded as too extreme and ill-disciplined—although others, including Jim Lane, made similar complaints about his tactics. Montgomery apparently resigned from Lane's militia service in late February 1858.[34] He planned to give up armed struggle, but was drawn back into it, as a man who would stand up against Border Ruffians and slavery, yet also could act as a moderating influence.

Among the first documented fatalities in this part of Kansas occurred on March 27, 1858. Border Ruffians attacked three farmhouses in the vicinity of the Little Osage River, wounding one anti-slavery man and killing two, Isaac Denton and a Mr. Dedrick.[35] The Squatter Court—from which Montgomery still claimed authority—tried and acquitted a man called Travis for the murders. Shortly thereafter, Travis and two companions were attacked, the latter being wounded, and Travis killed, apparently by a relative of Denton.

These events prompted free-state settlers to form a Protective Society, led by Montgomery, which confronted some of the more "obnoxious" pro-slavery settlers and demanded that they pull up stakes.[36] This brought Montgomery's force of 20 or fewer men into conflict with federal authorities on April 21, 1858. U.S. cavalry soldiers accompanied by a deputy marshal attempted to arrest him and his men on the prairie a dozen miles west of Fort Scott, and the two sides exchanged fire. Alvin Satterwaite, a soldier, was killed, and several of the Army horses were shot. One of the free-state men was wounded, but U.S. forces got the worse of the exchange, and Montgomery was able to withdraw his men without further trouble.

It is a point of embarrassment—at least to this biographer—that the first fatal casualty which can be certainly ascribed to forces under Montgomery's command was that of a United States soldier. When Montgomery himself served in the U.S. Army a few years later he never rose above the rank of colonel. Despite commanding a brigade in combat for significant periods, including at the battle of Olustee, and unlike hundreds of other officers in similar circumstances, he never became a brigadier general. Perhaps the ghost of an institutional memory of Alvin Satterwaite played a role in that non-event. The killing, to be fair, turned out to be the only one of a U.S. soldier or official which Montgomery was responsible for.

David S. Stanley, who served in Kansas in 1856–57 as a lieutenant and would later become a Union major general, wrote many years after in his memoirs that the U.S. Army was trying to interpose between the free-soil and pro-slavery forces to prevent violence.

> The Free Soil men had the enterprise and dash and the country, the slavery party could not hope to carry their laws there, and tried by favor of the general government and military demonstration, to force their institutions upon the territory. They failed, but the terrorism, the rowdy spirit of their own party, the uncertainty of life and property, have left their impression upon Kansas to this day. … The real sentiment of most of the officers and men was with the Free Soil Party, who were the real settlers. However, the [federal] Administration was desirous that Kansas be a slave state and our orders almost invariably favored the pro-slavery pretenders.[37]

While Montgomery continued his campaign of intimidation and expropriation against pro-slavery settlers, his opponents sharply escalated hostilities by perpetrating an atrocity in his own home county of Linn.

At the Marais des Cygnes massacre on May 19, 1858, a Missouri-based party of Border Ruffians led by Charles Hamilton (or Hambleton) rounded up 11 unarmed free-state men—apparently none of whom was connected to the violent conflict—and shot them, killing five and wounding at least another five. The next day, Montgomery was one of the leaders of a posse which went into Missouri in search of the murderers but failed to find any of them. (The Marais des Cygnes River flows from Kansas into Missouri. Its name, provided by French trappers, means Marsh of the Swans, and it was pronounced locally, according to a Civil War report by Union Major General Samuel Curtis, as "Mary de Zene."[38])

Montgomery's free state forces guarded the state border more rigorously following the massacre. They also stepped up a campaign against the Border Ruffians and pro-slavery settlers in Kansas, including Fort Scott, claiming to act only against those on the other side who were themselves guilty of violence and intimidation. After Marais des Cygnes, the increasing numbers of free-state settlers were more inclined to endorse Montgomery's aggressive tactics and leadership. A June 11 letter to Missouri governor Robert Stewart from James Hackney refers to "over 100 men who have been driven from the [Kansas] Territory by Montgomery's band. … the people are boiling over with rage."[39]

Yet Montgomery still did not commit himself to the kind of ruthless homicidal violence against civilians which John Brown had adopted at Pottawattamie in 1856, and which their opponents had adopted at Marais des Cygnes. Instead, in June 1858, he met and negotiated with Governor James Denver, and supported his efforts to bring peace to southeastern Kansas. The peace settlement largely negotiated at Fort Scott included withdrawal of federal troops and replacement of some pro-slavery local officials with anti-slavery men.[40] The troops were withdrawn from Fort Scott in August. Justice arguably was sacrificed, since Hamilton was never prosecuted for the Marais des Cygnes massacre, but Montgomery shared the current territorial governor's focus on the future.[41] The predominance of free-state voters in the Territory was being reinforced by new emigrants of the same political persuasion, which seemed to increase the likelihood of a peaceful settlement with the eventual establishment of a free state.

There was a complication in the return of Brown, whom Montgomery first met in late June or early July 1858.[42] Brown wrote to his son, also named John, on July 9:

> I am now writing in the log-cabin of the notorious Captain James Montgomery, whom I deem a very brave and talented officer, and, what is infinitely more, a very intelligent, kind, gentlemanly, and most excellent man and lover of freedom.[43]

Brown and Montgomery had much in common. Both grew up in Ohio of Scotch-Irish heritage and in the vicinity of anti-slavery sentiment, there becoming confirmed Protestant evangelical Christians.

Their characters had something in common with another Scotch-Irish-American Christian, the future Confederate general Thomas J. "Stonewall" Jackson, who came from the northern part of modern West Virginia, not far from the Ohio line. Brown and Montgomery, unlike Jackson, had each become increasingly convinced of the moral imperative of opposing slavery, no matter if that involved taking up arms even against the federal government. Both were family men who were widowed, remarried, and had children by both wives. Brown was more than 14 years the elder man, and much more famous, but that did not mean Montgomery was willing to acknowledge this outsider's leadership regarding the practical civil and military affairs of southeastern Kansas.

Brown and Montgomery both saw all human beings as equal in the eyes of God, which meant Blacks had inherent rights not to be kidnapped and enslaved. While some Southern Christians found justification for slavery in the Bible, abolitionists found the opposite, often comparing American Blacks to the Jews in ancient Egypt whom Moses led to freedom. (The epistles of Saint Paul provided ammunition both for the defenders and opponents of slavery.) And while Missouri is not the Deep South, the slave system there was by no means mild. An 1847 state law, for example, forbade slaves being taught to read and write.

Brown was an unluckier man than Montgomery. He had already lost one son in Kansas in the guerrilla warfare and would lose two more at Harpers Ferry in 1859. He had previously experienced the loss not just of a wife (as had Montgomery) but the deaths of about nine children caused by sickness. His family had often been blighted by poverty. Brown was a man marked by death, a less stable and more ruthless leader than Montgomery, quicker to violence, more willing to inflict and accept losses, to burn and to kill.

Brown had gone much further than Montgomery, both in the ferocity of his Kansas guerrilla warfare two years earlier, and, in 1858, in his desire for national civil war. He was already planning for a slave uprising in Virginia, which would lead to his Harpers Ferry operation the next year.

And although that would fail militarily, leading to the death of numerous family members and supporters as well as Brown himself, he accurately prophesied that it would help bring on the civil war he desired.

While Montgomery was not as radical as Brown, his willingness to work with him now, overlooking the Pottawatomie massacre of two years before, indicated he was closer to Brown's views than were conventional Republican politicians such as Lincoln and William H. Seward. Partly this was because Montgomery was prepared to take stern measures to prevent another massacre like the one at Marais des Cygnes, but there were also broader considerations. The prominent Republican politicians and most party members were anti-slavery, to be sure, but not at this stage abolitionists. The main reason for their caution was because they wanted to avoid the civil war which Brown eagerly anticipated. In Kansas, too, especially in the mid-1850s, many free-state supporters did not identify as abolitionists, and often, like Lane, even supported legislation to keep Blacks out of the state. Montgomery, if he ever had any sympathy for such views, no longer did so well before he associated with Brown. He, too, had become an unambiguous abolitionist—though not necessarily a supporter of the latter's most destructive tactical initiatives.

Brown, living under a different name to disguise his identity, started building a house near the Missouri line, but then became ill for some months.[44] His illness no doubt helped preserve the Denver peace treaty through the summer and into the fall. Another calming influence on the anti-slavery side was their movement's continuing success at the polls, with the Lecompton constitution being overwhelmingly rejected on August 2.

But the peace was falling apart anyway. On October 30, 1858, a dozen or more Border Ruffians again attacked Montgomery's home, firing into it at night, but withdrew without injuring any of the inhabitants or two guests.[45] The farmhouse west of Mound City had by this time been partly converted into what was called "Fort Montgomery." Built with thick, vertically and tightly placed oak and walnut logs, and only one small window high up.[46] It proved to be a defensible position and was then further strengthened with the aid of Brown's men.

In November, an ally of Montgomery's named Ben Rice was arrested and jailed at Fort Scott for the alleged April 1 murder of Travis, the man who had been acquitted by the Squatter Court of murdering Denton and Dedrick on March 27. Montgomery saw Rice's arrest as a violation of the Denver peace treaty.[47] He regarded his own potential indictment for the January ballot box destruction, which was apparently still contemplated, in the same light.[48]

Negotiations having failed, Montgomery invited Brown to join him on an expedition to free Rice. But when Brown advocated burning the town and killing anyone who resisted, Montgomery decided to exclude him from the raid so as to minimize violence.[49] Another reason was that Montgomery's military tactics differed from Brown's: "Montgomery seldom arranged his plan of attack in detail, leaving himself to shape his action as occasion might demand."[50]

At dawn on December 16, 1858, several dozen armed men led by Montgomery entered Fort Scott. Rice was found chained to the third floor of the Free State Hotel (an ironic name given its current role). Breaking his chains with an ax, the raiders freed the captive. John Little, a storekeeper, fired on the raiders, wounding two, and was killed by return fire.[51]

The raiders looted Little's store and the hotel, despite Montgomery's efforts to stop them,[52] and then withdrew from town with Rice and John Hudlow, another imprisoned jayhawker whom they had released.[53]

A few days later, Brown led a raid into Missouri which killed one slaveholder and freed about a dozen slaves, whom he brought back with him into Kansas and eventually farther north to freedom. Montgomery assisted Brown and the escaped slaves in the aftermath of this raid, being present at the house of his ally, Augustus Wattles, when the Brown raiders stayed there on their way north on the night of December 22.[54] He certainly did not want to see him arrested, or the Blacks returned to slavery. But he, Wattles and most free-staters also made clear their disagreement with Brown's tactics. The raid threatened to stir up more violence at a time when Kansas appeared to be advancing through politics and immigration into its eventual destiny as a free territory and state.

Montgomery set out his version of events in a January 15, 1859, letter in the *Lawrence Republican*:[55]

> We had, in this part of Kansas, from the first, a class of violent pro-slavery men, who came to the country determined to keep out all who were in favor of making Kansas a free State. It was no part of their policy to be peaceable. The plundering and driving of Free State men from the southern part of Kansas in 1856 is a matter of history. A sort of truce followed the advent of [Governor] Geary, during which many of the Free State men returned to their claims; but there was no real peace; outrages were frequent, and in Bourbon County, especially, Free State men were everywhere bullied and insulted. The Laws were not for Free State men; they were made for the benefit of the Pro Slavery party. The courts were controlled by the [pro-slavery party]. It was impossible to convict a pro-slavery man however guilty; and next to impossible to acquit a Free State man, however innocent. Under these circumstances, revolution was clearly our right. …
>
> The present difficulty was caused by the violation of the Denver compromise. … A few indictments were got up in both [Linn and Bourbon] counties, evidently for the purpose of asserting the right to drag us into the courts. … The attempt to assassinate me was planned in Kansas—a few Missourians being called in for the sake of appearance. Linn and Bourbon counties were both represented in the transaction. For Brown's doings in Missouri, I am not responsible. I knew nothing of either his plans or intentions. Brown keeps his own counsels and acts on his own responsibility. …
>
> The release of Rice was a popular movement, in which some of our former company were concerned. But many of those who participated in that movement, acted with me for the first time. … We desire peace, and no man will do more than I to obtain it on honorable terms. No possible good can be done by raking up the past and so the people have decided. Let the past be buried, and let the people choose their own officers, and all will go well.

On January 18, Montgomery agreed to submit himself to a potential trial in Lawrence for allegations of robbery and the murder of Little, and was released on bail. He then devoted himself to peaceful Republican Party politics, including speaking at public meetings in Lawrence and negotiating with the new territorial governor, Samuel Medary, who signed an amnesty bill (which the territorial legislature had passed) on February 11 or 12. Montgomery was no longer in legal jeopardy.[56]

Brown's departure helped peace, for the most part, prevail in Kansas for a while, even as the free state cause advanced. Montgomery was able to go home and plant crops—although in August there is a record of him protesting the kidnapping and demanding the return of a Kansas man, William Wright or Pickles. This became a legal border dispute between Kansas and Missouri authorities, which was settled through the intervention of the federal judge, Williams.[57]

On October 4, voters adopted the free-state Wyandotte constitution. Yet Montgomery was narrowly defeated in a November 8 contest for the territorial House of Representatives. Some of his allies thought he should contest the result on the grounds of fraud, but he declined to do so. Overall, he must have concluded that things in the Territory were moving in the right direction.

These Kansas events were dwarfed in significance by Brown's October 16, 1859, raid on Harpers Ferry, Virginia, the aim of which was to provoke slave rebellions in the South. While it does not appear that Montgomery had advance knowledge of the raid, it probably did not come as a complete surprise, and he did become involved in its aftermath. He and other abolitionists discussed mounting a military rescue mission but gave up the idea in part because Brown discouraged it, now seeing more value in dying a martyr to the cause and helping plant the seeds of civil war. This last goal of his was to prove far more successful than anything else he did.

Brown was the prophet of the Civil War, and there was a line to it from Bleeding Kansas to Harpers Ferry to Lincoln's election and Southern secession. But it was Montgomery who had and would further develop a more realistic grasp of how to fight against slavery. Only one of Brown's sons would serve in the war, playing a brief and minor role under the Kansas jayhawker Charles Jennison. While many more pacific abolitionists such as Garrison had themselves favored secession so that the North and West would not be tainted by slavery and its echoes in the U.S. Constitution, this was not Montgomery's view. As events would prove, only fighting through the coming war could turn it into a successful crusade to free the slaves. Not all abolitionists were willing and able to commit themselves to that hard road. Montgomery was able to make that commitment and would carry it through.

Brown was tried and sentenced to death in Charles Town, Virginia, and was hanged there on December 2. On the morning of his execution, he wrote that he was "now quite certain that the crimes of this guilty land will never be purged away but with blood." His prophecy would soon enough be fulfilled in the Civil War, which would cost far more American lives than any other war, before or since. The role played by Brown in Kansas and Virginia, and especially his well-publicized death, played a significant role in polarizing the country and causing the war.

Montgomery corresponded with Rev. Thomas Wentworth Higginson about a plan to rescue Albert Hazlett and Aaron Stevens, two of Brown's raiders who remained imprisoned in Charles Town. Montgomery knew both of the imprisoned men from their previous service on the free-state side in Kansas. Higginson, a Massachusetts Unitarian, was one of the "Secret Six" who financed and supported Brown's raid, and also had supported the Kansas free-state movement. Higginson and Montgomery had met in Kansas in 1856 and would go on to serve together during the Civil War.

Higginson's other claim to fame is as a friend, mentor, and posthumous literary agent of the poet Emily Dickinson. He and the other Northeastern abolitionists were for the most part literary-minded men and women, who valued and were prepared to support men of action with the same anti-slavery ideals. But they also tended to see themselves as coming from a higher class than men of the people like Brown and Montgomery—in which perception lay the seed of some future tensions.

Montgomery, traveling mostly by rail under an assumed name, brought seven men to meet with Higginson who had a dozen or so with him, on February 17, 1860, in Harrisburg, Pennsylvania.[58] While most of the men remained at Harrisburg, posing as cattle buyers, Montgomery took one, Silas Soule, with him to reconnoiter Higginson's proposed route to Charles Town, Virginia. They made their way through snowy mountain passes, and reached Charles Town, which they found on high alert. Nevertheless, Soule, feigning drunkenness, managed to get himself thrown into jail and into contact with Hazlett and Stevens, who told him they regarded rescue as hopeless and did not want to be responsible for lives lost in the attempt. This was accordingly reported back to Higginson, and, with other considerations such as another snowstorm, the upshot was the rescue attempt went no further.[59] Hazlett and Stevens were hanged on March 16.

Back home, Montgomery was elected as the Linn County delegate to the state Republican convention, which would send delegates to the upcoming national convention in Chicago. The state convention was held in Lawrence on April 11.

Meanwhile, the Kansas economy was getting worse. Some settlers moved west to seek gold in the Rocky Mountains, while others gave up farming in 1860 because of a bad drought and moved back east. Montgomery did not plan to move in either direction but looked to the northeastern states as a potential source of funding for Kansas, both to help his afflicted neighbors and to support the Republican cause.[60]

Montgomery headed east again around August 1, 1860, stopping first to see family (possibly for the first time in 23 years) in Ashtabula County, Ohio. From there he went to Massachusetts to meet abolitionist allies including George Stearns—who became a trusted, long-term friend and ally—Franklin Sanborn and Ralph Waldo Emerson. (It is possible he had first met Stearns earlier that year, after his trip to Harrisburg.)

Montgomery continued on to New York, where he met Horace Greeley, and then to Philadelphia. One significant personal connection he apparently made on this trip was with Harriet Tubman, the Underground Railroad leader originally from Maryland, who now lived near upstate Auburn, NY, not far from the main rail line from Ohio to the Northeastern cities.[61] Tubman also was a regular lecturer and visitor to abolitionist friends across the Northeast, and at that time was preparing for her last prewar expedition to free slaves in Maryland—so their meeting could have been at any of a number of locations. It may have been at an anti-slavery convention in Boston or New York City. In 1863, Montgomery, Tubman, and Higginson (whom he almost certainly saw on this trip) would serve together in the Civil War, raiding Southern plantations and conducting military expeditions from the Sea Islands of South Carolina and Georgia.

After returning home on September 8, Montgomery corresponded with his eastern connections on behalf of drought-stricken Kansans, seeking contributions of food, seed, and clothing for humanitarian relief, as well as arms to further the continued semi-military campaign against the slave power. Stearns was particularly helpful in that regard.

On October 6, 1860, with national tensions about slavery on increasingly high alert with the approaching elections, Montgomery wrote to Stearns:

> … butchering of those supposed to be free state men in Texas, and the preparations known to be making in Arkansas, for a like butchery there, together with the diabolical plot for robbing and destroying the free state men in southern Kansas … but at present everything is still: it is the calm that precedes the hurricane. … We have several fugitives [escaped slaves] on hand and more are expected. Some of them are from Missouri and some from Arkansas. … One of the fugitives: a fine fellow from Missouri, is staying with me. … We are organising our Republican Clubs, and preparing for the election.[62]

The Montgomery family's personal hospitality to liberated slaves would continue into the Civil War. "Montgomery himself kept one refugee in Linn County for three years and a dozen or more for nearly a year."[63]

Some of the Easterners saw him as a potential successor to Brown, but with the nationwide civil war Brown predicted seeming ever more likely, a successor was not necessarily required. And while Brown's actions, starting in Kansas, did help precipitate that war, many others, including Montgomery, could take credit for turning Kansas in the direction of freedom. Their success, with the corresponding failure of the slave power, played a major role in radicalizing the South and thus setting the stage for the war.

Stephen Douglas had been seen as the Democratic Party's most likely candidate for president in 1860 and would have had an excellent chance of victory had the Democrats united behind him. Douglas did run. But pro-slavery Democrats regarded his "squatter sovereignty" doctrine as having been discredited in Kansas, because men like Montgomery were winning the struggle there. The Democrats' Southern base thought Douglas' bright idea for Kansas was producing the wrong result. And since he stood by the basic principle, rejecting the Lecompton constitution and prepared to accept Kansas as a free state, they saw him as a betrayer of their cause.

The resulting Democratic split opened the way for election of the Republican candidate, Abraham Lincoln. He was a former congressman who had served only one term, and whose return to politics was spurred by Douglas' Kansas-Nebraska bill and the ensuing struggle there, which prompted him to run against Douglas and squatter sovereignty in the 1858 Illinois Senate race. Lincoln lost that campaign, but gained enough publicity to make him a plausible national candidate two years later against Douglas, John Breckinridge, and John Bell. After Lincoln took office as president, Douglas supported him and the Union in the early days of the Civil War, before dying on June 3, 1861. Montgomery was an active Republican who supported the winning presidential ticket in 1860.

The presidential campaign heightened tensions throughout the country, which reignited the already volatile terrain of southeastern Kansas, where threats turned into actual violence. On the anti-slavery side, the instigator was as much Jennison as Montgomery, but that does not mean the latter's role was benign.

Jayhawker is a term more associated with Jennison than Montgomery, although widely applied to both men and other irregular abolitionist fighters on the Kansas-Missouri border, including Lane. On November 12, jayhawkers probably led by Jennison and at least tacitly supported by Montgomery hanged a man called Russell Hinds (or Hindes) for the offense of returning a fugitive slave to his master in order to earn a reward—which action was not a crime in 1860, since the Fugitive Slave Law of 1850 remained in effect nationwide. Montgomery obviously regarded that law as an unjust dead letter, and did not object to the hanging, perhaps in part because Hinds was an old enemy. Hinds had tried to kill Montgomery in 1856, then was imprisoned by him and expelled from the Territory.[64]

Harpers Ferry and its aftermath moved Montgomery closer to Brown's radicalism, following in the abolitionist martyr's footsteps. This lent a ferocity to his fight against slavery now and in the early months of the Civil War. When the men were allies in Kansas in 1858, Montgomery—to some extent—criticized and declined to associate himself with Brown's extremism and ruthlessness. Like many abolitionists throughout America, he found it harder now to argue with Brown's ferocious prophecies. And unlike most Republican politicians, he was rarely inclined to let words be a substitute for what he saw as necessary action. He now assumed

Brown's mantle, willing to pursue the slave power in arms and help bring on the prophesied civil warfare.

Montgomery and Jennison and their followers joined forces shortly after Jennison's men had killed another pro-slavery man, Lester Moore, who had allegedly murdered two free-staters. They collaborated in capturing and hanging another pro-slavery man, Sam Scott, for the purported crime of returning to the territory after he had previously been expelled. While these killings were seen by many as amounting to murder, Montgomery was also actively involved in protecting and assisting slaves who were in flight from Missouri, Arkansas, and Indian Territory, and using funds and supplies sent from his connections in the East to relieve destitute people without regard to race.[65]

Meanwhile, Judge Williams had fled from Fort Scott. "In the court's absence," one historian sums up, "both factions administered their own kind of justice, hanging four men—two proslavery and two free-state. All settlers were intimidated by bands of night riders, who claimed to be free-state or proslavery"[66] but were sometimes mere robbers in the Kansas-Missouri borderland.

Montgomery tried to separate himself from men more interested in robbery than free-state principles. That would before long create a rift between him and the much younger Jennison, despite their future mutual service in the Union Army, in which both would serve as colonels. Their characters were very different:

> Montgomery was a teetotaler; Jennison drank heavily. Montgomery never swore, and chastised any of his men who did; Jennison often cursed a blue streak. Montgomery tried to restrain his men from excessive violence; Jennison often encouraged more violence. Not surprisingly, the two men eventually had a parting of the ways.[67]

Jennison's ruthlessness and inclination to plunder would be further demonstrated during the Civil War, and the relationship between the two men deteriorated further after it started. As an unsympathetic historian put it: "Montgomery was probably a sincere antislavery fanatic, but with Jennison, fighting against slavery was mainly an excuse for banditry."[68] Still, both men wound up doing good service in October 1864 at the battle of Westport.

Montgomery certainly supported taking supplies from pro-slavery Missourians and their Kansas allies, but he did not profit personally from these raids. Nor did he take funds raised from the East for purposes of poor relief or military supply and divert them for his own personal enrichment. Before and after the outbreak of the Civil War, Montgomery often sought to restrain his raiders. "He allowed no molestation of women, and he gave stolen horses away to needy Kansans when they were no longer needed. During the Fort Scott raid he let his men raid nearby stores for clothing but prevented them from having a go at the local bank's safe."[69] The Montgomery family would remain far from wealthy, close to the condition of their Kansas neighbors, which helped him retain the trust of those neighbors and lead them when necessary into danger.

Meanwhile, though, Jennison was regarded by Missouri authorities as a subsidiary desperado, with Montgomery as the chief and most dangerous threat. Judge Williams, who had fled to Clinton, Missouri, wrote on November 20 to Governor Stewart:

> The Abolitionists, under the command of Montgomery and Doctor Jennison [a medical doctor], to the number of from three to five hundred … have suddenly commenced a war of extreme ferocity on the law-abiding citizens of Southern Kansas, in the counties of Linn and Bourbon. ... has murdered Mr. Moore, a grand juror; Mr. Harrison, Mr. Samuel Scott, Mr. Hindes, and obliged all of the U.S. officers, including myself, to fly for our lives.

Williams' letter, as recorded in an appendix[70] to the 1861 Missouri legislative *Journal*, was followed in that document two days later by one from J. H. Leach, writing from Warsaw, Missouri: "Montgomery is at Ball's Mill—stole a number of negroes and murdered six or eight men." The circumstances of these alleged murders are far from clear, especially regarding Ball's Mill. It is likely (as Holman suggests, and several letters from Montgomery to Stearns in late 1860 support) that his activities in Missouri at this time were exaggerated. But if Leach was correct that some slave-owners and their allies were killed there, it is also certain he would have regarded them as having been "murdered" even if they were actually engaged in a firefight with Kansas jayhawkers.

It does, however, seem from his actions in November 1860, that Montgomery was becoming more willing to ignore not merely unjust laws but those that upheld public peace—along with, to some extent, the rules of civilized warfare and Christian injunctions to be merciful. It is also clear he now saw his mission as including the liberation of slaves.

"Residents of western Missouri reported that Montgomery was once again making war on them, 'kidnapping and freeing slaves, murdering slave owners, and destroying property.' A runaway slave from Bates County led one of his detachments."[71] Thus Montgomery was leading the way, as he would continue to do in the forthcoming war, not just in advocating abolition and liberating slaves, but enrolling Blacks to fight for their freedom. Such notions went far beyond what most northerners, including free-state Kansans and national Republicans, were at that time willing to accept—and of course were anathema to Democrats.

While Montgomery never became as famous as Brown, there were those on both sides of the slavery issue who now saw him as the dead man's ideological heir, with the ideology being active abolitionist revolution. This perception of Montgomery's conduct in late 1860 contributed to the accelerating nationwide political polarization, and the race to a Civil War. The *Richmond Enquirer* complained that it had expected Northerners to repudiate abolition fanaticism after Harpers Ferry. That had not happened. Instead:

> armed bands of traitors, in all the panoply of war, are openly invading the State of Missouri, murdering the people, burning the towns, and proclaiming the purpose to *free every slave in Southwestern Missouri*. How long—in God's name!—how long are we to suffer the humiliation of such insulting outrage?[72]

Exaggerations could have real-world consequences. Such articles helped sway public opinion in the South toward secession. Those sympathetic to slavery may have expected President-elect Lincoln, unlike Buchanan, to side with radicals like Montgomery. And the Southern fire-eaters' extreme rhetoric provoked an equal and opposite reaction among northerners, from radical abolitionists like Montgomery to moderate Unionists like Ulysses S. Grant, bringing them together in unity to support the Lincoln administration and the Union. Virginia, where the *Richmond Enquirer* was published, eventually seceded in April 1861, thus substantially increasing the strength of the Confederacy, and making the war more difficult for the Union to win. But Virginia's secession also made it more likely that in the event of the Confederacy's defeat, slavery would be abolished throughout the United States.

The notoriety Montgomery acquired would follow him into and influence his U.S. Army career, for better or worse. But in one way, at least, he was more like Grant than Brown: He would be seeking victory (or at least trying to avoid defeat), not martyrdom.

In December, Missouri Governor Stewart sent state militia Brigadier General Daniel Frost with 630 men to the contested borderland, where they found Montgomery had withdrawn from the state and was avoiding any confrontation there or in Kansas. Frost would soon become a Confederate general.

Montgomery's activities disturbed other governments, too, in Washington and Kansas, but all these administrations would be changing soon. He met in November with the new acting territorial governor, George M. Beebe, which helped calm the situation, but it was stirred up again by the return to office of Governor Medary, who sought to have the Linn County jayhawker arrested.

Medary, in December, sent Captain Nathaniel Lyon with a detachment of federal troops to do the job, but Montgomery evaded him too, and that governor soon departed for good. The Army captain was a free-state sympathizer, and probably did not look too hard for his quarry.[73] Lyon had less than a year to live. He would soon become a Union general, commanding an army against the Confederates at the battle of Wilson's Creek, where he was killed.

Beebe, back in control, left Montgomery in peace.[74] Much larger events were afoot.

CHAPTER 3

Civil War

James and Clarinda Montgomery's family had been growing throughout this time. The 1860 Census records them as living in Centerville, a hamlet giving its name to a rural area of Linn County, northwest of Mound City, Kansas. (Mound City itself being much less urban than its name might imply.) Jane Evans, Clarinda's mother, lived with them, as did James and Nancy, the two children from Montgomery's first marriage, and five children of their own: Evan, Mary Jane, John, Julia, and Hugh. Evan, Mary Jane, and John had been born in Kentucky in 1847, 1848, and 1851, respectively. Julia was born in 1854 in Missouri, and Hugh in 1858 in Kansas. Not included in the Census was Lewis, who was born in October 1860 in Kansas.

Clarinda, even more so than most frontier wives, had the primary responsibility of raising the family because of her husband's frequent absences from home. She also shared the risks of guerrilla warfare, with the Montgomery family home turned into a "Fort" near Centerville being more than once a target of violent attack. She had "proved a courageous and loving mate for him and a fond mother to his two bereaved children [after the death of his first wife], and an honored citizen of her new home in Linn County."[1]

That pattern would continue in the years to come, with Confederate Major General Sterling Price's great raid coming dangerously close to their home as late as the fall of 1864. The two elder Montgomery sons would serve in the war with their father on the side of the Union. The growth of the family was interrupted in these years when Montgomery spent much time away on active service. The few surviving wartime letters indicate his affection for and reliance on Clarinda. Their last child, Nellie, was not born until September 8, 1865, at Fort Montgomery, about 10 months after her father's Civil War career ended. It seems to have been a happy marriage.

Kansas became a state in January 1861, with its first governor, Charles Robinson, taking office in February (he had been elected in December). Finally, Kansas was governed not by an appointee of the pro-Southern Democratic President Buchanan, but by an anti-slavery man who was elected by the now solid majority of free-state Kansans.

Montgomery was active in the new state's political and then military affairs. He was elected a delegate to the Republican Congressional Convention in Topeka and helped send the abolitionist Martin Conway to the U.S. House of Representatives. He was also buying rifles with Stearns' money. In mid-April, after the attack and capture of Fort Sumter in South Carolina, and Lincoln's call for state militia volunteers, Montgomery served on Robinson's War Council with the rank of colonel and started raising a regiment.[2]

Despite having been a recent adversary of the federal government, avoiding arrest by one of its officers just a few months before, Montgomery was now prepared to serve in the U.S. Army. His experience in Kansas had proved his courage, commitment, and ability to lead, but unfortunately that was not all he brought with him into the national service. His occasional lack of discipline and disregard for the rules of civilized warfare would create problems, as was the case for other jayhawkers. Later in the war, both he and the Army moved in each other's direction. As they met in the middle, Montgomery would become a more effective soldier.

Lane was one of Kansas' new U.S. senators, and with Cassius Clay helped safeguard the White House during the first days of the Civil War. In June, Lincoln appointed him a brigadier general of volunteers. While Robinson and Lane were both for the Union and against slavery, they were soon at odds about key details regarding the organization and legal status of Kansas troops. The new state of Kansas was neither populous nor wealthy but put eight regiments in the field in 1861.

> Much confusion existed in the organization of these regiments, resulting from the action of the War Department at Washington in giving Senator James H. Lane authority to raise troops and organize regiments of volunteers in Kansas independent of state authority.[3]

Although some of his Eastern friends wanted him to start a slave insurrection across the South, Montgomery's focus at this time was more defensive, and close to home. He was concerned about potential attacks on southeast Kansas from pro-Confederate Missourians and Indians. Both Missouri and Indian Territory would be contested territory through most of the Civil War. Pro-Confederate Indians for a while dominated their Territory, which was situated in modern Oklahoma, on the southern border of Kansas.

Missouri is on Kansas' eastern border, north of Arkansas, and it was from the east that the threat to Kansas seemed and was most acute. Missouri, although it would be recognized by the Confederate government as one of its states, never formally seceded from the Union. It almost did, though, and in May 1861 its governor, Claiborne Jackson, appointed his fellow pro-secessionist Sterling Price as commander of the state militia, which would become part of the Confederate army. A 20th-century historian wrote:

> Should Missouri join the Confederacy, then Kansas would be practically cut off from the rest of the nation. Moreover, in case of war, Kansas would be exposed to attack from the Missourians, many of whom were known to be thirsting to avenge the raids of Brown and Montgomery.[4]

Further, Missouri was a much stronger and more populous state than Kansas, and would remain, off and on, on the front line until the defeat of Price's great raid in late October 1864.

A major complicating factor was that many pro-Union Missourians also supported slavery, which meant the fierce anti-slavery politics of people like Montgomery and Stearns would not, at least at this early stage of the war, necessarily be seen as helpful to the Union cause. Stearns was still funding most of Montgomery's supplies, including the Sharps rifles which would make his men better armed than their Confederate opponents. On June 21, Montgomery wrote to him:

> Events are thickening on us fast, and war now stares us in the face. An invasion of Southern Kansas is threatened from South West Missouri, and Western Arkansas, and besides this, they are endeavoring to Arm and enlist the Indians against us. They have been driving the Union Men out of Missouri; but they have changed the program now, and refuse to allow any non-Union men to leave. On the contrary, they compel them to swear allegiance to the State of Missouri, and draft them into the Rebel Army. In this state of things the Union men have called on me to head them; and I have promised to do so. I am going down with an active force to join them, and in so doing, I hope to keep them from our doors, by giving them something to do at home.[5]

At least one vital aspect of rural life was showing improvement. "Weather warm, crops flourishing," Montgomery wrote at the end of the letter to Stearns. His own farm had expanded to 320 acres, and his sons helped him plant crops there by the middle of May. He also continued to distribute relief supplies from the East to the poor, including to increased numbers of fugitive slaves. While some Kansans wanted them sent north out of state, maybe to Canada, Montgomery was not willing to pressure them to move north against their will. He had been a supporter and participant in the Underground Railroad for years, working in Linn County with several families who sent slaves north to freedom, and that commitment remained.[6] But his evolving abolitionism now viewed all African-Americans as entitled to make their way anywhere in American society. He helped find work for many on the farms of Linn County and had an idea that some would, before long, become eligible for service in the U.S. Army. In fact, before anyone else, Montgomery would use African-Americans in a military support role—as wagon drivers when his regiment picked up supplies from Fort Leavenworth in August 1861.[7]

On June 24, Governor Robinson, "reposing especial trust and confidence in the ability, integrity and diligence of James Montgomery," commissioned him as "Colonel of the Third Regiment of Volunteers for the United States Service."[8] The regiment would be a mixture of cavalry and infantry, and would serve in a brigade—including the fourth and fifth Kansas regiments—under Lane.

Montgomery, presumably with Lane's approval, almost immediately took about 180 men into action. (That was far from the strength of a full regiment; he was still recruiting soldiers, and one of the purposes of this raid was to find more volunteers.) He brought them into Missouri, as he had told Stearns he was going to do, and reported on how the raid went in a subsequent letter to him:

> Entering the state early in the morning of the 26th June, we marched to Bell's Mill (15 miles) where a company of the enemy was posted. They were attacked and quickly routed; but, with the life of one man wounded and one horse killed. The enemy was strongly posted, and under cover. They were so closely packed that they had not time to mount, thus leaving quite a number of horses and mules, ready saddled, which our footmen gladly appropriated. We took but one prisoner at this place, and can't claim that any of the enemy were hurt. We had two skirmishes earlier in the day, in which several prisoners, with their horses were taken, and one notorious villain (Bill March Banks) was killed. At Bell's Mill we learned, from a prisoner and other men (Union men), that we were driving into a force 8,000 strong, under General Rains retreating towards Arkansas before the U.S. forces. The next day a few of our boys acting with a small force of Union men attacked a superior number of Rebels on Walnut Creek, in Bates County, 11 miles east of this place, killing several men and horses without sustaining any loss theirselves. In another skirmish, since, two men of the enemy were killed.[9]

While Montgomery did not take the risk of putting it in writing to Stearns, his new official status in a national Civil War reinforced his inclination to discard any prior tactical inhibitions—or current political considerations and U.S. policies—about freeing enslaved Blacks. Some "contraband" slaves were liberated on this raid and accompanied Montgomery's troops back to Kansas. Many more would follow that freedom trail on subsequent expeditions to Missouri over the next several months.[10]

President Lincoln, however, had different priorities. He aimed to keep Missouri in the Union, which for now meant accepting slavery there. While Lane, like his subordinate Montgomery, wanted to use the freed Blacks as soldiers, that, too, was by no means federal policy at this time even in the rebel states, and certainly not in border slave states like Missouri and Kentucky. The priority of the administration in Washington, and of most higher-ranking officers and politicians on the northern side, was preserving the Union. While Montgomery was pro-Union, and determined to protect the new free state of Kansas, he did not endorse this cautious strategy. To him the war was about abolition, or it was hardly worth fighting. Abolition included freeing slaves in Missouri, and Lane's brigade continued to do that on smaller-scale raids from Kansas.

Montgomery's Third Kansas regiment came up to strength and was mustered in the next month. As second-in-command, lieutenant-colonel, he appointed James Blunt, who had been active in territorial politics on the free-state side. Blunt would go on to become a major general, and the most successful Union commander from Kansas.

Montgomery's regiment was picking up supplies at Fort Leavenworth in early August. The Black teamsters and wagon master he used were possibly the first African-Americans serving at least in a support role with the U.S. Army. They were mostly "contraband" slaves who had fled from Missouri and were recruited by Montgomery—who at this time made an abolitionist speech in the Kansas town of Leavenworth.[11]

The language of a 1792 federal law providing for the conscription of free White men into state militias had been interpreted as barring African-Americans from the national Army. But that was really a fig leaf covering prejudice and politics. The Lincoln administration was at this time very conservative on the issue, not wishing to alienate the many White Unionists who opposed abolition and the use of Black soldiers. Montgomery had no such reservations.

Lane was reluctant to commit the Kansas Brigade out of state, so it and Montgomery missed the August 10 battle of Wilson's Creek near Springfield in southwestern Missouri. This was a major Union defeat in which the commanding general, Lyon, was killed, and his army forced to retreat northeast to Rolla, while Price's Confederate militia occupied Springfield.

The Kansas Brigade was headquartered at Fort Scott, now again an official military base for the first time since 1853. Montgomery's regiment arrived there on August 20. Price sent a cavalry detachment west from Springfield to "clear the counties bordering upon Kansas of the marauding bands that infested that section of the state."

When the Confederate cavalry commander reported back with news of Lane's brigade being at Fort Scott, Price moved with about 8,500 troops in that direction. They encamped by the end of the month about three miles west of Nevada, Missouri, and about 15 miles east of Fort Scott, Kansas.[12]

A Confederate raid captured a hundred or so of Lane's mules (not from Montgomery's regiment), killing the man in charge of them.[13] The general ordered Montgomery with 450 troopers, mostly from the Fifth Kansas Cavalry, and one artillery piece to check out the Confederate force, to engage it unless it proved too strong, and to get the mules back. Montgomery's men moved into Missouri on September 2, as Price's larger force was moving toward Fort Scott.

The wooded terrain helped Montgomery's Fifth Cavalry to surprise Price's advance guard at Dry Wood Creek, south of Deerfield, Missouri, compelling it to retreat for about two miles. When Montgomery realized the larger numbers of Confederates he was up against, who were now trying to flank his position, he in turn retreated—without sounding a bugle so as not to alert the enemy.

Lane, getting the news about the strength of the Confederate force, abandoned Fort Scott and withdrew another 12 miles to the northwest, to what he called Fort Lincoln on the Osage River. He left Montgomery to cover the retreat—or as Lane reported to the regional headquarters at Fort Leavenworth, Kansas:

> I left my cavalry to amuse the enemy until we could establish ourselves here and remove our good stores from Fort Scott. … I am compelled to make a stand here, or give up Kansas to disgrace and destruction.
>
> If you do not hear from me again, you can understand I am surrounded by a superior force. I trust the Government will see the necessity for re-enforcing me. My loss so far [*i.e.* at Dry Wood Creek] is about 5 killed and 6 wounded. The enemy has suffered considerably.[14] Price reported that his losses were two killed and 23 wounded.[15]

Montgomery had performed well in his first significant combat operation of the war. Lane's alarm for Kansas proved unfounded at this time, as Price did not occupy Fort Scott but moved his army north in Missouri. This did not increase Lane's credibility with the U.S. Army or Robinson, the Kansas governor.

Price's army besieged Lexington on the Missouri River east of Kansas City and captured it on September 20. Meanwhile, though, his advance had opened the way for Lane's Kansas Brigade not just to reoccupy Fort Scott but to operate in the Confederate rear in southwestern Missouri—in

Confederate General Sterling Price, leading adversary of Union forces in Kansas and Missouri through most of the Civil War. (Negative probably made from original watercolor portrait held by DeGolyer Library, Southern Methodist University. Library of Congress)

a way which would further embitter the conflict with long-lasting damage for both sides.

Lane sent a message to Captain (or Major) William Prince at Fort Leavenworth stating his intention to operate behind Price's army in Missouri:

> I propose to pursue far enough to threaten their rear and confuse them. … the object of the pursuit is a hope that we will be able to cut off their train and recover the mules they have stolen from us.

Prince in his September 9 reply noted that he had been forwarding Lane's reports to Major General John Fremont, who commanded the Department of the West from St. Louis. But, Prince told Lane, his communications with Fremont were indirect and could be delayed due to the unrest in the state. And Prince urged Lane to:

> adopt early and active measures to crush out this marauding which is being enacted in Captain *Jennison's* name, as also yours, by a band of men representing themselves as belonging to your command ... Please have a formal examination into the plundering of private and public buildings which has recently taken place.

Jennison was raising what would become in October the Seventh Kansas Cavalry and had been leading raids independently into Missouri.[16] While Jennison, both before and during the Civil War, was one of the jayhawkers most likely not just to liberate slaves but to appropriate other "property" from those who supported slavery and secession, it is doubtful whether Lane or Montgomery was sympathetic to Prince's complaint.

Nor was the broader federal policy clear at this time. Fremont had on August 30 imposed martial law throughout Missouri, proclaiming: "All persons who shall be taken with arms in their hands within these lines shall be tried by court-martial, and, if found guilty, will be shot."[17] The proclamation also confiscated rebels' property and freed their slaves. Lincoln, concerned about alienating pro-slavery unionists in Missouri and other border states, controversially ordered Fremont to revoke the emancipation clause on September 11. No doubt Lane, Montgomery, and Jennison agreed with Fremont's tough policy, which influenced their actions.

Meanwhile, there were continuing raids and threats from would-be secessionists, including a September 8 Confederate guerrilla attack from Indian Territory on Humboldt, Kansas, 40 miles west of Fort Scott.[18] Sending Lt. Col. Blunt to deal with this and take command of troops left in Kansas, Lane led the rest of the Kansas Brigade—about 1,500 men—into Missouri.

The general distributed copies of the Fremont proclamation as he marched, and told his soldiers: "Everything disloyal, from a Shanghai rooster to a Durham cow, must be cleaned out." They were happy to oblige. There was a growing split in the Unionist ranks between hard-war abolitionist volunteers and their immigrant supporters, and the native-born, regular Army, sometimes slavery-supporting moderates, who did not want to alienate the White majority.

Lane stopped for a few days in West Point, Missouri, about 65 miles south of Kansas City, and tried to communicate with other Union forces. He learned of a small force of Confederates recruiting for Price in Morristown, about 20 miles north-northeast, and sent about 600 cavalry under Colonels Montgomery and Hamilton Johnson to deal with it. Johnson, like Montgomery, was a Protestant preacher (Methodist, in his case) whose religious convictions had led him to oppose slavery.

Early on September 17, Johnson, second in command, attacked first and prematurely, before Montgomery was in position. Johnson was killed along with Private James Copeland, with about six other Union soldiers wounded. The Rebels were driven east to Harrisonville. A few Confederates were captured along with about 140 horses and mules, 11 wagons, 15 tents, plenty of equipment, "a lot of store goods" and "an abundance of the best peaches."[19]

Montgomery, apparently enraged by the "murder" of his reckless friend Johnson (and prepared to ignore their purportedly shared Christian principles as well as the rules of war) was probably responsible for executing five prisoners, after a brief so-called court-martial. Two younger prisoners were released.[20]

While Price's militia had not yet formally become part of the Confederate army, and its supporters at Morristown might have been regarded as guerrillas, that would not justify their execution. The Kansas Brigade itself had a somewhat equivalent status on the Union side. It is possible that the executions were in retaliation for recent murders of captured Union soldiers in the area, although the evidence for that is unclear.[21] Nor is Montgomery's direct involvement in the September 17 executions definitively proven. If he was responsible, then he might have taken Fremont's August 30 proclamation as legal justification. Still, whatever their personal involvement in these and other outrages during the campaign, both Montgomery and Lane were also issuing orders demanding that their troops exercise restraint and comply with the rules of civilized warfare.

The ruthless acts at Morristown, and elsewhere, paved the way for even worse war crimes by Confederate guerrillas in Missouri such as Quantrill and "Bloody Bill" Anderson—just as Brown's Pottawatomie massacre in Kansas before the war was exceeded by the pro-slavery side's atrocity at Marais des Cygnes in Linn County.

On September 3, near St. Joseph, Missouri, pro-secession bushwhackers derailed a train on the Platte River. Up to 20 people were killed, mostly civilians. Pro-Union men were murdered, and their families driven away in Ozark County.[22] In Tennessee in 1861, pro-Union bridge burners were executed by Confederate authorities on orders from Richmond. Confederate guerrillas sometimes got similar merciless treatment from Union generals such as Gordon Granger and Philip Sheridan in Mississippi in the summer of 1862. That fall, the retreating Confederate army of Major General Edmund Kirby Smith hanged Unionists in Kentucky.[23] Two years later, Grant adopted the same policy in Virginia, ordering Sheridan to hang captured guerrillas commanded by John Mosby.

As Blacks were accepted into the U.S. Army—many of them recruited by Montgomery—they often found themselves in real danger of being murdered if they were incapacitated or tried to surrender in combat. An unknown but substantial number of his African-American soldiers suffered that fate after being wounded and left on the field by the retreating Union army at the Confederate victory of Olustee in 1864. Other Blacks were enslaved by advancing Confederate armies, and policies of execution and enslavement were endorsed by senior officials including the Confederate president and secretary of war.[24]

"Hard war" tactics were increasingly adopted as the conflict went on, especially in guerrilla conflicts such as Missouri, where taking no prisoners was a common procedure resorted to by both sides, including Lane and Blunt for the Union. In 1863, Union Brigadier General Thomas Ewing issued an order approved by Lincoln which depopulated and burned buildings in substantial portions of Missouri along the Kansas border, in retaliation for the murder of about 150 Union civilian males in Lawrence, Kansas, by Confederates under Quantrill.

Montgomery would follow the hard-war line a few days after Morristown by burning civilian houses at Osceola, and then again in 1863 when he burned a town in Georgia. It is still the indefensible executions at Morristown on September 17, 1861, which, if he was indeed responsible, mark the low point of his career. While others engaged in similar conduct and would do much worse as the war went on, that hardly amounts to an excuse. One reason for Montgomery's actions may have been his perception of the Union cause as desperately endangered, and that its peril, along with Fremont's proclamation and his own official position, entitled him to emulate the mercilessness of John Brown. Price's army had been victorious at Wilson's Creek and was advancing north through Missouri, while in the East the Confederates had won the battle of Bull Run.

But even in strictly military terms, the executions were not defensible over the long term. It was the strategy of more restrained and moderate Union commanders than Lane, Montgomery, and Fremont which, over the next six months, proved successful for the Union cause in Missouri and Arkansas—even though the Kansas Brigade did to some extent disrupt Price's offensive.

No executions are mentioned in the official report about Morristown, in which Lane said his troops "succeeded in routing the enemy, killing 7, capturing their entire camp equipage, tents, wagons, &c., some 100 horses and horse equipments. Our loss is 2 killed [Johnson and Copeland], 6 wounded."[25]

Lane, now concerned about threats to his own rear as well as disrupting Price's supply line, ignored an order from Fremont to march to Kansas City. Instead, the Kansas Brigade went in the opposite direction—southeast—toward Osceola, Missouri. His similarly incomplete report about events at Osceola says he ordered a forced march there:

> expecting to cut off the enemy's train of ammunition. The enemy ambushed the approaches to the town, and after being driven from them by the advance under Colonels Montgomery and Weer, they took refuge in the buildings of the town to annoy us. We were compelled to shell them out, and in doing so the place was burned to ashes, with an immense amount of stores of all descriptions. There were 15 or 20 of them killed and wounded; we lost none.[26]

Lane had come to rely on Montgomery as his second-in-command and pre-eminent fighting officer, and Osceola could be seen as a legitimate objective as a Confederate supply depot. But other evidence indicates that most of the town, which had a population of 3,000 (some undoubtedly Union loyalists) was deliberately looted and burned after its capture on September 24 after relatively light resistance, not accidentally set ablaze as a result of artillery fire.[27] Montgomery actively participated in the burning, following the orders of Lane, though he spared some buildings so women and children would have shelter.[28] He tried to destroy supplies of liquor, but many soldiers still left town drunk. (The teetotaling Montgomery was constantly trying to stamp out drunkenness in the ill-disciplined Kansas Brigade, and the problem would recur in subsequent commands.)

The brigade also took with them about 200 freed slaves, who were joined by many more fugitives as the general finally complied with Fremont's order and marched to Union-held lines near Kansas City. Also brought back were 350 horses and mules, and 400 cattle.[29] The fate of the Black refugees coming into Kansas would be a constant preoccupation of Montgomery for the coming years. He helped some find employment by the Army—eventually as soldiers—and others to get agricultural work.

Lane's campaign, including the theft of livestock, the sack of Osceola and the executions at Morristown, was inhumane, and alienated potential Union supporters. But it had some short-term positive effects. It contributed to Price's lack of supplies, especially ammunition. More important, it deterred him from making any move into southern Kansas. Simeon Fox–who served through the war with the Seventh Kansas, and much later became state adjutant general–said in his 1902 memoir that Lane's brigade, including specifically Montgomery's regiment:

> did excellent service along the Missouri border, and their presence there undoubtedly saved Kansas from rebel invasion when, after the dearly bought and doubtful victory at Wilson Creek, the Confederate general, Sterling Price, marched north to Lexington, in September, 1861.[30]

As Fremont moved west from St. Louis with a relief army, the secessionist state militia commander decided not to stand his ground. Price pulled out of Lexington at the end of September and retreated south. New recruits had not been forthcoming from slave-holding Missouri, and as he went south increasing numbers of his soldiers slipped away in desertion. His substantial tactical victories at Wilson's Creek and Lexington had not borne strategic fruit.

Actually, the Confederate victory at Wilson's Creek had been won by Price in conjunction with Brigadier General Benjamin McCulloch, who had since gone back to Arkansas. On September 25, McCulloch paid Montgomery a backhanded compliment (complete with inaccurate military promotion) in a message to Colonel (and future general) Thomas Hindman:

> I am just in receipt of information from Missouri stating that Generals Lane and Montgomery have defeated Colonel Hunter, of the Missouri forces, destroying his command—some 350 men. The same letter brings intelligence of their having burned Osceola, and that they are destroying the property of Southern men and taking them prisoners.[31]

Price's failure to attract support was interpreted by some Union leaders as another reason to reward and retain the confidence of middle-of-the road White Missourians, who, while not supporting Governor Jackson and secession, were not inclined to abolish slavery, either. These conservative Unionists saw people like Lane, Jennison, and Montgomery as radical abolitionists who were doing more harm than good to the Union cause. The abolitionists, on the other hand, justified their military tactics as successful, and regarded slaveholders' complaints about inhumanity and theft as hypocritical.

As the Kansas Brigade rested in camp near Kansas City, its lack of conventional discipline, along with Lane's acceptance of Indian troops and Black ones, too, at least in supply and support roles, was proving yet more controversial.[32] "Negroes and Indians mixed with the white rowdies" there, as a mid-20th century historian put it.[33]

Fremont, joined by Lane's brigade, pursued Price's retreating army and recaptured Springfield in late October. But Fremont was replaced in early November by Major General David Hunter, who on Lincoln's advice pulled back to Rolla and Sedalia, Missouri, leaving Price to reoccupy Springfield.[34] Lane's brigade with Montgomery moved back north along the border, accompanied by Brigadier-General Samuel Sturgis, a West Point-trained regular. Sturgis quarreled with Lane about the latter's freeing of slaves—and sometimes burning their owners' plantations. Lane organized the contrabands into a "Black Brigade" which he sent to harvest crops in Kansas. Montgomery's regiment alone brought 250 freed slaves out of Springfield.[35]

On November 19, Hunter was put in command of the new Department of Kansas, a job which Lane had wanted.[36] It was also in effect a demotion for Hunter, because Major General Henry Halleck took over from him

Major General David Hunter, who first became Montgomery's commander in Kansas, then brought him to the Department of the South. (Brady's National Photographic Portrait Galleries. Library of Congress)

the Department of the Missouri, a key border area whose boundaries stretched far beyond the state. Combat operations were more likely there than in Kansas. In Washington, the new general-in-chief was George McClellan, replacing Winfield Scott. Halleck and McClellan, unlike Fremont and Hunter, were not resolutely opposed to slavery, and had little sympathy for the radical irregulars commanded by Lane. Nor was Lincoln, despite his appreciation for Lane's support in Washington, much more sympathetic at this still early stage of the war. The president was more concerned to hold the support of pro-slavery Unionists, who outnumbered abolitionists in the border states. Fremont's activism on the abolition issue was one the reasons Lincoln had fired him.

Lane decided to return to the U.S. Senate, and in his absence, Montgomery led the Kansas Brigade regiments under the command of Hunter, who was told by Halleck to keep Lane's men out of Missouri.[37]

The brigade was held in Kansas, not far from Price's militia across the Missouri line, and supplies were becoming problematic. For the first but far from the last time in the war, Montgomery found himself commanding a brigade while remaining held at the rank of colonel. Hunter, however, was one regular Army officer who shared Montgomery's anti-slavery views and would be very helpful to the later military career of his tempestuous subordinate.

A December 1 letter to Montgomery from Captain E. E. Harvey, who was commanding "that portion of the 5th Reg now at" Osawatomie, Kansas, told a bleak tale of sickness and deprivation, including a lack of tents, blankets and clothing.[38]

Montgomery himself gave a grim report to Lane from Osawatomie on December 8, which began:

> Everything is going wrong here. What you and I feared at Springfield is coming to pass. The enemy is advancing [not for the moment west to Kansas, but north in Missouri, which] swarms with guerrillas, and this makes it difficult to procure information, [although Montgomery's scouts did provide some]. … The movement of the enemy evidently threatened Sedalia [Missouri], but I feared he would strike to the left [in the direction of Kansas] if he found Sedalia too strong. I informed General Hunter of the enemy's advance, and, without waiting for orders advanced to Osawatomie, to cover our trains and prevent the enemy from outflanking me. The enemy numbers full 10,000, and has twenty pieces of artillery, most of them rifled.

James Denver, the former territorial governor, was now a Union brigadier general, one more of Montgomery's superiors who were skeptical of his reports and willing to contemplate the breakup of the Kansas Brigade. Denver, Montgomery told Lane, issued an order:

> directing the Fourth Regiment to Wyandotte; Newgent's to remain at Paola; Jennison's to Leavenworth; Rabb's battery to Leavenworth; Third and Fourth to Fort Scott. I have kept Denver posted in the movements of the enemy; but I am coolly snubbed with the information that Price's advance is all stuff; that Price has no army; that his army is disbanded, &c.
>
> … You will see at a glance that I am in no condition to fight if the enemy comes in force. The measles are still raging in our camps, and our regiments are reduced to mere skeletons. One mountain howitzer and an 8-pounder gun, with 6-pounder ammunition, constitute my show for artillery. With such a show I must say I fear the worst.[39]

Although his intelligence about Price's movements was generally borne out by events, Montgomery received little credit for it or for his military responses—except, in backhanded form, from Price himself. In a December 6 message to McCulloch in Arkansas, Price reported that he planned to move north again soon to the Missouri River, and that,

> Predatory bands of the enemy, under such men as Lane, Montgomery and Jennison, supported by the United States forces, are not only desolating the country, but are committing the most barbarous outrages upon the people of that region. They at the same time effectually close the roads to the thousands of recruits who would join my army if they could get to it.
>
> ... I do, therefore beg me to give your instant and effective cooperation in a movement upon the Missouri River and also into Kansas if you shall concur in it.[40]

While Price referred to "predatory bands" of jayhawkers, Montgomery in the same month dispatched Major H. H. Williams to "to punish those marauding bands" of pro-Confederate guerrillas based in Missouri.

Price and McCulloch were increasingly at cross purposes. McCulloch had in fact left temporarily to confer in the Confederate capital of Richmond, Virginia, and Colonel James McIntosh replied for him to Price, saying no reinforcement from Arkansas was possible. So, in late December, Price retreated back to Springfield, where he established winter quarters. In February 1862, as a Union army commanded by Major General Samuel Curtis approached from Rolla, Price retreated to Arkansas.[41] There his and McCulloch's forces reunited under a new leader, Major General Earl Van Dorn, and were defeated by Curtis in early March at the battle of Pea Ridge—where McCulloch was killed.

Lane's Kansas Brigade, now led by Montgomery, would not be involved in this campaign, just as it had missed Wilson's Creek the previous year. Those were the two major battles fought in the theater up to this point, and their absence from them did not burnish the reputations of the leaders of the Kansas Brigade. Lane's war-fighting seemed only intermittently and tangentially connected with the main activities in the West of the U.S. armed forces. With his military career stymied, he devoted more attention to his political duties as a senator.

Montgomery, meanwhile, had to keep the troops left under his command reasonably well supplied through the winter. His Third Regiment was settled in by the end of December at winter quarters in "Camp Defiance," not far from the home of its colonel. There were small-scale raids back and forth across the border in December. Some pro-Confederate Missourians sought the return of fugitive slaves while "murdering and plundering"[42] in the Mine Creek area of Linn County, and some of Montgomery's jayhawkers retaliated and brought in supposedly "secesh" supplies, and more fugitive slaves, from Missouri.[43] It was the same kind of skirmishing, and in the same area, as his prewar raids and responses, but it was going out of style in this theater of the Union Army.

Montgomery continued to be the idol of some New England abolitionists such as Stearns' friend the writer Lydia Maria Child, who sent him a fulsome letter on December 26. But his political position at home was ever more precarious. Lane's absences and feuds further weakened political support for the Kansas Brigade and its jayhawking style of soldiering, and the result in early 1862 was the interruption of Montgomery's military career. Lane's military status was legally ambiguous—at times he appeared to have given up the Army in favor of his work in the Senate. Generals Halleck, Hunter, and Denver, along with Governor Robinson, did not place a lot of confidence in him—as a soldier, at least—or the remnants of his brigade, now led by Montgomery.

The upshot was that Robinson on February 20 ordered the Third Kansas Volunteers to be disbanded, which took several weeks to accomplish. Some of its members, and others from the Kansas Brigade, became part of the new 10th Kansas Volunteer Infantry Regiment, temporarily led by Montgomery.

Lincoln, in March, transferred Hunter to command the Department of the South, headquartered on the Sea Islands of South Carolina and Georgia. This put the general back in a real wartime command, where his abolitionist views might have political advantages—and where his feisty subordinate would before too long rejoin him. For now, however, Montgomery received an honorable discharge from military service in April 1862.[44] That same month Blunt, with Lane's support, "was commissioned a brigadier general and placed in command of the Department of Kansas"[45]—an appointment that Montgomery might well have thought should have been his.

Now a civilian, he was able to put in farm crops with his family—and would have time to harvest them that year. But he was far from done with the Civil War. Blacks in flight from slavery were continuing to come into Kansas from Missouri, Arkansas, and Indian Territory, and, as we have seen, Montgomery had already taken steps to include them into military units, as well as to assist them in finding work and in other ways. He now planned to recruit African-American, Indian, and White troops, including a new Black regiment which he hoped to lead.

In July 1862, Lane, still an influential politician, was appointed recruiting commissioner of the Department of Kansas. He began raising troops including, with Montgomery's support, Blacks—first listed as "laborers" but soon enough as soldiers in the First Kansas Colored Volunteer Infantry, who were sworn in at Fort Scott. These would become probably the first Black soldiers to actually fight for the Union, unlike the African-American teamsters recruited by Montgomery the previous year. Lane acted under what he claimed was oral authority from Lincoln. By October the Black soldiers were in combat in Missouri.[46]

But Montgomery would not be serving with them. On August 3, he had written to Robinson saying he had raised a regiment of Black troops and asking that he be appointed its colonel. He was the first choice of the men, he told the governor, and while their second choice was Jennison, Montgomery called his rival unfit for command as "an unmitigated liar, blackleg and robber."[47] Although Montgomery was on better terms with Lane than he was with Jennison, he increasingly felt abandoned by his old commander. Robinson was feuding with Lane and unwilling to favor those who had served under him—whom he could see from Montgomery's letter were also feuding with each other. So, the governor did not pick either Montgomery or Jennison to command the troops they had raised (including Indians, in Montgomery's case). There was also pushback from the Lincoln administration, which was not ready to have tempestuous Kansas jayhawkers like Montgomery, Jennison, and Lane lead the way in this very politically sensitive area.[48]

However, Lincoln was also at this time preparing an Emancipation Proclamation which would have the effect, for many people on both sides, of turning the war into a crusade to free the slaves. The final version, enacted on the first day of 1863, also authorized the freedmen's entry "into the armed service of the United States." The president had adopted a radical policy which was very controversial, and would remain so even in the North, for some time.

Montgomery had been pressing for abolition and Black enlistment since the war started, in his deeds more than his words, at a time when Lincoln was firmly opposed. The president had had practical reasons for that opposition, mainly military necessity, but he was also acutely aware of the need to build political support. In the 1860 election, Lincoln had won only 10 percent of the vote in Missouri. By 1864, 110,000 Missourians had enrolled in the Union armies, compared to 40,000 for the Confederacy.[49] In the latter year's presidential election in the state, Lincoln beat George McClellan by 70-30 percent.

It is certainly arguable that the Union's military successes in Missouri and Arkansas, such as the victory at Pea Ridge in 1862, were in part the result of the administration's conciliatory—*i.e.* to Union slaveholders—policies which were put into effect by generals such as Halleck. But ultimately it was the radicals' policies which were adopted by Lincoln and the United States. When Montgomery used Black teamsters in his regiment in 1861, he may well have been the first officer in the war to employ African-American troops. By early 1863, the administration had caught up with him, and he would soon be leading a Black U.S. Army regiment—but nowhere near Kansas or Missouri.

With Kansas politics proving a dead end for his ambition to return to soldiering, Montgomery began using his old and new Eastern connections to try to get back into the Army. What he aimed at and succeeded in doing was commanding one of the new Black regiments which the federal government would be authorizing to be raised and deployed in the Department of the South.

That department was commanded by the same Major General Hunter under whom Montgomery had served in Kansas. It was based on the Sea Islands of eastern South Carolina and Georgia, including Port Royal Island, St. Helena Island, and Hilton Head Island, all of which had been captured by the Union following the naval victory at Port Royal in November 1861. Most of the territory of those states would remain under Confederate control until the advance of William Tecumseh Sherman's Union army in 1864 and 1865. Meanwhile, though, the federal occupation of places including Beaufort and Hilton Head provided bases for the naval blockade. These places also had to be defended by the Army and provided opportunities for its offensive action.

It would take more than long-distance communication to confirm Montgomery's appointment. So, wrapping up his personal affairs and bidding his family farewell, he left Kansas for Washington, DC, arriving in December 1862. He immediately began lobbying the Senate, where his ally was not so much Lane but Kansas' other senator, Samuel Pomeroy (who had helped turn the town of Atchison against slavery before the war and became its mayor).

Montgomery also met briefly with Lincoln, who, he told Stearns, "received me very kindly." Crucially, he was backed by General Hunter, who was temporarily in Washington and "wants me to go South with him."

The upshot was that on January 13, 1863, Montgomery was authorized by the War Department "to raise, subject to the approval of the general commanding the Department of the South and under his direction, a regiment of South Carolina volunteer infantry, to be recruited in that State." Montgomery would waste no time in carrying out that mission and leading his new regiment into action.[50]

CHAPTER 4

With Tubman in the South

On January 20, 1863, Montgomery arrived by ship with Hunter at Beaufort, South Carolina. That state had been the first to declare itself out of the Union, in December 1860, issuing a "Declaration of Causes of Secession" which repeatedly mentioned the defense of slavery as justification for leaving the Union.[1] Its leaders, acting on instructions from Confederate President Jefferson Davis, had begun the Civil War by attacking and capturing Fort Sumter in April 1861.

Beaufort had been the home of the fire-eater Robert Barnwell Rhett, a former U.S. senator and Charleston newspaper editor who was a ferocious advocate for slavery. The Sea Islands area, including Beaufort, had been mostly populated by slaves living on profitable plantations, whose owners tended to be strong advocates of secession. Most of these rich and influential Whites had fled to the interior at the approach of Union forces, leaving more than 30,000 slaves behind in the Beaufort area. The latter were designated "contraband of war"[2] by Union forces, effectively confirming their freedom.

Montgomery began recruiting volunteers, African-American and mostly former slaves, for what would become the Second South Carolina Volunteer Infantry Regiment (Colored). So, some southern states would have regiments in both the Confederate and Union armies. Further confusing the issue, most of the Black regiments, including Montgomery's, would later in the war be redesignated as part of the U.S. Colored Troops.

The 2nd SC was the second Black regiment from South Carolina because the first had been raised in the latter part of 1862—and was commanded by Thomas Wentworth Higginson. The two friends and abolitionist comrades were now both colonels in the U.S. Army, with Higginson in the senior role.

Montgomery quickly discovered that Higginson's 1st SC regiment had already recruited most of the immediately available South Carolinians. But Hunter was not averse to going beyond the War Department directive, and Montgomery was soon installed on the USS *Cosmopolitan* bringing in recruits along the coast from as far as the southern tip of Florida, Key West. His regiment remained well under full strength, however.[3] It had 123 men in camp on Port Royal Island, south of Beaufort, on February 23, according to Higginson's account, and fewer than 150 when it went into action in early March. Montgomery and Higginson served under Brigadier General Rufus Saxton who, like Hunter, was a regular Army officer sympathetic to abolitionism. Saxton had been ordered the previous August by U.S. Secretary of War Edwin Stanton to raise regiments of "colored" troops in South Carolina.

In late January, Higginson led a three-ship expedition about 25 miles up the St. Marys River, which marks the boundary between Georgia and Florida, and brought back needed building materials and other supplies. His entry point was Fernandina Beach. A few miles south of there in northeastern Florida is the port of Jacksonville, where the wide St. Johns River provides a better pathway southward into the interior. Jacksonville was the main focus of Civil War activity in the state. It changed hands several times, including twice in 1862 before Montgomery arrived in the Department of the South.

Higginson was not the only friend to be found in Beaufort and nearby places such as Port Royal. That excellent harbor, in addition to serving as headquarters for the Navy's South Atlantic Blockading Squadron, gave its name to the budding Port Royal Experiment, in which "the region became the cradle of South Carolina's first Black schools and free labor initiatives."[4] It was becoming the national center of efforts to free, organize, and educate African-Americans.

Also there was Harriet Tubman, whom Montgomery had probably met in 1860 on his trip to the Northeast. Tubman and Montgomery were both well known as abolitionists who even before the war had moved beyond words to action by liberating enslaved people. They were both fierce Christians (in contrast to the more sedate Unitarian Higginson), which was a key part of their commitment to the emancipationist cause. Tubman, as she grew into a young woman, had "experienced an intensification of her Christian faith, a deep and abiding spiritual foundation that remained with her throughout her life."[5] Montgomery and Tubman also had been friends and comrades of the most famous and warlike Christian abolitionist in America, John Brown.

Brown, who was hanged before the war broke out, had dubbed her "General Tubman," and now she was traveling regularly on U.S. warships by virtue of passes issued to her by actual generals of the U.S. Army. Her functions ranged from senior intelligence operative to nurse and laundress, and her contacts from the highest to the humblest. So, it was to be expected that she and Montgomery would seek each other out very soon after his arrival in South Carolina and become firm allies.

Tubman became famous in the Underground Railroad in the decade preceding the Civil War, helping slaves escape captivity and leading them to freedom. Her version of Christian belief and practice, as with Montgomery and Brown, had some of the harder side of the biblical Old Testament about it. Tubman was known as "the Moses of her people," which was the subtitle of her first biography, by Sarah Bradford, written and revised while its subject was still alive.

Tubman, like Montgomery, was sometimes prepared to be ruthless. Once when leading north a party of escaped slaves (according to a modern biographer's version of an incident that Bradford relates), a man in the group "said he was going to turn around and take his chances back on the plantation. Tubman warned that he could not leave. It would compromise the entire operation. He would have to stay with the group—to which he had agreed at the outset. The other fugitives tried to coax him to keep on going. But when it was time to move forward, he refused." Tubman pointed a revolver at his head, telling him to "move or die."[6] He moved, and with the rest of the party went on to Canada and freedom. (It should be noted that there is no evidence of Tubman actually using her weapon against an escaped slave, which, given the increasingly ruthless nature of the conflict around slavery, redounds to her credit.)

Despite her fame—or notoriety, as the Confederates saw it—Tubman was able to work undercover and, according to a 20th-century account:

> deceive the enemy during her missions. Dark complexioned, short and stooped, with a bandanna wrapped around her head, she resembled a typical plantation woman. General Rufus Saxton, in charge of volunteers, wrote that she "made many a raid inside the enemy's lines, displaying remarkable courage, zeal and fidelity."[7]

While Tubman did go on dangerous raids, including up the Combahee River with Montgomery, her most important intelligence function was as an analyst, organizer and planner, gathering information from escaped slaves and other African-American scouts and agents, and communicating it to senior Union officers.

Harriet Tubman, photographed in 1868 by Benjamin Powelson in Auburn, New York. (Library of Congress)

Montgomery's lack of prejudice enabled him to take Tubman seriously, to see what he and she had in common. He came to understand that she could serve their mutual cause not only as a source of guidance and information, but that they could be fellow fighters for freedom—which they would become in early June on a very successful military mission up the Combahee.

Like Montgomery, Tubman had pulled political strings to get herself into the Civil War. She was sent South in May 1862 by Massachusetts Gov. John Andrew, "to act as spy and scout for our armies, and, if need be, to act as hospital nurse, in short, to be ready to give any required service to the Union cause."[8]

She was part of the "Port Royal Experiment," tending to and training African-Americans in the vicinity of Beaufort. Nor was she the only woman so engaged. A more famous nurse, Clara Barton, arrived in April, and women schoolteachers were there, too, determined to uplift the freed slaves.

Many Black soldiers learned to read and write. Almost all men from the 1st North Carolina, later to serve bravely under Montgomery at Olustee, learned to a greater or lesser extent, according to Frances Beecher, wife of its colonel, James C. Beecher, when the regiment was formed: "Whenever they had a spare moment, out would come a spelling-book or a primer or Testament, and you would often see a group of heads around one book."[9] (Colonel Beecher was half-brother to Harriet Beecher Stowe.)

Tubman was not qualified to teach school but helped train freed women in productive work such as nursing, cooking, and laundry. She was also a key source of military intelligence for Montgomery and his superiors, encouraging them to return to and go beyond Jacksonville, Florida, and to expect freed slaves there to volunteer to join the U.S. Army.[10] (Higginson's January foray up the St. Marys River, while in other ways successful, had not brought in many recruits.)[11] Montgomery was "well known" to Tubman and "trusted as one of John Brown's men."[12]

Later that summer, after Hunter was replaced by Brigadier-General Quincy Gillmore, Montgomery wrote to the new commander: "I wish to commend to your attention, Mrs. Harriet Tubman, a most remarkable woman, and invaluable as a scout. I have been acquainted with her character and actions for several years."[13] This letter is evidence that Tubman and Montgomery did meet on his trip East in 1860.

As Hunter conferred with his senior officers, including Higginson and Montgomery, he decided on a new, somewhat larger, and considerably more ambitious expedition to Florida. As a result, on March 5, 1863, Saxton ordered Higginson (Montgomery would be second-in-command) on a mission to recapture Jacksonville and proceed up the St. Johns River. They were "to carry the proclamation of freedom to the enslaved; to call all loyal men into the service of the United States; to occupy as much of the State of Florida as possible"—which would not be much, since they brought with them fewer than one thousand soldiers.[14]

Montgomery had only about 120 men in the 2nd SC, and, incredibly, the Army had not up to this point even provided them with weapons. This deficiency was now finally remedied *en route* to Florida aboard the USS *Burnside*, on which they were issued muskets and ammunition. "Montgomery ordered that they be given some quick instruction in handling and loading the weapons and then allowed them to fire a few practice rounds from the ship's deck. This might be all the musketry training they would have before going up against the enemy ..."[15]

The Black troops, accompanied by one Navy and one Army gunboat (another Navy ship had temporarily gone aground downriver) surprised and swiftly occupied Jacksonville on the morning of March 10. According to Higginson's account,

> ... by previous agreement, I steamed to an upper pier of the town, Colonel Montgomery to a lower one; the little boat-howitzers were run out upon the wharves, and presently to the angles of the chief streets; and the pretty town was our own without a shot.[16]

William L. Apthorp, a captain in Montgomery's regiment, said resistance had been anticipated, but "We found everything quiet. A few mountain pickets skedaddled and a few secesh ladies who came down to welcome us, seeing the dusky hue of our men, followed the example of the pickets."[17]

Montgomery went with his men to set up a defensive line on the outskirts of Jacksonville. The next day, when he was back in town conferring with Higginson, the 2nd SC came under attack from about 200 rebel cavalry. Apthorp said:

> We waited there for fire and received it, … One man fell severely wounded. … Our men returned the fire with some effect, [then fell back. Moving forward again, the regiment found themselves outnumbered by Confederate infantry. Another retreat brought them near the harbor where Union gunboats could engage in the skirmish, and] the repulse began by us was turned by a few shell and shrapnel into a rout [of the rebels. Apthorp reckoned this encounter taught the Confederates] that a black man could stand up and pull a trigger and that a bullet from his rifle was as deadly a thing to receive as if a white man had fired it.[18] [They were probably using rifled muskets.]

Montgomery arrived as the rebel infantry were advancing. According to a modern historian:

> With disaster looming, Montgomery suddenly appeared. He had heard the gunfire and come out to investigate. He called to the fleeing men of the 2nd. They rallied around him and once more began to return the enemy's fire, resolutely, if not expertly, loading, aiming, and firing as they had been taught to do just three days ago. Montgomery's presence steadied them, even when at one point he dropped flat on the ground to take cover as the Rebels loosed a heavy volley. … Two men of the 2nd had been wounded, and one, Private Bristol Walker of Company A, had been killed. [The retreating Confederates took away their fallen comrades, so the number of their killed and wounded is uncertain] … but the soldiers of the 2nd were sure they had inflicted more than a dozen casualties.[19]

The detail about Montgomery dropping to the ground is telling. He was certainly courageous, but that did not to his mind involve unnecessary exposure to fire, which helped him—and perhaps his two eldest sons when they joined him in the Army—survive the war unscathed. But that style of warfare did not necessarily impress more traditionally trained officers.

Higginson consolidated his position in Jacksonville, expanding the picket lines and building two forts named after their regimental commanders. Then he deputed Montgomery to raid up the St. Johns River, which upstream goes south—at a width of about four miles[20]—into the Florida interior:

> In Colonel Montgomery's hands," Higginson recalled, "these up-river raids reached the dignity of a fine art. His conceptions of foraging were rather more Western and liberal than mine, and on these excursions he fully indemnified

> himself for any undue abstinence demanded of him when in camp. I remember being on the wharf, with some naval officers, when he came down from his first trip. The steamer seemed an animated hen-coop. Live poultry hung from the foremast shrouds, dead ones from the mainmast, geese hissed from the binnacle, a pig paced the quarter-deck, and a duck's wings were seen fluttering ...[21]

The St. Johns was Montgomery's introduction to the opportunities presented by the lush, green, flat river deltas of the deep South—a very different landscape from southern Kansas and Missouri. In Florida, South Carolina, and Georgia, he would negotiate his way upstream through their maze of estuaries, swamps, shoals, and some military defenses to targets which presented themselves—or which agents like Tubman had told him about.

His "several major raids"[22] on the St. Johns River were sanctioned, within limits, and these limits, as Montgomery now acknowledged, included recognizing the rights of prisoners. But he was now free to lead slaves into freedom, and recruit some of them into the Army. This was a nightmare for Southern plantation owners, and those in Florida quickly became aware of the threat he represented and withdrew away from the river into the interior, taking their most valuable slaves with them. This reduced the opportunity for recruiting, and Montgomery only got about 30 new soldiers from Florida.[23]

When he was in Jacksonville, Montgomery helped to guard, fortify and defend the place. There was minor skirmishing on the outskirts, and Hunter sent in two White regiments of reinforcements. Higginson described Montgomery in a journal entry as "splendid, but impulsive & changeable." The two colonels remained on good terms throughout this Florida campaign, although their relationship would deteriorate after they returned to South Carolina.

Apthorp, unlike Higginson, unambiguously supported Montgomery's hard-war tactics, stressing the importance of economic warfare, to deny the rebels "surplus resources for the support of an army. The alternative choices of capitulation or starvation will soon stare them in the face, and the victor can dictate terms."[24] It is undeniable that this strategy—when adopted by the highest levels of the Union's military establishment—did contribute to the ultimate defeat of the Confederacy.

Montgomery led one raid upriver on March 14, and another three days later. The March 17 raid, Apthorp said, stopped at the "plantation of a Colonel Bryant in the Rebel service," who was captured along with much of his livestock. The soldiers considered capturing Mrs. Bryant, too, after she stated how "she despised and abhorred them. She hoped every one of them would go to hell that they would sink down into the bottomless pit." But the men obeyed orders to leave her behind.[25]

On March 25 Montgomery led a longer expedition, planned for several days with a march into the interior of Florida. It went "seventy-five miles up the St. Johns to Palatka and returning laden with wagons, mules, cotton, forage, freed slaves, and fifteen prisoners."[26] One prisoner, a lieutenant, escaped. Higginson says there were 13 prisoners, whom Montgomery, leading a landing party, found sleeping.

> [He] … took all their guns then shook one on the shoulder to wake him. "What is it?" quoth the sleeper. "You are prisoners" said Montgomery. "No," said the man explaining, "we belong to Westcott's company" (a noted guerrilla force). "Yes" said Montgomery, "*but we don't*." So they were all taken, with all their horses and arms."
>
> [The lieutenant, however], "… escaped by aid of a crowd of female friends who came to take farewell. He crawled away behind their skirts, then ran & would not stop though Montgomery raised his pistol. But M wouldn't shoot, for he said he couldn't kill him in his sister's presence—a very characteristic touch. His revolver is unerring—the other day he shot an alligator in the eye, the only part visible." [A 21st-century historian says there were 15 prisoners, minus the escaped lieutenant].[27]

Palatka is where the very wide river bends, then narrows some distance upstream, and the forest looks like a jungle to northern eyes. Montgomery had with him about 120 men from his regiment along with some from the 1st SC.[28] The purpose was exploring as well as raiding, he and Higginson having in mind the establishment of military posts on the river. But Confederate resistance stiffened at Palatka on March 27, after Montgomery landed troops ashore at several points. Two of his men, Lt. Col. Liberty Billings and a Black private, John Quincy, were wounded. They were both from the First South Carolina. Quincy, a lay preacher, had family enslaved near Palatka, and was about to set off on an expedition with Billings and other soldiers aiming to look for and liberate them.

He would die from his wound back in the Beaufort contraband hospital on April 16.[29]

The skirmish at Palatka called off the search for Quincy's family, but not the whole mission. It was later that night of the 27th to 28th that Montgomery captured the rebel prisoners. But the next morning, of the 28th, before he could proceed further, he was precipitately recalled by Higginson, who had sent the *John Adams* upriver to find him.[30] The reason was an order from Hunter immediately withdrawing the whole federal force from Florida, pulling it back to the Sea Islands. Jacksonville, for the fourth time, was being abandoned to the Confederates. Higginson was upset at the order to withdraw, and Montgomery very likely shared in a general indignation at it.

Still, Lincoln had been paying attention to this somewhat obscure campaign, telling Hunter "I am glad to see the accounts of your colored force at Jacksonville. … It is important to the enemy that such a force shall not take shape and grow and thrive in the South, and in precisely the same proportion it is important to us that they shall."[31] They were laying the groundwork of the large-scale recruitment of Black soldiers, which would help win the war. In fact, the good performance of the two Black regiments in Florida may have persuaded Lincoln in late March to commit to raising many more.[32] And Montgomery's deep penetration of the Florida interior would prompt further Union efforts along these lines, in which he himself would often participate in his continued service in the Department of the South.

The military aims of these early expeditions included securing supplies for the Union occupation of the Sea Islands. A year later, when the U.S. Army returned to northern Florida in much greater force for what became the Olustee campaign, the strategic goal was more to prevent Confederate supplies such as cattle being sent north out of Florida to feed the main rebel armies. But even in March 1863, the Union campaign was disrupting the Confederate supply chain and engaging enemy troops, and so can be plausibly seen as contributing to the war effort in more important spheres of operations.

Hunter, however, had changed strategy in the course of March, fearful that it was too risky to establish a permanent outpost in Florida. Higginson

Thomas Wentworth Higginson in later life. A prewar abolitionist ally, he was Montgomery's military commander in the 1863 Florida campaign. (Photo by Notman, Boston. Library of Congress)

partly blamed Hunter's chief of staff, Brigadier General Truman Seymour, whom he did not regard as sympathetic to the abolitionist cause. Hunter's attention was also directed in the opposite direction, north, to the much closer and more important target of Charleston, South Carolina, where the Confederacy had been born and the home of its most extreme supporters. Capturing Charleston was the key but ever-elusive objective of the Department of the South, as far as most political and military leaders in Washington were concerned. But a major naval attack on the heavily fortified Charleston harbor failed on April 7.

Montgomery's expedition returned to Jacksonville from Palatka on March 28. Much of Jacksonville was burned during the evacuation the next day, but it was apparently done by some of the White reinforcements, members of the 8th Maine and 6th Connecticut, not the Black troops in Higginson's and Montgomery's regiments. After being delayed by a storm, Higginson's little army returned to South Carolina a few days later. The Confederate prisoners captured by Montgomery's men came with them, impressing some of the White soldiers in Beaufort and raising their estimation of Black troops.[33]

Regarding the subsequent coolness between Higginson and Montgomery, it seems the result of the former regarding the latter as too undisciplined and unwilling to follow strict military rules. The deterioration in their relationship can be seen in Higginson's *Journal*, which, unlike his 1870 book *Army Life in a Back Regiment*, was not published until many years after his death.

Higginson wrote in May:

> [Montgomery] … is very ambitious, and impatient constitutionally in regard to system and order, for which I am rather a stickler. Our whole method as to discipline is so different that perhaps we are as well apart. In carrying on war we should not differ much, except that my plans would be more tenaciously adhered to, less flexible …. As it is, he [Montgomery] will never rise above a brigand. His hatred of control makes it hard for him to believe that a regiment which is well drilled can be fit for action. Whereas I believe that want of self-control will demoralize our men and want of drill will unfit them for regular warfare when needed. He thinks me strait-laced and red-tapish—I think him fitter to command a hundred men than a thousand …. [Not sharing Higginson's own] notions of civilized warfare. He had one of his men shot without trial, the other day, for desertion, & was about to shoot two more when Dr. [Seth] Rogers' wonderful power of influence made him change his plan. Yet he is not a harsh or cruel man, but a singular mixture of fanaticism, vanity, and genius.[34]

Clearly, there is something to Higginson's criticism, but it is notable that even at his most critical, his last word of description for Montgomery is "genius." Montgomery's lack of discipline could at times (*i.e.* at Morristown) amount to something even worse than harshness or mere cruelty, and many of his fellow soldiers and regular Army officers—with whom the upper-class Higginson increasingly found common cause—regarded him as difficult to deal with. Yet Montgomery was learning to restrain his worst instincts, and in this period was also devising and executing the spectacularly successful Combahee River raid. And unlike the more senior Higginson, he was advancing to brigade command, in which he would prove a capable combat leader. Montgomery regarded

Higginson as too refined and conventional to be an effective warrior—and there is something to his view, too.

One curious contrast between the two men is that they both happened to befriend women who would become much more famous than they. Higginson became the first editor of the reclusive poet Emily Dickinson. Montgomery was the champion and ally of the African-American freedom fighter Harriet Tubman.

After returning from the Jacksonville expedition, Montgomery's unconventional approach drew him into even closer consultation with Tubman, whom some of his fellow officers would not have regarded as a fit person to give military advice or to serve alongside soldiers on active duty. However, the commanding general, Hunter, was in touch with her and sympathetic to the abolitionist cause, and Montgomery had Tubman's confidence more than any other officer. The three of them planned new raids up rivers into the interior. There is some evidence that Montgomery led a raid in early May up the Ashepoo River in South Carolina, northwest of Beaufort and closer to Charleston, which freed a number of slaves.[35]

But a bigger, more spectacular raid to free many more slaves was being planned up the nearby Combahee River into the Confederate heartland of "low country" South Carolina, considerably west of Charleston in an area where plantations continued to be operated, and some planters felt relatively safe from such attacks. The objective, in addition to liberating slaves and finding among them potential recruits for the Army, was to "take up the torpedoes [mines] placed by the rebels in the river, to destroy railroads and bridges, and to cut off supplies from [*i.e.* to] the rebel troops." Tubman would personally accompany the mission, "with several men under her."[36] Prior to the raid, she also had overseen African-American "scouts familiar with the interior," with "considerable knowledge as to the location of supplies and the disposition of the Negroes in the region."[37] Those scouts, including Walter Plowden, told Tubman in May that the Confederates had withdrawn troops and guns since the last major Union scouting expedition in February.

The location of torpedoes and channels in the river would obviously have been useful information. Montgomery's gunboats did avoid any mines on the expedition from June 1 to 3, guided by Plowden, Tubman "and two of her pilots, Charles Simmons and Samuel Hayward, both of whom were familiar with the area."[38] Nevertheless, one of the transports went aground not long after leaving Beaufort, and had to be left behind. The soldiers were transferred to the other two boats, which would put a physical limit on the raid's great success: There would not be room for all the enslaved people who wanted to escape.

The raid up to Combahee Ferry and beyond, almost 50 miles west of Charleston, was a courageous venture for Tubman, placing herself at risk of death in battle, or in the event of capture being murdered, executed, or sold back into slavery. There is now a historical marker there, along with a bridge named after her which brings Route 17 east across the swirling Combahee River *en route* to the city.

This was not the first time she had risked all during the war. It was not just the scouts she directed who gathered intelligence for Montgomery and Hunter, but she herself "was often sent into the rebel lines as a spy, and brought back valuable information"[39]—although there is no direct evidence of her playing that role before the Combahee expedition.

The Black soldiers and White officers of Montgomery's regiment faced similar or worse risks, of which they were aware. A proclamation issued by Confederate President Davis on December 24, 1862, had started off by denouncing the Union general Benjamin Butler as "a felon deserving of capital punishment," and went to threaten similar drastic punishment against "armed slaves in insurrection" and their officers, which meant Montgomery's entire regiment and their civilian allies like Tubman.

The policy was formalized on May 1, 1863, by a resolution of the Confederate Congress, signed by Davis. Captured Black troops were to be dealt with by state law, which meant being returned to slavery or possibly executed. The latter threat was explicitly applied to their White officers. Part of the resolution said:

> That every white person, being a commissioned officer, or acting as such, who, during the present war, shall command negroes or mulattoes in arms against the confederate States, or who shall arm, train, organize, or prepare negroes or mulattoes for military service against the confederate States, or who shall voluntarily aid negroes or mulattoes in any military enterprise, attack, or conflict

> in such service, shall be deemed as inciting servile insurrection, and shall, if captured, be put to death, or be otherwise punished at the discretion of the court.[40]

In Washington, meanwhile, the Lincoln administration was following the way set out by leaders like Montgomery, Fremont, Hunter, and Frederick Douglass, and in May established a national system of raising Black regiments to be known as United States Colored Troops. Almost 200,000 African-Americans would end up serving in the U.S. Army or Navy, with almost 40,000 losing their lives, mostly from disease.[41]

Montgomery, in consultation with Hunter, was now prepared to be more destructive of property held by rebels—and had no inhibitions whatsoever about freeing their "property" of enslaved labor. This was in part economic warfare, a policy designed by Hunter to drive Confederate supporters inland, leaving their most productive fields and workshops untended. The planters now brought their slaves with them, but Montgomery was prepared to follow them deep behind enemy lines.

While Montgomery might burn buildings and crops, he did not respond in kind to the explicit Confederate policy which threatened his own and his fellow soldiers' lives if they were captured. He did not revert to the ruthlessness of the Kansas-Missouri border war. He no longer executed prisoners.

Montgomery made a June 3 report to Hunter about the Combahee River raid but it is apparently lost—at least not included in the Official Records.[42] According to a 21st-century historian:

> Montgomery's plans were simple and effective. At every landing, his troops would disembark, push back any Confederates and then hold the area. Being on a peninsula, he had little to fear from a flanking movement of the Confederates. … With each stop, the Union forces would open a new front … Once Montgomery's objective had been reached and the destruction done, [he] would pull back downriver, removing his men and the fleeing slaves as he went. The men on shore would slowly pull back to the landings, preventing the Confederates from bringing up any effective artillery. The overall strategy was to make a lightning-fast strike upriver, throw the Confederates into confusion and then, before an effective counterstrike could be made, pull off out of reach of the Confederates.[43]

Hunter on the same day sent a copy of Montgomery's lost report to Stanton, and paraphrased it in his own message:

> … Colonel Montgomery, with 300 men of his regiment and a section of the Third Rhode Island Battery … penetrated the country of the enemy 25 miles, destroyed a pontoon bridge across the Combahee River, together with a vast amount of cotton, rice and other property, and brought away with him 725 slaves and some five horses. … Colonel Montgomery with his forces will repeat his incursions as rapidly as possible in different directions, injuring the enemy all he can and carrying away their slaves, thus rapidly filling up the South Carolina regiments in the department, of which there are now four.

Actually Hunter's—or Montgomery's—initial estimate of the liberated slaves was on the low side, and the real number exceeded 750. Tubman said it was 756, Higginson (in a June 10 letter to his mother) 800, and Apthorp more than 800.

Hunter's description of Montgomery's activities came too late to convince Stanton that he was being a sufficiently aggressive departmental commander, and later that very same day of June 3 he was relieved and ordered to report to Washington after handing over the command upon the arrival of his designated replacement, Brigadier General Quincy Gillmore. Abolitionists had been hoping—unrealistically—that Higginson or Montgomery would be promoted to succeed Hunter, while lobbying against Seymour, whom they saw as sympathetic to slave-owners or even "a strong proslavery man," and hostile to the use of Black troops.[44] Instead, the young outsider Gillmore was brought in. A regular who graduated first in his West Point class, he was an expert gunner. As a captain in 1862, his direction of artillery played a key role in the capture of Fort Pulaski, Georgia, which closed Savannah to blockade runners. From then on, his promotion was swift. By 1863, he was a brigadier general in Kentucky, where in his first independent command on March 31 he won a cavalry skirmish at Somerset.

There was some Confederate resistance to the Combahee River raid, but no casualties from Montgomery's force. The most detailed extant military report comes from the Confederate side, an inspector of cavalry named Captain John F. Lay. He reported on June 24 that "Major Emanuel, with his squadron of cavalry" and a "company of light artillery" had been stationed in the area for defensive purposes, after the Confederates received intelligence about a raid being planned. Possibly the earlier Ashepoo River raid had alerted them about what to expect. But despite the advance warnings, the Confederate military proved no match for the well planned and executed operation. As Montgomery's troops landed at various points, one handful of outnumbered Confederates retreated. Others exchanged fire with the Union soldiers but devoted more energy to trying to prevent fleeing slaves from joining Montgomery's boat. They used dogs for this purpose, and a Confederate lieutenant apparently killed "a negro girl … he shot her down." Montgomery's soldiers then fired on the lieutenant from a boat, but without hitting him. (If Montgomery did not witness this action, it would have been reported to him—and probably to Tubman, too, if she did not see it.) Then a party of Union soldiers were confined to a mill by Confederate small-arms fire, but before the rebels could bring up an artillery piece Montgomery's men were rescued by gunboats.

When Emanuel was bringing up artillery to fire on one of the boats, "he was surrounded by the enemy in ambush on both sides of the road, delivering a cross-fire" and mortally wounding one Confederate. Emanuel retreated. Lay's report is critical of Emanuel's defense for,

> allowing a parcel of negro wretches, calling themselves soldiers, with a few degraded whites, to march unmolested, with the incendiary torch, to rob, destroy, and burn a large section of country. … it is my duty to report the results of this raid as mortifying and humiliating to our arms … This raid by a mixed party of blacks and degraded whites seems to have been designed only for plunder, robbery, and destruction of private property; in carrying it out they have disregarded all rules of civilized war, and have acted more as fiends than human beings. Fortunately the planters had removed their families, who thus avoided outrage and insult. The enemy seem to have been well posted as to the character and capacity of our troops and their small chance of encountering opposition, and to have been well guided by persons thoroughly acquainted with the river and the country. Their success was complete … They also successfully carried off from 700 to 800 slaves of every age and sex.

In the aftermath of Montgomery's operation, the Confederates sent reinforcements to the area.[45]

This account, while obviously not the way Montgomery or Tubman saw things, is nonetheless revealing. No allegation was made that the Union troops attacked civilians or killed anyone except one Confederate soldier in combat. The report acknowledged without embarrassment that the Confederate troops attacked the fleeing slaves, apparently killing one girl. The extravagant denunciations of the Union tactics appear to be not so much about what they did, burning buildings and food supplies, for example, as to who was doing it, i.e. Black troops commanded by "degraded" White officers. If the Confederates had known Tubman was aboard one of the gunboats, that use of a woman on a combat operation would no doubt have confirmed them in their contempt, yet they felt no shame about killing a young female civilian who was running away. In such an atmosphere, it is perhaps unsurprising that Montgomery's attitude toward destruction of rebel property did not soften in the immediate future. The Confederate version does not confirm that the raid destroyed explicitly military supplies such as mines, guns, and ammunition, which is claimed in some Union-friendly accounts.[46] But Montgomery regarded all stores including food as potential supplies for the Confederate army defending Charleston and the rest of the South.

Montgomery stood alongside Tubman in the lead boat, the USS *John Adams*, "with Walter Plowden, the local scout who helped direct the ships around the mines. … Montgomery and his small force made their way to the plantations where Tubman and her scouts had identified Confederate warehouses and stockpiles of rice and cotton."[47] Some Union troops landed on the roads to Ashepoo while the rest continued upriver. As most of the Confederate soldiers were driven off or withdrew, a larger number of slaves approached Montgomery's men and were informed about what was going on and invited to board the boats for freedom. Whistles were blown from the boats for the same purpose. "Overseers, plantation owners, and managers tried in vain to keep the slaves from running away; though they brandished whips, guns, and pistols, their threats of punishment and even death were almost useless against the mass desertion. Several slaves were killed or wounded, however, by rebel soldiers and others."[48]

According to Apthorp, the burning and destruction had an immediate and positive military effect:

> Smoke soon appeared in the direction of Colleton. Smoke rose also in our rear, and for an extent of fifteen miles along the river the country was in flames. Aside from other considerations this was our only course of safety. The rebel force,

> consisting mainly of artillery and cavalry and only a few miles distant, greatly outnumbered us, but seeing such an extent of country occupied and judging our strength from our audacity they thought the whole force of the Southern Department was upon them and [they] sat still in astonishment and indecision. …
>
> That part of our men thrown out farthest up the river was attacked, but repulsed their assailants without loss to themselves, though at least one of the enemy's saddles was emptied. One contraband was killed while crossing the fire of both parties on his way to the boat. … Meanwhile we heard the guns of the *John Adams* and saw by the columns of black smoke the party at Colleton had not been idle.

The troops had destroyed a "place with a large amount of property valuable to the rebels, and [burned] a pontoon bridge across the river. We had a sharp skirmish with the enemy but repulsed them, killing a few."[49] The Navy ships also fired on the rebels.

The raid was, like Montgomery's other operations in this theater, largely an African-American affair. While he and other officers were White, the

The Combahee River raid, from *Harper's Weekly*, 1863. (Library of Congress)

vast majority of the Union soldiers were Black, as were civilian scouts like Tubman and Plowden. Tubman, as quoted by her 19th-century biographer, gave the most detailed account of how the slaves reacted.

> [She] describes in the most graphic manner the appearance of the plantations as they passed up the river; the frightened negroes leaving their work and taking to the woods, at sight of the gun-boats; then coming to peer out like startled deer, and scudding way like the wind at the sound of the steam-whistle. … But the word was passed along by the mysterious telegraphic communication existing among these simple people, that these were "Lincoln's gun-boats come to set them free." In vain, then, the drivers used their whips in their efforts to hurry the poor creatures back to their quarters; they all turned and ran for the gun-boats. They came down every road, across every field, just as they had left their work and their cabins; women with children clinging around their necks, hanging to their dresses, running behind, all making at full speed for "Lincoln's gun-boats." Eight hundred poor wretches at one time crowded the banks, with their hands extended toward their deliverers, and they were all taken off upon the gun-boats, and carried down to Beaufort.[50]

Sometimes Tubman's role in working with Union forces had been to reassure African-Americans that they would be safe with them, and "quiet the doubts and silence the fears of these slaves regarding stories they had heard about the 'Yankees' and what they would do to the Negroes in the South; and through her efforts, many slaves were led to safety within the Union lines."[51] By this time on the Combahee raid, however, while Tubman's calming influence remained valuable, Montgomery's force and the Blacks they were trying to rescue had the opposite problem, which they could not entirely overcome.

A Philadelphia *Inquirer* newspaperman who accompanied the raid reported that there was not room enough on the boats for all who wanted to come aboard.

> This was the saddest sight of the whole expedition—so many souls within the sight of freedom and yet unable to attain it. But the transports were filled to their utmost capacity; they looked more like slavers than the harbingers of liberty; and as they turned away from the river-bank, and started homeward bound, moist eyes were on those decks, for they saw in the distance those whom a cruel fate had left behind. The song of liberty floated upon the river, but the wail of despair went up from the dismal shore. … This expedition reflects great credit upon Col. Montgomery and the men of his command. He has destroyed

> property of the enemy estimated at a million of dollars, proved himself a capable commander, and that the negro troops can be made efficient soldiers. He has also provided his regiment with two additional companies, deprived the rebels of seven hundred and twenty-seven negroes, and accomplished the most successful raid in this department.[52]

It would remain the most successful raid in the Department of the South for the duration of the war.

Tubman described a scene of jubilation, song, and laughter, including Montgomery who called out to her by the name "Moses"—which she had earned years before on the Underground Railroad—as rowboats took the slaves to the gunboats. Meanwhile, "The masters fled; houses and barns and railroad bridges were burned, tracks torn up, torpedoes destroyed, and the object of the expedition was fully accomplished."[53] Despite some wishful modern depictions, as at the end of the 2019 film *Harriet*, of an armed, disembarked Tubman leading soldiers while carrying and preparing to fire a rifle, there is no evidence that actually happened. That's a pity, because Tubman's life was quite sufficiently dramatic and heroic not to require such mythologizing embellishment. The movie, like *Glory* before it, has many positive elements, but its Combahee River scene at the end is not accurate historical representation. In one way though, it marks an improvement. While *Glory* maligned Montgomery, *Harriet* merely fails to mention him.

Montgomery and Tubman both addressed the troops and the freed slaves during a gospel-singing service at a Baptist church upon their return to Beaufort. Most of the Combahee refugees soon moved to what was called Montgomery Hill in Port Royal, and about 150 joined the U.S. Army—most of them in his 2nd South Carolina Infantry.

Tubman's involvement in this action was highly irregular, and it showed how Montgomery's impatience with military formalities could sometimes have positive, rather than negative results. The number of enslaved people freed on this raid was at least twice and probably several times as many as the total number Tubman had brought to freedom on the Underground Railroad before the war.

Tubman dictated a letter about the raid to Franklin Sanborn:

> if he didn't think we colored people are entitled to some credit for that exploit, under the lead of the brave Colonel Montgomery? We weakened the rebels somewhat on the Combahee River, by taking and bringing away seven hundred and fifty-six head of their most valuable live stock, known up in your region as contrabands, and this, too, without the loss of a single life on our part, though we had good reason to believe that a number of rebels bit the dust.[54]

Sanborn wrote later that Higginson was frustrated with Tubman as well as with Montgomery, and for much the same reasons. She performed some of "her best service in S. Carolina; but her direct way of interpreting orders, and Montgomery's soldierly way of acting under general orders, offended the more fastidious Col. Higginson, and led to censures by him of both Montgomery and Harriet."[55]

This tiny (under five feet), illiterate, epileptic—the result of a head injury inflicted by an overseer in her youth—middle-aged, dark-skinned Black woman, born, raised, and physically abused in slavery, provided valuable intelligence on multiple occasions to Montgomery and other Union officers, risking her own life and freedom. She also served additional roles through most of the war to assist Union soldiers and freed slaves, primarily as a nurse but also as laundress, cook, practical teacher, and mentor. After a leave and a temporary return to the North in the late fall of 1863, Tubman may or may not have accompanied Montgomery on the Union expedition to Florida in early 1864.[56] Like him, she would return home from South Carolina that year, but also like him, would return to national service, speaking to African-American troops and then becoming matron of the Colored Hospital at Fortress Monroe, Virginia, near the end of the war. Montgomery's friendship and respect for Tubman show his ability to overcome the prejudices of the time in service of their common cause.

Northern abolitionists and newspapers rejoiced at the success of the Combahee raid. Even Higginson called it "a most brilliant success," though adding that he did not favor "burning private houses."[57]

Higginson and other critics had a point. Montgomery may have been following Hunter's orders in destroying buildings on four plantations (including a large private library), burning and flooding crops, but some who disapproved saw him as carrying out the harsh orders remorselessly, even gleefully.[58] That was in part because South Carolina was seen by many Unionists as the heart of secession and slavery, where White civilians as well as soldiers were guilty of starting the war. That's the way Sherman's soldiers treated it when they entered the state almost two years later. Montgomery, however, would soon do worse in Georgia.

It's true that his destruction of property cannot be weighed in the same judgment scale as enslaving human beings. Nor was it as bad as the execution of prisoners earlier in his career. Nor were any of his actions in the war worse than those done by superior officers such as Sheridan. Nonetheless, amid the glorious success of the Combahee raid there was a hint of the moral ambiguity that attaches to all warfare and most human lives.

That eventful June 3, when Montgomery and Tubman returned from the Combahee River and General Hunter was given notice he was being relieved, was also the day the 54th Massachusetts Volunteer Infantry arrived at the Union base in Beaufort. Like Montgomery's 2nd South Carolina and other African-American regiments, the 54th was commanded by White officers. Montgomery and his men attended a welcoming ceremony, at which he was presented with a regimental flag for the 2nd South Carolina made by a lady in Connecticut. Accepting on behalf of his troops, he told them the now raised flag symbolized the fact:

> that you have a country and a home. … The ground over which you march, the fields on which you fight are to be your own. … You are to be as free as the winds of Heaven that now kiss these ample folds. But all depends upon your courage, your obedience to orders, and your constancy in the work of crushing this rebellion.[59]

The 54th Massachusetts was led by the young Boston Brahmin Col. Robert G. Shaw, whose commission was of later date than Montgomery's. Accordingly, and in light of the recent success of the 2nd SC, Hunter placed Shaw under Montgomery's command, which was then stationed about a hundred miles south at St. Simon's Island, Georgia.

Luis Emilio was a captain of the 54th who was aged only 18, seven years younger than Shaw and 30 younger than the new brigade commander. Emilio, who wrote a postwar memoir of the regiment, describes Montgomery at this time as "a man of austere bearing, cool, deliberate, and of proved courage. In personal appearance he was tall, spare, rather bowed, with gentle voice and quiet manner."[60]

He was also very busy, despite (or perhaps because of) Hunter's impending departure. On June 6, Montgomery led the 2nd South Carolina on "an expedition from St. Simon's up the Turtle River to Brunswick and beyond, and destroyed a span of the railroad bridge over Buffalo Creek."[61] That was a few miles west of Brunswick, Georgia, which is close to St. Simon's. He planned his next inland raid a little to the north, but still within Georgia, at Darien, on the Altamaha River.

Before he set off, and shortly before Hunter handed over the reins to Gillmore, the commanding general sent a message to Montgomery clarifying the rules of engagement under which he was to operate.

Hunter's June 9 message[62] began by referring to and transmitting a copy of a new Union policy developed by "an international and military jurist, Dr. Francis Lieber," and revised and endorsed by Halleck, the War Department and Lincoln. He cautioned Montgomery that:

> it is peculiarly important, in view of the questions which have heretofore surrounded the employment of colored troops in the armies of the United States, to give our enemies (foreign and domestic) as little ground as possible for alleging any violation of the laws and uses of civilized warfare as a palliation for these atrocities which are threatened against the mean and officers of commands similar to your own. If, as is threatened by the rebel Congress [referring to the May 1 resolution], this war has eventually to degenerate into a barbarous and savage conflict, softened by none of the amenities and rights established by the wisdom and civilization of the world through successive centuries of struggle, it is of the first moment that the infamy of this deterioration should rest exclusively and without excuse upon the rebel Government.

Hunter told his subordinate to:

> … avoid any devastation which does not strike immediately at the resources or material of the armed insurrection which we are now engaged in the task of suppressing.
>
> All fugitives who come within our lines you will receive, welcome, and protect. Such of them as are able-bodied men you will at once enroll and arm as soldiers.

This instruction implies that the freed slaves were subject to conscription, as Hunter had favored for some time, and Montgomery was prepared to resort to the draft when volunteers did not step forward.[63]

Hunter continued:

> You will take all horses and mules available for transportation to the enemy; also all cattle and other food which can be of service to our forces. As the rebel Government has laid all grain and produce under conscription, to be taken at will for the use of its armed adherents, you will be justified in destroying all stores of this kind which you shall not be able to remove … All household furniture, libraries, churches, and hospitals you will of course spare.
>
> That the wickedness and folly of the enemy may soon place us in a position where the immutable laws of self-defense and the stern necessity of retaliation will not only justify but enjoin every conceivable species of injury is only to be too clearly apprehended; but until such time shall have arrived, and until the proof, not merely of declarations or resolves but of acts, is unmistakable, it will be both right and wise to hold the troops under your command to the very strictest interpretation of the laws and usages of civilized warfare.
>
> Expressing the highest confidence in your courage, skill, humanity, and discretion, I have the honor to be, colonel, very respectfully, yours,
>
> D. Hunter, Major-General, Commanding.

The letter may have reflected second thoughts by Hunter about the degree of destruction inflicted on the Combahee raid, in light of the new Lieber principles. But it is "questionable"[64] whether Montgomery actually saw it before departing on his Darien raid. Whether he did or not, he did not live up to Hunter's instructions on that expedition. Nor, however, did he inflict "every conceivable species of injury," or revert to the merciless killing of the Missouri campaign.

On June 10, most of the 54th Massachusetts soldiers,

> were at work pitching camp and clearing the ground, when a steamer came to the wharf. Colonel Montgomery was on board, and hailing Colonel Shaw from the deck, said, "How soon can you be ready to start on an expedition?" Colonel Shaw replied, "In half an hour, and at once caused the … roll to be sounded." Hurried preparations were at once made, and at 6pm eight companies of the regiment embarked.[65]

Additional troops on the expedition, all under Montgomery's command, included five companies of his Second South Carolina, and gunners from the Third Rhode Island Artillery. The two transport boats went aground, causing a delay as they waited for the incoming tide. At 1am on June 11 the small Union flotilla entered the Altamaha River until they reached the town of Darien. "Then the gunboats searched it with their shells and fired at a few pickets seen east of the place."[66]

The troops landed without resistance, finding only a handful of civilians present. The inhabitants, according to Emilio, were now living "a few miles inland. Some fifteen or twenty men of the [Confederate] Twentieth Georgia Cavalry, under Capt. W. A. Lane, picketed the vicinity, but had retired."

Apthorp said:

> The burning of this place has, I believe, called forth peculiar indignation from our enemies at the north, while our friends have been almost weaned from us by the perpetration of such an atrocity. Passing over the difficulties of finding the channel over the bar on the right, and the worse than corkscrew winding and twisting of the yellow stream—full of alligators—up which we wormed our way next morning, I will give a simple account of that act of vandalism. Approaching the town we shelled the woods ahead of us well, and drove away guerrillas we could plainly see from their hiding places. Thus we cleared the town and by dint of several well-aimed [shots from the gunboats], cleared [from] a fine sheltering knoll of butternut [trees], a band that was skulking behind it, and proceeded on land. The 54th Massachusetts, brave but unfortunate, were with us in their fresh fullness, and eager for work. The town was quickly explored and picketed on all sides, and then we searched it. It had been a good while deserted and used as a rendezvous for guerrillas, and belonged entirely to full-blooded rebels all in arms against us. What better warrant did we need for its destruction? After removing such articles as combined value and portability, we applied the torch, in this case Lucifer matches, and at evening left a fine bonfire. In the mean time, however, there was an important by-play which resulted in the capture … of a fine schooner and eighty bales of cotton, a little father up the river.[67]

The Confederate cavalry captain, William A. Lane, filed his own report on these events. (No such report by Montgomery appears in the *Official Records.*) Around noon on June 11, Lane said:

> two steamers and two gunboats made their appearance in Doboy Sound, and without halting proceeded with great rapidity southward along the channel known as the inland pass from Savannah to Brunswick. … When they reached the Altamaha, however, instead of proceeding southward they turned in the direction of Darien, and in a few minutes were vigorously shelling our pickets just east of the town, and in thirty minutes from the commencement of the shelling the town of Darien was being burned. The position of said picket being open and exposed, they retired … out of sight of the gunboats.[68]

The gunboats continued shelling the woods outside Darien, and a Union landing party heavily outnumbered Lane's force, which retreated at their approach.

Darien, according to Emilio, was a town of 75 to 100 residences, with "three churches, a market-house, jail, clerk's office, court-house, and an academy," and storehouses and mills along the river. The soldiers were ordered to "secure from the houses such things as would be useful in camp … Soon the plundering thus legitimized began."[69] They took cotton and other supplies, including live cows and sheep, aboard the boats. "Lumber, resin, grain, salt pork and other foodstuffs filled the holds of the Yankee ships."[70]

Then, as Shaw related in a letter, Montgomery declared to him:

> "I shall burn this town." He speaks in a very low tone, and has quite a sweet smile when addressing you. I told him I did not want the responsibility of it, and he was only too happy to take it all on his own shoulders. … The reasons he gave me for destroying Darien were that the Southerners must be made to feel that this was a real war, and that they were to be swept away by the hand of God like the Jews of old. In theory it may seem all right to some; but when it comes to being made the instrument of the Lord's vengeance, I myself don't like it. Then he says, "We are outlawed, and therefore not bound by the rules of regular warfare." But that makes it none the less revolting to wreak our vengeance on the innocent and defenseless.[71]

Montgomery's reversion to an Old Testament mode of warfare was partly the result of the threats made against Black troops and their White officers by the Confederate government. These men were not yet fighting the bloody battles which so many Union soldiers had experienced in other theaters of operations, but they were at more risk of death should they be captured, which made the colonel little inclined to be merciful to their enemies. So, the town was burned, with "Montgomery applying the torch to the last buildings with his own hand. Fanned by a high wind, the flames eventually destroyed everything but a church, a few houses, and some lumber-works."

According to another account, "… a Negro Methodist church, a free Negro's cabin and several small houses were spared."[72] A blockade-running schooner was captured with 55 bales of cotton, along with another 25 bales on a barge.

Shaw, in the brief period of life that remained to him, wrote two letters to superiors protesting Montgomery's action. However, according to his subordinate Emilio's memoir, Shaw "ascertained that Colonel Montgomery acted in accordance with General Hunter's orders."[73]

This is confirmed in a letter Shaw wrote to his mother about the public controversy, saying:

> I see by the papers, what is thought of the destruction of Darien, and it provokes me to have it laid on Montgomery's shoulders, when he acted under orders from Hunter. I, myself, saw Hunter's letters referring to it. I am sorry if it is going to harm the negro troops, but I think myself it will soon be forgotten.[74]

He also wrote to his father, asking him to tell Gov. Andrew that Hunter, not Montgomery, was to blame.

Yet, from another perspective, to men like Shaw and Higginson:

> James Montgomery was a primitive patriarch uninhibited by any effete Eastern notions of the rules of civilized warfare, and his Old Testament style of warfare was completely at odds with the Harvard notion of fair play. To New England romantics, war was a kind of game, played according to definite rules. Montgomery, with fanatic realism, made his own rules. Higginson, the romantic, had raised money to send Sharps rifles to Kansas in the fifties. Montgomery, the realist, had used them.[75]

Nor did all northeastern abolitionists agree with Shaw about Darien. Frederick Douglass, for example, defended Montgomery, as did Tubman and other African-Americans, including at least two members of Shaw's own regiment, Corporal James H. Gooding and First Sergeant George Stephens.[76] (Two of Douglass' sons were serving in the same regiment.)

The controversy has rumbled on through the years, and most of those who have written about it, including the screenwriter of *Glory*, have taken Shaw's side over Montgomery's. In defense of the latter, he was neither the first nor the last to have adopted such tactics. In fact, by the end of the war, they would be adopted by the most senior Union commanders, notably Generals Ulysses S. Grant, William T. Sherman, and Philip Sheridan. Sooner than that, in the Department of the South in the summer of 1863, Gillmore would authorize the prolonged bombardment of Charleston.

Economic warfare did play a role in destroying Confederate morale, bringing the war to an end, and diverting troops from defending important strategic targets such as Charleston was a legitimate objective. However, despite ongoing efforts from 1863, in some of which Montgomery was involved, Charleston did not fall until 1865 when its defenders were about to be cut off by Sherman's advancing army. Still, even though its troops were outnumbered through most of this period, the Confederacy could ill afford the men and resources it was forced to commit to South Carolina, and to other states including Florida, to defend against the Union's Department of the South. The Union siege of Charleston also enhanced the effectiveness of the naval blockade, which was put in place in 1861 by the Navy Board and old General Winfield Scott's Anaconda Plan to cut off trade to the Confederacy. Union operations drastically reduced Charleston's effectiveness as a port—along with other ports such as Savannah—which could supply the Confederate war effort. The Department of the South was undeniably not a main theater of the war, and arguably did not use the Army and Navy in the most strategically useful way. But those who served there like Montgomery, as well as allied civilians such as Tubman, did play a role in winning the war, as did those in the other "sideshow" theater where he was involved, in Missouri and Kansas. The Union soldiers who gave their lives in such places, whether in combat or from disease, did not die in vain.

Montgomery defended setting fire to Darien by pointing to similar harsh tactics adopted elsewhere by the enemy, as well as the Confederate threat to execute captured White officers such as himself, Shaw, and Emilio, who commanded Black troops. Emilio said the inhabitants of the town were mostly living elsewhere. Ironically, many Darien residents in the 18th century had resisted the introduction of slavery, and in 1863 the most famous person associated with the area, who had not set foot there for a generation, was the English writer, actress, and abolitionist Fanny Kemble.

Lane's report said, "There were no white people living in Darien," and according to another Confederate cavalry captain, W. G. Thomson, some of the Blacks left with Montgomery.[77] The great majority of slaves appear to have been withdrawn into the interior by plantation owners—who may have learned a lesson from the Combahee raid. In any case, even for those who were made homeless, no one in coastal South Georgia was likely to freeze to death in the middle of June. And Shaw himself, despite his criticisms over the Darien incident, retained positive views about Montgomery, as he wrote to his mother: "I can't help feeling a great respect for him. He is quiet, gentlemanly, full of determination, but convinced that the South should be devastated with fire and sword."[78]

It must be stated explicitly that Montgomery's depiction at Darien in the film *Glory*, largely based on the book *One Gallant Rush: Robert Gould Shaw and His Brave Black Regiment* by Peter Burchard, is in important respects inaccurate. The book says Montgomery was born in Kentucky, when in fact he was born and raised in the abolitionist-heavy northeastern corner of Ohio, and remained in that free state until he was over 21. Some contemporary accounts wrongly suggest that Montgomery moved as a child to Kentucky, so Burchard's error is hardly unique.[79] It's true that Montgomery did move to the slave state of Kentucky, and the fact that he chose to do so as an adult may indicate that his opposition to slavery was not as strong then as it later became. But, as discussed in the "Westward Bound" chapter above, it was still possible to openly oppose slavery in Kentucky at the time Montgomery moved there, and many people such as Cassius Clay did so. There is no evidence for Burchard's unsourced and incredible claim that Montgomery owned slaves while living there.[80] It is probably based on Shaw's statement in a letter that Clarinda Montgomery had been the daughter of a slave-holder. The letter to his mother said, "His wife is the daughter of a Kentucky Slave-holder." While this apparently referred to Montgomery's current wife, it may have been based on a misunderstanding by Shaw. According to Holman, it was Montgomery's "first marriage" that was "to the daughter of a slaveholder."[81] It is hardly likely that both wives came from slave-holding families, and Shaw seems to be the sole source of the claim that Clarinda did. Most Whites did not own slaves, especially in Appalachian locales like Morgan County, where Clarinda was from.

In a much more famous case, the fact that Julia Dent Grant was the daughter of Missouri slave-holders did immensely complicate the life of her husband, Ulysses, who lived for several years with his in-laws and briefly owned a slave, although he set the man free before the Civil War and would later become a champion of Black civil rights. But there is no evidence that Montgomery was similarly caught up in the slave system, and what can be established about his life and career makes any such suggestion highly unlikely. And while Julia Grant may have held slaves into the Civil War, well before then Clarinda Montgomery—whatever her childhood experience had been—was exposing herself to danger by standing with her abolitionist husband.

The film-makers then went beyond their inaccurate source to invent a scene of Montgomery killing one of his own insubordinate soldiers at Darien.

These and other libels have damaged Montgomery's historical standing, and not just because there has been no biographer, until now, to refute them. It is true that Montgomery was a hard-war man, and could be equally hard on his own men, willing to have deserters shot, and not always any more racially enlightened than other Union officers. On June 28, he had a man from the 2nd SC shot for desertion, which Emilio in his memoir called an "illegal action." As noted above, Higginson also had serious reservations about this execution.

But Higginson had had his own problems with desertions and tolerated almost equally stringent measures to eliminate them. On January 3, before Montgomery arrived at Port Royal, three men deserted from the 1st SC and were pursued. According to regimental surgeon Dr. Seth Rogers, one "would not halt at command" and as a result was shot and brought back mortally wounded. "The feeling through the regiment in regard to the fatal result is that the deserter received his just punishment," Rogers said in a letter.[82]

Emilio and Shaw, whose regiment consisted largely of free Black volunteers from Massachusetts and elsewhere in the Northeast, regarded Montgomery's treatment and direction of his "contraband" freed-slave soldiers as on occasion harsh or worse. They and later chroniclers like Burchard were not necessarily wrong about that. Shooting men for desertion was especially problematic because there could be a thin line between volunteers and conscripts in the Department of the South. In early February, when Montgomery had been recruiting his regiment at Key West, "Orders from General Hunter authorized him to seize every able-bodied male contraband on the Key, whether willing to be a soldier or not, but Montgomery found that volunteers came forth readily." Hunter had told the officer in charge of Key West that "every adult male Negro between the ages of fifteen and fifty, who is capable of bearing Arms, to be found within your Command" must be shipped up with Montgomery to Port Royal.[83]

By now in the wider war, both sides were using conscription to fill their thinning ranks, which increased the risk of desertion. How to treat this problem was a vexed question for everyone in the military chain of command, including Lincoln, who often pardoned deserters but sometimes permitted their execution. It does not appear that Montgomery extended such harsh discipline to the 54th or other regiments under his command beyond the 2nd SC, but the negative pattern with that regiment does not reflect well on his leadership. (Nor would his handling of the unequal pay issue be free from racial insensitivity.)

Yet even in the 2nd SC, execution was not the usual punishment for desertion. Private Cuffie Heyward, for example, enlisted in the regiment on March 3, 1863, was reported to have deserted on July 6 of that year, then rejoined ("joined from desertion") in October, and was "discharged on certificate of disability on Dec. 2, 1863."[84] And Shaw himself provides evidence of the magnitude of the problem Montgomery was trying to address, and the fact that the great majority of soldiers who deserted or otherwise absented themselves without leave from the regiment did not face execution.

For Shaw's judgments of Montgomery's most controversial actions—not just the Darien conflagration—were by no means as simple or as negative as has sometimes been portrayed. In a July 7 letter to his wife, Shaw noted that Montgomery is "not the only" Union officer who has ordered towns burned:

> [General John] Foster destroyed three towns in North Carolina without reason, and Blufftown, in this Department, was burnt the other day by white troops. Montgomery's previous reputation has been such that he attracts attention. Many people here blame him for having had one of his men shot without trial. According to Regulations, it was wrong; but the court-martial in this case would

Colonel Robert G. Shaw in Boston in 1863, not long before he led the 54th Massachusetts to the Department of the South. (Photo by John Whipple. Gladstone Collection, Library of Congress)

> have been a technicality, for the man's guilt was unquestionable, and before he could have been tried Montgomery's regiment would have been dissolved. He had lost seventy men by desertion, in two days. Since the execution not one has gone, but thirty or forty have secretly returned in the night. Of course such a power cannot be allowed to a Colonel, as there would be murders without number under the name of execution; and I do not believe Montgomery has heard the last of it. Nevertheless, as the right and wrong of the matter, he only violated a clause of the Regulations, and the result is extremely beneficial.

Shaw then related a probably exaggerated tale of the ruthless pre-war border killings in Kansas involving the man who was now his brigade commander, commenting "… I wonder Montgomery has not become a *wild beast* instead of a reasonable man. He commands the respect of all his superiors, and is undoubtedly a man gifted with some great qualities. You cannot talk with him long without discovering that he is in reality a tender-hearted man."[85]

Montgomery was a significantly flawed hero, as is generally the case with heroes. But those flaws also laid the groundwork for negative fables to stick to his later reputation, unfairly tarnishing it beyond what the facts show. This is a common process, which also happened in the case of the vastly (and justly) more celebrated Grant, whom Lost Cause-influenced mainstream historians in the 20th century would often and unfairly describe as a corrupt, drunken butcher.

Still, despite any excuses, Montgomery's burning of Darien is hard to defend. There was no immediate military necessity for it, and it must have contributed to the impoverishment of civilians. It further embittered the war.

The controversy over the operation quickly became public, which would eventually embarrass the new department commander, Gillmore. The Confederate general commanding in Charleston, Pierre Gustave Toutant-Beauregard, wrote him an indignant protest letter on July 4, with heavy emphasis on the Combahee and Darien raids, and "the atrocious consequences which have ever resulted from the employment of a merciless, servile race as soldiers."[86]

On June 15, Gillmore still envisaged Montgomery in a raiding role, telling Halleck in Washington: "Colonel Montgomery, with 1,500 colored troops and some artillery, now occupies Saint Simon's Island, and will be directed to make raids from that point, and occupy the enemy in that direction. He will be able, I think, to keep many, if not all, of the Georgia troops in that quarter."[87]

Halleck, however, no admirer of Montgomery from his Missouri days, may have had other ideas. At any rate, Montgomery's regiment, the Second South Carolina Colored, was moved north, closer to Charleston—first to St. Helena Island and then to Folly Island, where it was put to work constructing fortifications.[88] The focus of the Department of the South (10th Corps in the U.S. Army) was shifting away from raiding and toward capturing Fort Wagner—on Morris Island northeast of Folly Island. The real target of course was beyond the fort to the harbor and Fort Sumter, and beyond it the city which the forts were protecting, Charleston, where the Confederacy had been born. These longer-term military efforts would prove to a large extent unsuccessful, but their failure cannot be blamed on Montgomery.

Gillmore maneuvered around Fort Wagner, launching an unsuccessful attack on July 11. Meanwhile, in a diversion, he moved the 54th back with the 2nd SC as part of Montgomery's Third Brigade of Brigadier General Alfred Terry's First Division, which on July 8 landed on James Island northwest of Morris Island. While he had previously commanded troops from other regiments, including the 54th, this was Montgomery's first formal brigade command.[89] He would remain a brigade commander—albeit one never promoted to brigadier general—for most of the next year in the Department of the South.

As Gillmore reported much later:

> The demonstration up the Stono [River] was commanded by Brig. Gen. A. H. Terry and was eminently successful. A large part of the Morris Island garrison was drawn to James Island by it.
>
> The attempt to cut the railroad was intrusted [*sic*] to Colonel Higginson, First South Carolina Volunteers … It signally failed, with a loss to us of two pieces of field artillery and a small steamer.[90]

Thus did the careers of Higginson and his former subordinate continue to diverge, with Montgomery becoming the more competent officer.

Montgomery's brigade was engaged in a "demonstration" on James Island on July 10, and then in a more serious engagement on July 16 at Grimball's Landing. The Confederates suddenly attacked and were repelled largely by the 54th Massachusetts, which suffered by far the heaviest casualties of any Union regiment: 14 killed, 17 wounded, and 12 captured or missing. Montgomery's brigade was covering the Union retreat to Grimball's Landing, and from there down the Stono River to Cole and Folly Islands.[91] While many of Terry's troops were evacuated by boat down the river, Montgomery's brigade and the 10th Connecticut Infantry Regiment (whose retreat had been covered by the Grimball's Landing engagement) had to make a difficult march in rainstorms—much of it by night—for most of the way.[92]

Terry in his report on the skirmish lauded:

> the steadiness and soldierly conduct of the Fifty-fourth Massachusetts Regiment, who were on duty at the outposts on the right, and met the brunt of the attack.[93] [Gillmore reported that he] evacuated James Island on the 17th, as I required

> more men here [*i.e.* on Morris Island], and did not consider General Terry's position longer tenable.[94]

The 54th was for the time being transferred away from Montgomery's control—in large part due to Shaw's prior request, which had been backed up by Massachusetts Gov. Andrew in a June 29 message to Stanton. Andrew said "Higginson, the senior colonel …, although a brave and chivalrous gentleman of high culture, has never seen much service, and never any in the field until he went to South Carolina. Montgomery, the next in rank, undoubtedly a valuable man and very useful as a good bushwhacker, is hardly a competent brigadier."[95] Whatever Shaw's complicated view of Montgomery, the primary change he sought was to put his regiment into the forefront of active service, which was at last granted.

So, the 54th was placed under the command of Seymour and Brigadier General George Strong. Shaw, as he told his mother, had written to Strong "& expressed my wish to be in his Brigade. Though I like Montgomery, I want to get my men alongside of white troops, and into a good fight if there is to be one."[96]

While the 54th would perform well and bravely in the imminent battle, the command change did not lead to success. The regiment led the heroic yet failed frontal attack on Fort Wagner on July 18. Among the casualties were Shaw, who was killed, along with two other officers and at least 31 enlisted men, with another 146 soldiers from the regiment wounded and 92 captured or missing.[97] Total casualties were higher among the supporting regiments. General Strong suffered a mortal wound, and General Seymour, too, was injured, putting him out of action until October. After the battle, Montgomery assigned Tubman to the hospital where the wounded Black soldiers were being cared for in Beaufort.[98] Barton tended wounded White troops on Hilton Head. Other hospitals were opened in Beaufort as casualties continued to mount during the siege.

Gillmore had proved a more aggressive departmental commander than Hunter, but not, so far, a successful one. His failure to storm Fort Wagner was in part the fault of his superiors in Washington, such as Stanton, who had pushed for a more aggressive campaign against Charleston.

They had previously, in April, pressured Rear Admiral Samuel DuPont into a failed naval attack on the city's defenses.

Gillmore now settled back into his area of competence, gunnery, and siege warfare. The target remained the Confederate-held Fort Wagner, on Morris Island. Montgomery, back in regimental command with the 2nd SC, was moved with Terry's division to Morris Island, serving in Col. Joshua Howell's Second Brigade. The Confederates, meanwhile, who had reoccupied James Island, fired artillery from there and other locations, including Fort Wagner and Battery Gregg (a short distance north on Morris Island), and Fort Sumter in Charleston harbor, against the Union besiegers of Fort Wagner. Union artillery fire was directed against the rebel forts and batteries, especially Wagner and Sumter, and from August 22 on the city of Charleston. The latter bombardment was dubiously justified by Gillmore on the undoubtedly true grounds that the city was a supply base for the forts. Sumter, of course, had stumbled upon lasting worldwide fame in 1861, precipitating the war itself as a U.S. fort requiring defense and reinforcement. Its fall at that time turned it into the key to the Confederate defense of Charleston, and thus a prime target for U.S. forces on land and sea.

Ground for the artillery had to be won by Union infantry, including Howell's brigade, advancing their entrenchments, building artillery positions, hauling logs, guns, sandbags, and supplies. They often worked by night, trying to avoid Confederate fire. Howell himself was wounded in the head by a Confederate shell on August 16.

Montgomery's professional competence in the siege of Fort Wagner was recognized on August 24 by his restoration to an expanded brigade command by Gillmore. It was the 4th Brigade of Terry's division, later designated the 3rd Brigade.

This time, in addition to the 2nd SC and 54th Mass., his "colored brigade" included the Third Regiment, U.S. Colored Troops.[99] The latter regiment had been newly mustered-in at Philadelphia, Pennsylvania. The U.S. government was finally committing itself to raising Black regiments, following in the footsteps of Montgomery and others. By the end of the war, there would be 175 regiments of United States Colored Troops, comprising a significant fraction of the U.S. Army.

Major General Quincy Gillmore in front of his tent on Morris Island, South Carolina, in 1863. (Photo by Haas & Peale. Library of Congress)

As the siege continued, another of Terry's brigades overran rebel rifle pits, which enabled artillery to be brought closer to its targets.

The Confederates increased their artillery fire from James Island and Fort Wagner, causing casualties. More men fell ill—in summer heat aggravated by lack of fresh water and the near presence of the corpses of soldiers and horses killed earlier in the conflict, the men having been buried in shallow graves. The average percentage of Black soldiers out sick during the siege was almost 14—but it was above 20 for the White Union troops.[100] Army reports indicate that Montgomery's camps were generally well kept up with sanitary measures enforced, which must have contributed to the relatively low Black casualties.[101]

Mines ("torpedoes") were a problem, as was friendly fire. But the advance also enabled heavier Union bombardment of Wagner and Gregg, which toward the end of the campaign reduced the return fire from there.

In late August, Montgomery was joined by his eldest son, also named James, who was 20 or 21 years old, and had become a junior officer with the 2nd SC. Montgomery wrote about this to Clarinda on August 25:

> My Dear Wife: God be praised! My life and health are still spared. James arrives safe, and is now commanding a company. The men seem pleased with him. I took him to the front, immediately, and gave him a little experience in dodging cannon balls. He performed first rate. He will make a fine officer. Our heavy artillery opened on Fort Sumter on Monday Aug. 17th and for seven days and nights our monster bolts and shells were hurled against its walls incessantly. The work had been greatly strengthened since the attack by the Iron-clads last spring; and showed a power of resistance truly wonderful; but, thank God? It is now a mass of unsightly ruins. It refuses to surrender, and keeps its flag flying, but its guns are all disabled, and she has not one that she can fire.

He wrote to her again on August 29:

> Still, the work goes on. At all hours of the day and night are heard the heavy booming of mortars and cannon, and the bursting of shells. Our men in the trenches are protected by splinter proofs, and other contrivances, and 'cover' when they see a shell coming. Yet with all their activity in dodging, many are hit; and we lose, on an average, ten or twelve men every day.
>
> Of course, we see many sad, sickening sights: men with heads, legs and arms torn off. Others dashed all to pieces;—One poor fellow with both arms torn off, and both eyes blown out lived several weeks. Such is war. God grant that this, the greatest war of the world, may be one among the last. …
>
> Last Wednesday evening, while acting as General Field Officer of the day, I was ordered to storm the enemy's Rifle Pits, in front of Fort Wagner. For this purpose, 275 men of the 24th Mass. (white), and as many more of the 3d New Hampshire Regts. were placed in the advanced trenches; the Massachusetts men in front, and the New Hampshire men in reserve.
>
> A Mortar Battery was ordered to shell the rifle pits rapidly, to keep the enemy close under cover. When all was ready, the Mortars were ordered to cease firing, the signal to charge was given, and away went the Mass. men with a dash that quickly put them in the enemy's works. We captured 67 prisoners with but a trifling loss on our part.
>
> As soon as the works were carried, the Mortars were ordered to open on Wagner with shells, and the long guns with solid shot, to prevent the Rebels from attempting a recapture, and give our men time to intrench themselves, which they were very quick to do; and the works are now fairly ours. The matter went off very much to the satisfaction of the commanding general, who complimented me very highly. He was all the better pleased from the fact that a similar attempt the night previous had been a failure.
>
> One thing may need a little explaining. You might ask how I came to be in command of White troops. The explanation is this: There are brigade commanders on this island. These are each in turn, General Field officers of the day for one

> day at a time. The General Field Officer is for that day commander of everything in the field, and ranks next to the commanding general.
>
> Our trenches are now pushed almost to the very walls of Wagner, and the capture of that place by storm would seem to be possible.
>
> James is out with his company in the trenches, tonight, where he is pretty sure to see something interesting.—More tomorrow

He did write as promised the next day, August 30:

> James had a rough experience in the trenches last night. Twenty-four men were killed or wounded close round him, while he himself, was knocked down by the concussion of a shell which burst over him; his face was burned twice, by shells exploding near him; but God be thanked he is not seriously injured; though once his hair was twisted by a rifle shot grazing his head. None of his men were seriously injured, though all had their narrow escapes. They were moving a battery of Mortars forward from the 3d parallel to the 5th, close up under the walls of Fort Wagner. The full moon shone brightly, and they were exposed to a terrific fire of rifles, from the ramparts of Wagner and grape shells and canister from Wagner, Gregg, Moultrie, Johnson, and James Island batteries. A detail of men from the 3d Regt. of my brigade had seven men killed and wounded last night. Lt. Col. Purviance of the 85th Pennsylvania, was killed this morning by one of our own shells. I have just been notified that my turn has come to act as Genl. Field Officer of the Day. This gives me the command of all the operations in front, for the next 24 hours, beginning at 6 o'clock this evening. This is an honorable but very dangerous service. It is nothing else than going into a 24 hours battle, in which the number of killed and wounded is likely to be large in proportion to the numbers engaged. The cannonade going on at this moment, would be terrible to persons not used to it.
>
> Whether I will be ordered to storm Wagner or not, is more that I can say, but I have my suspicions. The Genl commanding has got it into his head that I have the courage necessary, for desperate undertakings. Let us hope that the good Lord who has been my guard and shield, will still protect and deliver me. "O God! In thee do I trust, let me never be confounded."

In this and several other surviving letters written to Clarinda from Morris Island, he also includes instructions and advice about farm management and household finances, often using his Army salary to pay back debts. The next letter, on August 31, said:

> The night, just closed, has been very hot on our men in the trenches. The fire was truly terrific, and that of Wagner, especially, was so close as to give little time for covering. There were no changes needed last night, and I had only

> to visit and inspect the different lines and see that everything was in working order. While I was in the advanced trenches, four men were severely wounded, and one slightly. One had a foot cut entirely off, besides being wounded in the hip. One of the wounded men belongs to the 3d U. S. Regt. of my Brigade. This regt. has suffered severely during the week.
>
> My South Carolina Regt. which has seen more service than either of the others, has lost but one man, killed, and three wounded. Only one has been seriously hurt, since we came to the siege of Charleston.

On September 4, his letter ended: "I think you had better have your chimney torn down, before cold weather. Build that west end up solid, with rock, so as to hold the building steady; and dig the foundation to the rock, so the rats can't undermine it."[102]

On September 6, orders were issued for a third attempt to capture Fort Wagner the next morning. Montgomery's brigade did not have the lead role, but was ordered to:

> move up and occupy the trench south of the Beacon House before light. These troops and all others must be kept carefully concealed from view, and perfectly quiet. No man will be permitted to leave the ranks during the assault, to assist the wounded or for any purpose whatever. The wounded can be taken care of when the affair shall be over. All commanding officers will caution their men upon this point.[103]

Fortunately, Beauregard had recognized the hopelessness of his position on Morris Island and abandoned it overnight, giving up Fort Wagner and Battery Gregg on September 7 without further bloodshed. This Union success, however, did not lead directly to the capture of Fort Sumter, let alone the city of Charleston, both of which would hold out until 1865.

The siege operations from July 18 to September 7 cost the Union army 358 casualties, including some from Montgomery's regiments: Six men were killed and 12 wounded in the Third U.S. Colored Troops; and at least three were killed and five wounded in the 54th Massachusetts.[104] (Including deaths from disease would raise this total.)

Gillmore and Rear Admiral John Dahlgren launched a bungled joint operation on September 8 which failed to capture Fort Sumter.

Montgomery's brigade remained on Morris Island, helping turn the captured positions into Union outposts which could effectively return the continuing Confederate artillery fire.

At this time, the unfortunate controversy over pay for the African-American troops came to a head, in a way which has cast a shadow over Montgomery's modern reputation. As with some other such shadows, his conduct, while properly subject to criticism, is not, in context, beyond defense. That does not, however, make the basic Union policy—of paying Black soldiers less than White ones—defensible.

"Black soldiers were initially paid $10 per month from which $3 was automatically deducted for clothing, resulting in a net pay of $7. In contrast, white soldiers received $13 per month from which no clothing allowance was drawn."[105] Actually, the situation for the serving Black troops was even worse, because it was in June 1863 that Stanton actually cut their pay to these levels, in a belated interpretation of the Militia Act of July 1862. "Higginson, Montgomery, and many other officers of black regiments joined in protesting the gross unfairness of this policy, as did many of their men."[106]

Congress and the rest of the U.S. government, including the Army, would by fits and starts remedy this situation by the spring of 1865[107]—when the war was ending. By then, it had also become possible for a very few African-Americans to be commissioned officers. But for most of the war, Black soldiers could neither become officers nor receive equal pay.

The political reasoning behind these policies was to appease the presumed racism of most of the Union population, notably in the key border states where slavery remained legal, and in the Army where leaders like George McClellan wanted no part of an abolition war. In 1861 and through most of the next year, public opinion and the administration proclaimed a war to save the Union, not to abolish slavery, and those generals like Fremont and Hunter who sought to make it more about the latter goal were disavowed by Lincoln.

Even in 1863, after the enactment of his Emancipation Proclamation, the president was careful not to get too far ahead of public opinion. The impression was created that the newly enlisted Black troops would be used largely on guard duty in rear areas, and so could be given lower

Black Union soldiers with White officers in South Carolina during the Civil War. Some officers, but not Montgomery, brought their wives to the Department of the South. Other White and Black civilians served in roles such as nurse, teacher and chaplain. (Library of Congress)

wages. In fact, however, they soon found themselves in combat, and more likely to be murdered if wounded and captured, or else returned to slavery. For some who had actually been slaves—those, for example, liberated and recruited by Montgomery—their lower-level status in the U.S. Army may not have seemed so onerous. But that did not apply to the mostly free Blacks from the Northeast, many of them more or less middle-class, who filled the ranks of the 54th Massachusetts.

"Military pay for black soldiers had been an issue since the very first black regiments had been formed. … Many black regiments, including the 54th Massachusetts, refused to accept the lesser pay."[108] In that refusal, the men of the 54th had been supported and joined by their now heroically slain commander, Robert Shaw.

Montgomery, now again in brigade command of the regiment, was no less of an abolitionist than Shaw had been, sharing none of the unsympathetic attitude toward Black advancement which was demonstrated by officers like McClellan or Halleck. On Hunter's say-so, he had promised his Black recruits equal pay at the beginning of 1863, and was embarrassed to discover that was not what they would actually be getting.[109] He did not, however, have Shaw's charismatic connection and shared geographic origin with the soldiers of the 54th—nor, obviously, that officer's martyred reputation. But Montgomery was not wrong to see a discipline problem brewing, and one that he could not afford to indulge when his troops were in line against the enemy.

So, when the regiment's noncommissioned officers rejected overtures from the paymaster on September 27 and then again on September 30, Montgomery addressed them on the latter date. Emilio, who wasn't there, got his account of the speech from Sgt. Stephens of Company B, an account "in substance as follows", but one that when taken up by later historians has sometimes been inaccurately put between quotation marks and purported to be the exact words of Montgomery.

Those alleged words included liberal use of what in the 21st century must be referred to here as the n-word. Its unvarnished usage was much more common in the Civil War era, especially in areas of the mid-South where Montgomery had spent most of his life, and was not necessarily associated, as it would be today when used by Whites, with racial ill-feeling.

On the substance of the matter, Montgomery berated his soldiers, and said their refusal to take the pay as apportioned could be construed as insubordination and mutiny, meaning they could be court-martialed and shot. "The colonel," Emilio commented, "seemed to be unaware that his remarks were insulting, and most of the men he addressed [were] born free." The Black soldiers were acting on principle, and were becoming increasingly embittered as they risked their lives for their country and freedom with no pay, with the result that many of their families back home were becoming increasingly impoverished. Some of them likely felt that they had seen more combat than Montgomery, whom they regarded as more of a raider than a battlefield commander.

Montgomery was more aware of these circumstances than Emilio presumed and did not actually carry out his dire threats. He may well have regretted coming on too strong, speaking too harshly. But he was trying to assert the necessity of military discipline. And his leadership of the regiment was far from ineffective. It would perform well under his brigade command, especially in the 1864 Florida campaign, although some of its soldiers including Emilio would hold on to a grudge against him. Yet the pay issue remained unresolved during that time. After the regiment was removed from Montgomery's command and sent back to South Carolina from Florida, the pay and discipline issues resurfaced as an even bigger problem.

In the late spring of 1864, when Montgomery was no longer connected with the 54th Massachusetts, the grievances came to a head. In May, the regiment's senior White officers threatened Black soldiers with pistols in order to get them to obey orders just to go on guard duty. And after a separate incident in June, a Black soldier was executed for mutiny.[110] Whatever may have been Montgomery's failings as brigade commander of the 54th, things got worse under his successors.

There was in fact a link between the pay issue and desertions by—and occasional executions of—Black soldiers. As Brigadier General William Birney wrote in April 1864 to Major W. C. Foster, chief of the Colored Bureau in the adjutant-general's office in Washington:

> How legislators can imagine that we can raise [Black] troops, as a permanent thing, at $7 a month I cannot see. The man must have $2 for himself, and he cannot support his family on the other $5. Hence the great number of desertions in this department. The black soldiers deserted by the score because their families were starving. Colonel Montgomery shot two men, but that did not stop desertion. Congress can stop it by giving the black soldier enough to support his family.[111]

Montgomery himself tried to get Congress to do just that. He supported and lobbied for full equality of pay, backdated to the start of a soldier's service. As he stated in a January 1864 letter to U.S. Sen. Henry Wilson of Massachusetts, chairman of the Committee on Military Affairs:

> I can certify, most conscientiously, that the troops under my command have been second to none in efficiency; while their loyalty and fidelity might put to the blush some who boast of white skins. Could Honorable Senators have seen, as I

> have seen them; toiling in the trenches before Wagner, mounting guns, digging, carrying shot and shells for weeks and weeks together; and this under a storm of shot and bursting shells, I know they could not, and would not, withhold so simple an act of justice.[112]

Montgomery's brigade that fall and winter joined in the bombardment of Fort Sumter and Charleston, while the Confederates stepped up their artillery fire from Fort Moultrie against the Union positions on Morris Island. Sumter was reduced to ruins, but the rebels hung on there.

On November 23, Montgomery's "colored brigade" in Terry's division had a name change from 4th to 3rd, containing the same three African-American regiments.

While the pay issue continued to fester, action was taken on another front to reduce racial discrimination. Gillmore's order of November 25 noted that he "has heretofore had occasion to rebuke officers of this

GENERAL BEAUREGARD.—(From a Photograph furnished by E. Anthony.)

Confederate General P. G. T. Beauregard, capable defender of South Carolina, Georgia and Florida. 1861 *Harper's Weekly* engraving from photo furnished by E. Anthony. (Library of Congress)

command for imposing improper labors upon colored troops. He is now informed that the abuses sought to be corrected still exist." Montgomery was probably one of the people informing the general and lobbying for him to issue this order.

"Colored troops will not be required," Gillmore's order continued, "to perform any labor which is not shared by the white troops, but will receive, in all respects, the same treatment and be allowed the same opportunities for drill and instruction."[113] In other words, Black regiments could parade, guard, and train like any other. They would no longer be stuck with hauling, digging, or other "fatigue" work by Terry, the division commander, or other White officers who sought to spare White troops such labor—segregate them from it, one might say.

Soon after, Thanksgiving was celebrated. The brigade stayed on Morris Island into the new year, exchanging artillery and other fire with the Confederates. On December 17, Terry's troops were drawn up at his orders to witness the execution of a deserter. This was none of Montgomery's doing—the soldier was White, from the 3rd New Hampshire Infantry Regiment, and did not belong to his brigade.

The troops celebrated Christmas "with apple dumplings, minced pies, beefsteak, mutton, and ham added to the usual fare," while New Year's Day brought "far grander still" parades to celebrate the first anniversary of the enactment of the Emancipation Proclamation.[114]

Soon, many of these men would be shipped to a new field of battle, while to others, including Montgomery, the change would mark a return to a state where they had fought the previous spring. Another, much larger, Florida campaign was coming up.

CHAPTER 5

Olustee and After

Over the winter of 1863–64, Lincoln and his private secretary, John Hay, considered a plan to occupy Florida and reconstruct it back into the Union. In January, Lincoln sent Hay—who a generation later would serve as U.S. secretary of state—to Hilton Head to confer with Gillmore. Halleck, still the Army's general in chief, and Stanton, the secretary of war, were not so enthusiastic about the plan, but Gillmore came around to it—since he was apparently not going to be able to capture Charleston in the near future. (Soon, Grant would be placed in charge of the U.S. war effort, and such strategic diversions would cease or wind down.)

While Lincoln's motive was in substantial part political, there were also military and strategic reasons to pursue a Florida campaign, in accordance with retired General Scott's Anaconda Plan. Florida had become an increasingly important source of supply for rebel armies in the south of the Confederacy commanded by Beauregard and Joseph Johnston. Florida's cattle supplied their beef, and its hogs their bacon. Beef was of particular importance, and production was increasing in Florida as Georgia ranchers, threatened by invasion, sent their cattle south.[1] Salt was another Florida staple, along with beans, potatoes, citrus fruit, lumber and cotton. Cutting off such supplies—and directing them to the Union, instead—would weaken the Confederate military and economy. And any gain in Union-controlled territory would increase the opportunity to recruit more Black soldiers for the U.S. Army.

So, on January 28 Montgomery's brigade was ordered to Hilton Head to prepare for embarkation as part of the new, stronger expedition to

Florida which would be dispatched in early February. Gillmore would be in direct command initially but planned to hand over to Seymour. The army had four brigades—three infantry and one cavalry—each led by a colonel. Thus, Montgomery's plight of being a colonel, rather than a brigadier general, who commanded a brigade, was not at all unusual in this particular campaign.

Union troops occupy Sanderson, Florida, before the battle of Olustee. Engraving from *Harper's Weekly*, 1864. (Library of Congress)

The regiments were, however, under-strength and were reorganized in Florida, with a sizable part of Montgomery's brigade being detached for scouting and to join the cavalry. This would leave him with just two African-American infantry regiments: the 54th Massachusetts and the 1st North Carolina[2] (the latter soon to be redesignated the 35th U.S. Colored Infantry). The confused command arrangements at the brigade and regimental level reflected more damaging confusion at the top, with Gillmore later trying to direct events from out of state, and Seymour determined to go his own way. That mismatch between Gillmore and Seymour, and the latter's blunders, would be key factors in the failure of the campaign.

The Union forces, including Montgomery's brigade, soon reoccupied Jacksonville against light resistance. They advanced 20 miles west to Baldwin, and then farther west to Sanderson and Lake City, where cavalry skirmished and withdrew. Gillmore on February 11 temporarily broke up Montgomery's brigade, sending most of the 54th Mass. to Baldwin while the colonel and three companies of the 2nd SC were dispatched up the St. John's River (where they had campaigned the previous March) to scout, gather supplies and attack any rebel pickets they found.[3]

Montgomery's troops freed some slaves, who left for Jacksonville. Gillmore ordered Seymour to fortify Jacksonville, Baldwin, and Palatka, which with Fernandina and St. Augustine would be the core of the Union position, confined to the northeastern part of the state. In the middle of February, Gillmore departed from Florida to return to department headquarters at Hilton Head. Seymour, left in command, decided to ignore Gillmore's cautious instructions and pursue a more ambitious agenda, advancing westward toward the Suwanee River and Lake City, and asking Gillmore to distract Beauregard in Georgia to prevent him from sending reinforcements south. Gillmore, aghast, sent a staff officer south to rein Seymour in, but it was too late. On the morning of February 20, the latter general "initiated a colossal blunder that led to losses of tragic proportions at the battle of Olustee."[4] Since Seymour and Gillmore had the previous July also launched the failed and costly assault on Fort Wagner, it is perhaps not surprising that their joint efforts the next year should have resulted in further failure and heavy losses of U.S. soldiers, many of them African-American. Seymour had been wounded at Fort Wagner, and again demonstrated personal courage at Olustee. But that admirable quality would only help to alleviate the disaster for which his own incoherent strategy and tactics were largely responsible.

Before the battle, Beauregard reinforced the Confederates under Brigadier General Joseph Finegan, who established a camp near Olustee Station, 13 miles east of Lake City, digging trenches to protect it.

Any Union move west of Baldwin was unauthorized by Gillmore, and Seymour seemed to oscillate between bravado and timidity, between thinking he could conquer northwestern Florida—including the state capital of Tallahassee—in battle, or that he had better retreat to Jacksonville. He was "advancing on his own initiative, and now that he had done so, it seems that he was beginning to lose his nerve."[5] Like his friend George McClellan two years before, Seymour at times exaggerated in his own mind the number of Confederates in the opposing army. But unlike McClellan, he was also prone to suddenly changing his view and underestimating the enemy threat.

Gillmore, too, had changed his mind about the campaign, at first proposing to move west to the Suwanee, then becoming more cautious. Montgomery's brigade, which had been in the rear, was sent west by Gillmore, who was on his way out of Florida, to reinforce Seymour,

Major General Truman Seymour commanded the Union army at the battle of Olustee. (Library of Congress)

who was retreating from Sanderson. Montgomery joined Seymour at Barber's Station. As Seymour there consolidated his army, which had met little effective resistance so far, he again grew confident—fatally overconfident—and determined upon a renewed advance.

Seymour marched his men quickly west from Barber's Station, following a rail line between Jacksonville and Tallahassee, on the morning of February 20. One of his objectives was to destroy the railroad bridge over the Suwanee, which he never reached.

Montgomery's reduced brigade was in the rear of Seymour's army. The 54th Massachusetts, unlike some other regiments, exhibited high morale on this fine day, singing songs such as "We're Bound for Tallahassee in the Morning" and "Old Folks at Home" as they marched along.[6]

But the reinforced Confederates, while not as numerous as Seymour had previously feared, more or less matched the Union army. And they were well prepared for its advance, which they surprised and ambushed in front of their defensive lines. The battlefield would be on flat land among scattered pine trees and between swamps, eight miles west of Sanderson.

The Confederates were under Finegan who was supported by Brigadier General Alfred Colquitt, commanding the reinforcements sent down by Beauregard from South Carolina. Beauregard was Gillmore's equivalent, in overall command of the theater, but not present at the battlefield. The Confederate victory was in large part due to Finegan (supported by Colquitt) and Beauregard outgeneraling Seymour and Gillmore. Seymour was expecting the Confederates to remain behind their defenses, failed to adequately reconnoiter, and was surprised by the rebel attack on his advancing army.

Union Colonel Joseph Hawley's brigade collapsed in the fighting, and Colonel William Barton's came under severe pressure. Montgomery, hearing the battle, sent his adjutant to seek orders, but decided not to wait for them and "started to march his brigade toward the sound of the guns."[7]

Montgomery, riding at the head of the 54th Massachusetts, received orders from Seymour confirming that his brigade should advance. As the situation at the front deteriorated, Seymour came to realize that the battle was lost and that Montgomery's men, his last reserves, were needed

The battle of Olustee. 1894 lithograph by Kurz & Allison. (Library Company of Philadelphia)

to stabilize the battlefield and cover a retreat. On the march, the men discarded inessential equipment as they came up double-quick to battle, the 54th Mass. ahead of the 1st North Carolina.

> Hundreds of wounded stragglers streamed past … making their way to the rear. The 54th was greeted with discouraging statements made by the retiring troops, who announced, "We are badly whipped!" or "You'll all get killed!" The men pressed on, undaunted by the words.[8]

The 54th was only about 500-strong at this engagement, some of its soldiers having been detached for garrison duty in Jacksonville. According to the report from its colonel, Edward Hallowell:

> the regiment moved forward at the double-quick about 2 miles, where it was formed in line between the railroad and dirt road, under a sharp fire from the enemy. In this formation it advanced some 200 yards through a swamp, driving the enemy from some guns, and checking the advance of a column of the enemy's infantry.[9]

The arrival of Montgomery's brigade encouraged the New York regiments still fighting and prevented capture of a field hospital. The regimental band of the 54th began to play patriotic tunes, including the national anthem. At this point it was late afternoon, and the brigade's task was to hold the line until dark.

Montgomery placed his two regiments in a wide V formation, at an angle of about 120 degrees. The 54th Massachusetts was on the left and the First North Carolina on the right. "Montgomery took a position in the middle of the line and directed the action while sitting on the stump of a tree. ... Both regiments were immediately engaged by the Confederates, who sought to brush them aside and rout the Federal army."[10] Seymour's entire force was in imminent danger of destruction.

The remnants of Hawley's brigade were at first in the middle, as he reported:

> Colonel Montgomery's brigade had come up. The Fifty-fourth Massachusetts, Colonel Hallowell, went into action on our left. The First North Carolina, Lieutenant-Colonel Reed, on our right, between us and Barton's retiring brigade, went up into the field, halting and firing fiercely, with its right well forward, so as to form an angle of perhaps 120 degrees with the line of the Fifty-fourth, with full space for us between.

The reserve brigade's advance enabled Hawley to withdraw the 7th Connecticut and the remnants of his other two regiments, leaving it to Montgomery's men to hold the line against the oncoming Confederate army.

According to Robert Broadwater, a modern historian of the battle, "Half the color guard of the 54th fell, including Corporal James Gooding, a whaler from New Bedford, who was shot in the thigh." Gooding survived the battle, one of the black wounded not killed there, only to die in July as a prisoner at the notorious Andersonville camp in Georgia. (Gooding was one of the black soldiers who had defended Montgomery's actions at Darien the previous June.) Also wounded was Sgt. Stephen Swails, who later became the first Black to be commissioned as an officer in the 54th.[11]

Hallowell described Swails as acting sergeant-major, who "deserves special praise for his coolness, bravery, and efficiency during the action; he received a severe but not mortal wound in the head."

Montgomery had moved from his position at the center to be with the 54th, where he and his staff were "freely exposing themselves to the enemy fire and steadying the men to their purpose." Seeing the Confederate effort to flank them from the direction of the railroad, Montgomery began "shouting 'Fire to the left! Fire to the left!'"[12]

The 54th was able to hold on, but in the turmoil, Hallowell became separated from most of his men, leaving Lt. Col. Henry Hooper in effective command of the regiment. Ammunition was getting low, and Seymour was not now in contact with Montgomery's brigade, although he was reforming other troops to cover a retreat. Darkness was coming on, which meant the 54th had held on long enough. Montgomery, according to Emilio's account, suggested that imminent withdrawal might be necessary with each man making his own way back as best they could.

While Emilio praised Montgomery's courageous conduct in the battle up to this point and did not personally witness the purported proposal that "Each man take care of himself" in precipitate withdrawal, he saw it as an unwelcome example of the brigade commander's "bushwhacking" and, by implication, cowardly style of warfare. It was not, however, seen that way by either Montgomery's immediate subordinate, Colonel Hallowell, or their superior General Seymour, both of whom were still on the battlefield.

When it came down to it, the brigade commander went along with the relatively junior Hooper, who thought the position could be held long enough to organize an orderly withdrawal; Montgomery could have overridden him but chose not to. The men were told to fix bayonets, and withdrew in good order, turning occasionally to fire a volley at the enemy, who were not following closely.[13] According to Hallowell, who was able to rejoin the main body of the 54th, it was Montgomery who ordered them back to form "a new line … on the right of the dirt road, where the regiment staid till after dark." And Seymour's report, as we shall see, had only praise for his conduct.

Montgomery, however, had found a more urgent task on the right of his line, where the First North Carolina's fate proved less fortunate than that of the 54th Massachusetts, though no less heroic. It came under heavier fire and suffered higher losses. The 1st NC's colonel, James Beecher, was away in the North (either on leave or carrying dispatches), and it was commanded on the battlefield by Lieutenant-Colonel William N. Reed. He was partly Black, being described as a "mulatto" by a Union major in a letter to Gillmore.[14] That means Reed was the highest-ranking African-American soldier in the U.S. Army.

The 1st NC had begun by obeying Seymour's order to charge the enemy, forcing the Confederates back a few hundred yards. But after a pause in the action, "A second advance, by a reinforced rebel battle line, forced the First North Carolina to give ground, which they did in good order, pouring a destructive fire into the ranks of the gray line."[15] They were, however, taking severe losses. Reed was mortally wounded. Major Archibald Bogle took command of the regiment, then fell wounded along with seven other officers, and Captain Charles Jones was killed. A Black soldier who tried to rescue Bogle was killed; Bogle would be captured and survive Andersonville. Artillery fire smashed trees to pieces, with their falling limbs wounding some of the troops. The regiment suffered some 230 casualties in two-and-a-half hours—most of them, of course, African-Americans like Julian Williams, a former slave from Camden County who was killed.[16]

The regiment was finally forced to withdraw, though not in a headlong flight. Soldiers were able to keep firing as they went back, to hold off the Confederate pursuit.[17] Montgomery joined his previously inexperienced and now battle-battered North Carolina regiment to help keep it together and guide its retreat, in the absence of its fallen leaders.

The upshot was, according to a contemporary account, that Montgomery's "two colored regiments had stood in the gap, and saved the army!" Toward the end of the battle, the Confederates were attacking on both the right and left. "… Both flanks were thus being folded up, and slaughter or capture would have been the inevitable result. [But] We fell back in good order, and established new lines of battle, until we reached Sanderson."[18]

Seymour, for all his strategic failures leading up to the battle, and his unimaginative tactics of feeding in reinforcements piecemeal, was not lacking in courage or honest observation of what his men did and did not do. He joined in the fight to stave off disaster, and in his official report gave credit to Montgomery and both of the regiments in his brigade.

Seymour wrote:

> … the Fifty-fourth Massachusetts had replaced the Eighth U.S. Colored Troops and a rapid fire was opened, the influence of which was soon visible. The left of the enemy's line was forced backward, and … the First North Carolina was brought up to the right of Barton's brigade by Lieutenant Colonel Reed in the most brilliant manner. The entire force was now hotly engaged.

Seymour praised the performance of Barton's brigade and its leader, then said: "Colonels Hawley and Montgomery, also commanding brigades, conducted their troops with great personal intelligence and valor. … The colored troops behaved creditably—the Fifty-fourth Massachusetts and First North Carolina like veterans."[19]

It is notable that Seymour singled out the "colored" troops as fighting well, and Montgomery's brigade as the best of them, since he himself was an experienced combat soldier, having fought in the Mexican War and, in 1862, in several battles under his West Point classmate McClellan. And, like McClellan, he had had the reputation of being dubious about employing Black soldiers and their radical abolitionist officers like Montgomery.

Yet Seymour's March 25 report made a point of saying that the defeat was not the fault of the African-American troops, "but in the unanticipated yielding of a white regiment from which there was every reason to expect noble service, and at a moment when everything depended on its firmness." The unnamed regiment was the 7th New Hampshire Infantry, in Hawley's brigade. Command confusion seems to have contributed to the collapse of this and the severe losses inflicted upon another of Hawley's regiments, the 8th USCT. But the two in Montgomery's brigade remained steady until the loss in combat of the First North Carolina leadership, which resulted in the brigade commander taking charge as the men fell back.

As a reliable observer in personal command of the battlefield, Seymour's praise is convincing evidence that Montgomery had evolved into a capable and brave leader of a Civil War brigade. He was also the brigade commander whose outnumbered troops held up best at the end of the day. Finegan had come up with his reserves to take personal command of the rebels, and it was Montgomery's brigade which fended off their whole army long enough to save Seymour's from complete disaster. Even more than the Combahee River raid or later at the battle of Westport, it was his greatest day of public service—although this time in the desperate circumstances of a battlefield defeat.

Montgomery's own brief report on the battle notes that his brigade was in the rear of the Union army's advance, guarding the baggage train, when he first heard gunfire ahead:

> Thinking it might be a demonstration intended by the enemy to draw us away from the train, I immediately disposed my force so as to protect it, at the same time sending an aide to the front for orders. The aide was hardly out of sight when the fight thickened so rapidly that I moved forward with the Fifty-fourth without waiting for orders, leaving the First North Carolina to guard the train. We soon met the aide with orders to bring up both regiments. The Fifty-fourth Massachusetts was placed on the left of the line, while the First North Carolina moved directly forward. Fresh re-enforcements of the enemy came up at this time, and the fight, which had slackened a little, broke out again in all its fury, and continued till sunset, when the troops retired slowly from the field. The Fifty-fourth, commanded by Colonel Hallowell, lost 1 captain and 2 lieutenants wounded, and 84 men killed, wounded, and missing. The First North Carolina lost in killed, wounded, and missing, 199 men and 10 officers.[20]

The report, dated March 15, is notable for its understatement and lack of vainglory. While not all the details of what he did in the battle are clear, it is undisputed that his decision not to wait for orders before marching to battle saved crucial time, enabling his brigade to play a vital role in saving the army from destruction. Montgomery's actions at Olustee are similar to those of Major General Gordon Granger at the battle of Chickamauga exactly five months before, when the latter's bringing up the Reserve Corps without orders helped save the Army of the Cumberland from annihilation.[21] Both battles were Confederate victories in which Union reserve troops vigorously counter-attacked and then held on defensively until nightfall, enabling an orderly retreat. Chickamauga, obviously, was much larger and more strategically significant, but there is nonetheless a genuine parallel, including the limited Civil War combat experience at the start of these battles of both Granger and Montgomery.

After Olustee, the 54th Massachusetts (joined by some men from the First North Carolina) initially covered the Union retreat to Sanderson, until Seymour replaced them as rearguard with the 7th Connecticut and the cavalry brigade, as the army continued to withdraw. Montgomery accompanied most of the harder-hit and leaderless 1st NC on the grim, exhausting march back toward Jacksonville.

Seymour's report described thus the end of the battle and its aftermath: "The struggle continued until dusk, and ended with cheers of defiance, and finding it hopeless, under existing circumstances, to advance farther, the troops were withdrawn in perfect order to Sanderson and then to the St. Mary's." They were in fact withdrawn past the St. Marys River to the vicinity of Jacksonville, and Seymour's formulation may be regarded as putting a positive spin on his army's situation. The purportedly "perfect order" of the retreat was achieved in difficult circumstances by soldiers including Montgomery, who was bringing back the 1st NC. Lieutenant Colonel Reed died from his wounds about a week after the battle.

The 54th Mass. encamped about halfway from Baldwin to Jacksonville, then on the next morning of February 21 was ordered by Seymour back to Baldwin, 10 miles west, to rescue a broken-down train filled with more than 300 Union wounded, in danger from the approach of Confederate cavalry. They brought in additional wounded stragglers, putting them on the train, too, and pushed and pulled it, using rope, vines, shoulders, and muscle—with some help from horses and mules near the end—back to Jacksonville on the evening of February 22.[22]

Seymour's casualties were heavy, especially compared to his total strength—evidence of the battle's ferocity. He reported 203 killed from his 5,500-strong army, 506 missing and 1,152 wounded. Casualties would have been much heavier but for the stalwart performance of Montgomery's brigade.

"Olustee would be one of the smaller battles of the war, with only approximately 10,000 men participating in it from both armies combined," according to a 21st-century historian. But for those soldiers, "... it was as fierce a struggle as any fought on this continent during the four years of Civil War... In a battle that lasted only about four hours, the casualty rates were appalling." Confederate casualties were about 17.5 percent "of the force engaged, while the Union army sustained losses of 35 percent, greater than those suffered at Gettysburg or Chickamauga. Many veterans of Gettysburg, and other hotly contested fields of the Army of Northern Virginia, who fought at Olustee proclaimed that it was the hottest fight they had been involved in during the war."[23]

Many wounded Black troops were killed on the field by the Confederates. The commander of one of Finegan's cavalry regiments, Lt. Col. A. H. McCormick, had announced in advance that "I shall not take any negro prisoners in this fight,"[24] and there is ample evidence that at least 50 wounded Black prisoners, and probably more, were murdered. Some prisoners were sent to Andersonville.

A letter written more than seven months later by Brigadier General John Hatch, then commanding the District of Florida, to Major General E. A. Hitchcock, commissioner for exchange of prisoners, throws some bleak light on what happened immediately after the fighting:

> Soon after the battle of Olustee, in Florida, a list of our wounded and prisoners in the hands of the enemy was forwarded to our lines by the commander of the rebel army. The very small number of colored prisoners attracted immediate attention, as it was well known that the number left wounded on the field was large.
>
> It is now known that the most of the wounded colored men were murdered on the field. These outrages were perpetrated, so far as I can ascertain, by the Georgia regulars and the Georgia volunteers in Colquitt's brigade.[25]

An early 20th-century memoir by a Fourth Georgia Cavalry soldier, William Frederick Penniman, confirms that many Black wounded prisoners were deliberately killed by their captors.[26]

A battlefield monument erected in 1936 by the United Daughters of the Confederacy extols Colquitt as "Hero of Olustee" and adds: "This decisive engagement prevented a Sherman-like invasion of Georgia from the South." Another monument put up there by the same organization says the Confederates fought for the cause "of liberty and state sovereignty."

The official records of casualties for Montgomery's regiments listed 22 killed at Olustee from the 1st NC, including its commander, 131 wounded and 77 missing.[27] The 54th Mass. casualties are listed as 13 killed, 65 wounded, and eight missing.

It seems likely that most of the missing and many of the wounded Black soldiers did not survive the war. Many of the evacuated wounded were shipped up to hospitals in Beaufort, South Carolina. Casualties for the 54th Massachusetts were lighter than those of the 1st North Carolina because the latter regiment, after fierce fighting, was forced off the field, whereas the former remained in good order throughout the battle and retreat.

It is also notable that the total casualties for Montgomery's brigade, 316, were notably lower than the losses for the brigades commanded by Colonels Barton, 824, and Hawley, 587. This is another indication of the cohesion and successful performance of his two regiments as they fought in desperate circumstances.

Casualties for the 54th Mass. at Olustee were much lower than at Fort Wagner the previous year, when Shaw was killed, and the regiment was not under Montgomery's command. And while at Fort Wagner its sacrifice bore no military fruit, at Olustee it, along with the 1st NC, played the key role in saving Seymour's army.

Finegan reported Confederate casualties as 946, with 93 killed and 847 wounded.

Florida, like Texas, was not a major front of the Civil War, but it was a dangerous one for Union troops, who were often at a disadvantage against Confederate soldiers defending, as they saw it, their home states. And in Florida, at least, that "defense" involved merciless treatment of African-Americans.

The heroic conduct of Black soldiers in the Olustee campaign, notably those in Montgomery's brigade, did not go unremarked. While the lost battle prompted widespread criticism of Union military and political leadership, and the atrocities inflicted on Black soldiers also drew attention, Olustee did not discourage African-Americans from volunteering to fight for the Union and a free country, but had the opposite effect. Black soldiers had proven again at Olustee, more clearly than ever, that they could fight as bravely and effectively as their White comrades. This accurate perception contributed to a nationwide increase in Black recruitment, helping provide the U.S. Army with the necessary manpower to finally win the war.[28]

The battle had an equally significant effect on White opinion, including Lincoln's. "There have been men who have proposed to me to return to slavery the black warriors of Port Hudson and Olustee to their masters to conciliate the South. I should be damned in time and eternity for doing so." So said the president on April 19.[29] Those very serious words marked Lincoln's firm new commitment, and that of his party, to abolishing slavery. That commitment would be endorsed by voters in November when Lincoln led the successful Republican ticket, results which assured and cemented the gains being won on the battlefield by Union soldiers.

But such climactic effects lay in the future. Meanwhile, in the wake of the Union defeat, Jacksonville was partly besieged by Finegan. The city was quickly fortified with telegraph wire, a moat, and a vertical-log stockade with artillery. The 54th was put on the left on the front line of defense.

Swails' promotion to second lieutenant was initiated soon after the battle but was blocked on racial grounds by the War Department for almost a year—by which time Montgomery had long since been removed as brigade commander of the 54th.

On February 25, Montgomery became commander of the Third Brigade in the First Division, under Brigadier General Israel Vogdes. His new brigade did not include the regiments which had fought under him at Olustee. Instead, he had his old Second South Carolina, soon to become the 34th U.S. Colored Troops, plus the Third South Carolina and another regiment fragment to be consolidated into the 21st USCT, along with a light artillery battery.

Gillmore returned to Florida, insisting on a defensive strategy anchored on the St. Johns River. The Lincoln-Hay plan to reconstruct Florida was abandoned as a result of the military setback at Olustee, but there would be no more evacuations of the state. Forts were built outside the walls of Jacksonville, protecting the entrance gates. Both the Union and Confederate sides sent in reinforcements, and the rebels, too, constructed fortifications designed to prevent another Union offensive into the interior. Confederate torpedoes did damage to Union shipping on the St. Johns, with four men lost on April 1 when an Army transport was sunk. Palatka was threatened by Finegan's advance.

Seymour was replaced in late March as District of Florida commander by Hatch, who then replaced Gillmore as department commander at Hilton Head before being replaced by Major General John Foster—Hatch, however, remaining in the department. In Florida, Hatch was replaced by Brigadier General George Gordon, who was replaced by Brig. Gen. William Birney.

Montgomery had to deal with all these passing-through superiors, and more. In late March he was ordered to reinforce Palatka. With only river transport for one regiment, he went with the 34th USCT up the St. Johns River through the night of March 30/31.[30]

Palatka was abandoned on April 12, as the tide of reinforcements shifted into reverse. Gillmore was preparing to move troops out of state, north to Hilton Head and beyond. Montgomery's men held on briefly across the St. Johns River, on the east side at Picolata, where they fortified a defensive position which would remain in Union hands.[31] But on April 13 Gillmore ordered his brigade, along with other troops including the 54th Massachusetts, back from Florida to Folly Island south of Charleston in South Carolina.

The intense focus of both sides—with Grant's influence now dominant in Washington—was shifting north, to the war's main fronts in Virginia and Georgia. They both started sending troops to Virginia from Florida and the rest of the Union-designated Department of the South, which was becoming ever more of a backwater where neither side had ambitious plans. In early May, Gillmore would follow Seymour north to Virginia from the Sea Islands, bringing with him an army corps.

Before that, however, amid the constant change in the department's senior ranks, but before the departure of Gillmore, Montgomery lost his brigade command. On April 30, he was listed as commanding the 34th USCT on Morris Island, the site of Fort Wagner, north of Folly Island and closer to Charleston. He was in a brigade commanded by another colonel, William Gurney.[32] The 34th USCT was, of course, the former

2nd SC, the first regiment that he had recruited in the South at the beginning of 1863. As we shall see, he would be restored temporarily to brigade command to fight in a hard skirmish in July, but most of the rest of his wartime service was as a regimental colonel.

Why did Gillmore do this, effectively demoting Montgomery by removing him from brigade command, rather than recommending his promotion to brigadier general? It can't just have been expedience and the press of changing events and reconfigured military formations.

According to Emilio, his Colonel Hallowell of the 54th Massachusetts assumed command of Morris Island on April 20 and was relieved by Montgomery the next day when the latter arrived with the 34th and 21st USCT. Colonel Gurney arrived with his New York regiment on April 23, and relieved Montgomery. It is possible, even likely, that Montgomery's commission as colonel was officially regarded as dating from January 1863, not from 1861 when he served in Kansas and Missouri under Lane (having been commissioned by Governor Robinson). Thus, Gurney may have been regarded as senior, and took charge for that reason. Gurney had commanded a brigade and briefly a division in Virginia but had less combat experience than Montgomery.

Seymour had reported Montgomery's good conduct at Olustee, but Gillmore blamed Seymour for that defeat, so was not persuaded by his version of events. The department commander was a conventional officer who was more than a decade younger than Montgomery; they had little in common. Nor was Montgomery known for a tactful approach to his military seniors, although he got on well enough with some of them such as Hunter, Terry, Birney, and Hatch. He had formed a low opinion of Gillmore,[33] which was probably reciprocated.

Gillmore was by now a frustrated man, inclined to blame his troubles on other officers. He commanded the Department of the South for almost a year in 1863–64 and accomplished very little, being bested at every turn by his Confederate counterpart, Beauregard. They both moved north to Virginia at about the same time in 1864 and faced each other again, Gillmore serving under Major General Benjamin Butler. The outnumbered Beauregard won that campaign, too, while Gillmore feuded with Butler. It is a melancholy and embarrassing fact that Gillmore, who was a major general for the second half of the war, experienced the peak of his career at his first-place West Point graduation, and made his most positive military contribution in April 1862 as a captain at Fort Pulaski. Montgomery, by contrast, learned as he went on how to be a good soldier.

He also got moved around the department—not always to the delight of more senior officers. In May, Hatch ordered Montgomery and his regiment to Saint Augustine, Florida, on the east coast south of Jacksonville. But Gordon, the District of Florida commander, pushed back in a May 19 message urging Hatch to rescind the order. This was because Gordon didn't want to see his current subordinate, Colonel William Noble, and his Connecticut regiment replaced by Montgomery's 34th USCT—an opinion heavily colored by the races of their respective troops, and, apparently, his perception of what was needed in their commander.

> Colonel Noble is a man of experience, a lawyer as well as a soldier, a statesman and a gentleman. He has a regiment of white troops whose influence and whose presence is much more favorable to the Government in winning back loyalty settlers and refugees than could Colonel Montgomery with his colored regiment. [Replacing the White troops with the Black] would be exceedingly injudicious.[34]

Gordon's protest didn't work, and Montgomery's regiment was shipped down to Saint Augustine. But the colonel's May 22 message from there back to Hatch's adjutant general—one of only a few entries by Montgomery in the *Official Records*—indicated that things weren't exactly running smoothly.

"I arrived at this place last evening," Montgomery's message began, "and today we are ordered on an expedition into the interior by General Gordon." (This was probably to do with protecting shipping on the St. Johns River, where that morning a Confederate attack had destroyed the USS *Columbine.*)

> Colonel Noble says he has not received the order to turn over the command of the post to me, and that he waits to receive it through the proper official channel. My leaving Hilton Head on the night of the 20th was more hasty than I liked, but in the high state of excitement in which I found my men, it seemed to be a matter of the first importance to get away with them as quickly as possible. The sight and conduct of the women had thrown them into such a

> state of excitement, bordering on mutiny, as I never saw before, and hope never to see again. It was all over with them as soon as we got away, and they are now as gentle as ever. I have put a few of them in arrest, and have reduced one of the sergeants for refusing to assist in quelling the disturbance. … PS—The men had found liquor somewhere, but from whom they obtained it I have not been able to learn. Some of the men were intoxicated, and much, if not all, of the mutinous conduct can, I think, be attributed to that cause.[35]

While Montgomery was being honest with Hatch and not sugar-coating his problems, such a message was hardly calculated to reassure the department commander that the situation was well in hand. It also indicates that Montgomery's methods had not secured good discipline even in his original regiment, the only one now remaining under his command. On the other hand, he no longer felt he needed to resort to extremely punitive actions, such as execution, when faced with serious indiscipline.

Montgomery had stopped at Hilton Head to pick up supplies on his way down to Florida from Morris Island. He found more than he bargained for there in the civilian community which had sprouted up next to the military base in this rear-echelon, headquarters area, in the way of whiskey and sexually available women—not that he was subject to temptation in that regard, but some of his men were. "He swiftly gathered his regiment from the streets of Hilton Head, placed them aboard his transport and steamed away from the island, the whiskey, and the women as quickly as possible."[36]

Montgomery and his regiment were recalled from Florida to Tybee Island, Georgia, to be part of an expedition headed by Birney up the Ashepoo river in South Carolina. The goals included cutting a rail line. But this would not prove as successful as similar forays the previous year. In fact, it proved something of a disaster for Montgomery's regiment which suffered significant casualties for no gain, although no blame was attached to its colonel.

Birney ordered Montgomery to rendezvous with the expedition at the mouth of the Ashepoo and follow the lead transport boat upriver. Some White cavalrymen accompanied the 34th USCT on the transport steamboat *Boston*. Very unfortunately, it was led on the night of May 23/24 about eight miles past the designated disembarkation point, went aground, and came under artillery fire in the morning from Confederate

Fort Chapman. The *Boston* was destroyed, and 13 of Montgomery's soldiers were killed, the rest being evacuated by other transports. No wounded were recorded in official records. The fatal casualties were the result of drowning, according to Private Simon Payos, while "All of the horses were burned up."[37]

One of Montgomery's officers, 21-year-old Lt. George W. Brush, won the congressional Medal of Honor for his role in commanding a small boat which took "a large number of Union soldiers on board the stranded steamer *Boston*, and with great gallantry succeeded in conveying them to shore, being exposed during the entire time to heavy fire from a Confederate battery."[38] (Both Brush and Payos survived the war.)

The expedition then withdrew to Hilton Head and Port Royal without accomplishing its goals.

An Army court of inquiry blamed the colonel of the 9th USCT, Thomas Bayley, in the lead transport, and he was accordingly court-martialed at Hilton Head in August, but acquitted. Foster, who had replaced Hatch in command of the Department of the South, also blamed Birney. Partly it was bad luck that Montgomery's boat was stranded within artillery range of a rebel fort, and partly a sign of efforts made by Beauregard and others to toughen Confederate defenses. Wherever the fault, the blundering attack was the antithesis of the Combahee raid the year before, and a bleak finale to Montgomery's career as a coastal raider.[39]

Birney, unlike Gordon, was a firm supporter of employing African-American soldiers, and was more personally sympathetic to Montgomery. On June 5, after succeeding Gordon in Florida, Birney was requesting that Montgomery and his regiment "shall be sent to me." However, a reply the next day on behalf of Foster said "one regiment of white troops will be stationed at Saint Augustine"—which would rule out Montgomery's regiment. Foster's message also withdrew more troops from the state and told Birney to stay on the defensive.[40]

So, Montgomery stayed in South Carolina, where little progress had been made by the Union army during his Florida sojourns.

Foster, in part because he had received naval intelligence about an imminent rebel effort to break the blockade, in June developed a complex plan of attack around Charleston involving his subordinate Generals

Hatch, Birney, Saxton, and Alexander Schimmelfennig. On June 1, Foster steamed away from Hilton Head with more than 5,000 troops. He left most of them, under Hatch, on Seabrook Island, SC, with orders to head to Johns Island and beyond, to threaten Charleston from the west. Foster, meanwhile, took Birney's brigade, including Montgomery's regiment, several miles up the North Edisto River, landing it at White Point. Birney ran into Confederate resistance and did not advance to Foster's satisfaction, failing to cut the Charleston and Savannah Railroad.

Birney recommended withdrawal, so his brigade was sent to James Island to support Schimmelfennig, where it and the other troops were engaged in light skirmishing on July 5. On July 6 Birney was ordered back to Florida. This was in part because Foster had completely lost confidence in him, and partly because there was a surplus of generals engaged in the South Carolina operation, but none at all in Florida. That large district, in Birney's absence, was being commanded by Colonel Noble.

Birney's departure left Montgomery to once again—and for the last time in combat—assume brigade command. He had his own 34th USCT plus two other colored regiments, the 7th and part of the 35th USCT, and perhaps 100 other troops whom Birney had been commanding, for a total strength of between 1,200 and 1,300 men.[41] (The 35th USCT was the former 1st NC, which had fought under Montgomery at Olustee.) They were sent to support Hatch on Johns Island—which is west of James Island (and Morris and Folly islands), and southwest of Charleston.

The reinforced Confederates would counter-attack there and had to be fended off before the Union force withdrew. Hatch's report says the Union troops, after running into resistance, had been "re-enforced by Montgomery's brigade" on July 8, with the main fight taking place the next day.

This was a temporary return to brigade command for Montgomery due to the contingencies of combat and the musical-chairs rotation of higher command. And he performed well in the skirmish, which is sometimes called the Battle of Bloody Bridge, or Burden's Causeway.

Hatch's report for July 9 said:

> At daybreak the enemy drove in my pickets. At 5:45am, he attacked my line in force with great spirit, but was easily repulsed in about fifteen minutes. At

> 6:30am, he again attacked with a larger force. There was no wavering in our lines, while the infantry poured in a deadly fire. … the enemy flying in confusion in ten minutes from the opening of our fire. Our loss in these two attacks was trifling, while that of the enemy was undoubtedly severe. … The total [Union] loss during the occupation of John's island was 2 officers and 9 men killed, and 2 officers and 69 men wounded. The number missing I have not yet received. It is, however, very small. …
>
> Colonel Montgomery, commanding brigade, and Colonel Slidell, commanding One hundred and forty-fourth New York Volunteers, also deserve notice for their skillful handling of their troops and gallantry in action.[42]

But the Union troops were withdrawn from Johns Island after the fight. Montgomery and his men were sent back to James Island, then south to Coles Island, farther away from Charleston, then back to Beaufort, farther still.

Foster's elaborate operation had accomplished nothing strategically toward the capture of Charleston, and while the main fighting was on July 9, most Union losses took place in the build-up. The total casualties were hardly insignificant: 33 killed in combat, 133 wounded, 143 missing (most of them captured), "3 sunstruck, and 18 drowned by the upsetting of a boat."[43] Troops under Montgomery suffered few of these losses prior to the July 9 skirmish. At the skirmish near White Point when Birney was still in brigade command, the general reported that four men in Montgomery's regiment suffered minor wounds.

While Foster's offensive may have discouraged further reinforcement of rebel armies on the war's main fronts, Virginia and Georgia, and helped prevent the Confederates from exporting cotton out of Charleston, and while he was cavalier to describe any losses as "trifling", it was all of minor importance compared to what was happening elsewhere.

Nor did Montgomery's good performance in the defensive engagement on Johns Island do anything for his own career. He was listed at the end of the month as being once more just a regimental colonel, of the 34th USCT. Foster, another regular West Pointer, probably lumped Montgomery in with Birney as another abolitionist volunteer officer in whom he had little confidence.

Some of the soldiers in the 34th had been with Montgomery for a year or more. Privates Butler Williamson and Jack Aiken, for example, had joined the 2nd SC in June 1863, Aiken being one of those liberated on the Combahee River raid. They both would survive and serve through the war. Not so fortunate was Israel Knabb, who enlisted in Florida on March 29, 1864. Private Knabb was killed in action on December 9 that year, being shot in the stomach at Deveaux, South Carolina.[44] But by then Montgomery was no longer with the regiment.

Higginson, suffering from chronic diarrhea, had left the Department of the South for New England in May, subsequently resigning his commission. Clara Barton had left in the winter to rest, then returned to service in Virginia in 1864.

Tubman (who may or may not have participated in the Olustee campaign) had departed for the North in June[45]—though she would return to serve in Virginia near the end of the war. She had arrived in Beaufort eight months before Montgomery and had previously returned home temporarily to Auburn in the fall of 1863 before coming back to South Carolina.

Montgomery had had no such leave, and now that Tubman had gone home again, he must have thought all the more about his own family in Kansas, most of whom he had not seen since 1862—although he was still serving with his eldest son, James, from his first marriage. James the younger would—as Montgomery wrote to Stearns on December 10 of that year—remain serving with the 34th USCT after his father left for home.[46]

The Department of the South was not a healthy posting, especially for front-line troops encamped in the summer in places like Morris Island, where disease took a heavy toll. General Schimmelfennig would accept the surrender of Charleston in February 1865, when the Confederates abandoned the city because of Sherman's offensive in their rear. He also contracted tuberculosis in that vicinity, which would cause his death that September at the age of 41.

Montgomery, at 49, was a generation or more older than not just his own son, but many of those with whom he had served. Emilio, for example, shared his December 22 birthday, but was a full 30 years younger. Montgomery was tired, in seriously poor health from asthma and other causes, and probably frustrated that despite achieving more success than many a brigade commander, he had not been promoted to brigadier general.[47] He was stuck in an obscure department where not much was going on, and where he felt he had done enough. He applied for and was granted sick leave, at first in Beaufort and then for 30 days back home in Kansas.

In addition to asthma, it is likely that Montgomery shared the digestive complaints of most Civil War soldiers. "Nearly three-quarters of Union soldiers suffered from serious bowel complaints in every year of the war; by 1865 the sick rate for diarrhea and dysentery was 995 per thousand."[48]

In early August, off the coast of Alabama, Admiral David Farragut's fleet defeated the Confederates and, working with the Army, blockaded Mobile Bay, shutting down a key port. In early September, Sherman took Atlanta, Georgia. Grant was engaged in what would become the very long siege of Petersburg, Virginia, south of Richmond. Lincoln's re-election and Union victory were looking more likely—and the president and his party were now explicitly calling for the abolition of slavery. The good cause seemed relatively safe. Montgomery resigned his commission in September.

Writing about these events to Stearns, he said:

> My health became very poor, while I was in the South, and I came home on sick leave, about the first of August. When my leave expired I was worse instead of better; and seeing no prospect of being soon fit for service, I sent in my resignation and got my discharge.[49]

An Army surgeon in South Carolina had confirmed the seriousness of his condition (without getting into specifics of what it entailed). According to a modern Linn County, Kansas, historian:

> The activity and climate of the South had crippled his health and Montgomery would never fully recover. ... Arriving in Kansas in August Montgomery's health did not improve and on the day he should have returned to South Carolina he sent a letter of resignation and requested a discharge from the army. By September 23, 1864, when he received his discharge, his health had improved somewhat.[50]

By then, Confederate Major General Sterling Price's Army of Missouri had already entered that state from Arkansas. Montgomery was not home long.

CHAPTER 6

The Westport Campaign

While Montgomery's most significant military service was in Florida and South Carolina, his last arena, in the fall of 1864, brought him back to Missouri, where he had first fought in the Civil War; and at last, he returned even to his own home county in Kansas. Here, too, he would make a difference, especially at the campaign's decisive battle. And unlike a few earlier occasions, his military performance in trying conditions could not be faulted.

Jim Lane, his somewhat disreputable commander in 1861, was involved this time, too, but only as a staff officer to a more professional soldier, Major General Samuel Curtis, an anti-slavery man who had won the battle of Pea Ridge in 1862, and now commanded the Department of Kansas. Curtis would command the Army of the Border in the upcoming campaign. Montgomery's old subordinate James Blunt was now another major general, serving under Curtis. The two generals had fought the rebels hard in the first years of the war but were deemed too abolitionist-minded for moderate Missouri Unionists to put up with, and were outmaneuvered politically by the rising young West Point general John Schofield. Then the latter was moved east to take a more prominent part in the war under Major Generals William T. Sherman and George Thomas.

Curtis and Blunt were sent in the other direction, west to defend settlers against Indians—until Major General Sterling Price reminded everyone that the Confederacy was not dead yet. Jennison was still a colonel but would command a small brigade at the forthcoming battle of Westport. He would fight well there, but also in the course of the campaign resorted to his old tactics of executing prisoners and looting civilians.[1] Blunt took notice, which the next year resulted in Jennison's dishonorable discharge from the U.S. Army.

A Kansas militia regiment en route to the Missouri border in October 1864 to fight the oncoming Confederate army. Painted lantern slide by Samuel J. Reader. (Library of Congress)

Montgomery, by contrast, who started this new campaign as a mere private before suddenly and unexpectedly rising to command a regiment and other troops, was now a more professional officer. He was no longer inclined to the ruthless jayhawking of the early 1860s. For most of these men and many others, the upcoming campaign would be the culmination of a decade-long conflict along the Kansas-Missouri border.

The Union soldiers on the Kansas side would be joined by a contingent from Missouri in Price's rear, commanded by cavalryman Alfred Pleasonton, another major general serving under a more senior one, William Rosecrans. The military and political entanglements of command on the Union side would immensely complicate the campaign. The intrusion of Kansas electoral politics by Governor Thomas Carney (who had replaced Robinson) and his allies would become a particularly egregious factor.

On the Confederate side, Lieutenant General Edmund Kirby Smith, commander of the Trans-Mississippi Theater, had been unable to obey orders to send troops east, because the U.S. Navy controlled the Mississippi River and the Gulf of Mexico. So instead, still conferring with Richmond, he adopted another plan to try to relieve the increasingly hard-pressed Confederacy. Price, Montgomery's old adversary and now a major general, was sent north to raid—or capture, if he could—Missouri. During the course of the raid, on the other, east side of the Mississippi, Confederate armies under Generals John Bell Hood and Nathan Bedford Forrest were also moving north, headed ultimately for Tennessee and, they hoped, beyond. It was all part of the last major strategic offensive by the Confederacy, and Montgomery played a minor but solid role in stopping it. His main contribution was at Westport, the largest and decisive battle of the Missouri campaign, in modern-day Kansas City. Price's army, too weak to capture St. Louis, had followed its backup plan of veering west toward Kansas, where, retreating south from Westport, it would come uncomfortably close to Montgomery's home.

Price was no great military leader, but he had competent subordinates including Generals John Marmaduke and the formidable Jo Shelby, the latter saving the rebel army on several occasions in late October.

Price also collaborated with the unsavory guerrilla leaders Quantrill and Anderson. They were not for the most part fighting with his army but coordinating with it and him. They were part of the broader Confederate campaign, forcing Rosecrans to deploy more troops against them, and making some Kansas militia soldiers want to stick defensively close to home rather than going boldly into Missouri to defeat Price, which was what Curtis wanted them to do.

In September, according to Rosecrans' report, "Anderson's gang attacked a railroad train on the North Missouri road, took from it twenty-two unarmed soldiers, many on sick leave, and after robbing placed them in a row and shot them in cold blood. Some of these bodies they scalped and put others across the track and ran the engine over them. On the 27th this gang, with numbers swollen to 300 or 400, attacked Major Johnston with about 120 men of the Thirty-ninth Missouri Volunteer Infantry, raw recruits, and, after stampeding their horses, shot every man, most of them in cold blood."[2] Montgomery had never contemplated committing atrocities on this scale, although arguably his earlier methods of ruthless warfare contributed to the escalating savagery in Missouri. (Anderson was killed in a skirmish on October 26.)

Price's army had set off from southern Arkansas in August, evading federal troops there and entering Missouri on September 19, 1864. "It was a cavalry raid, covering 1,488 miles of Trans-Mississippi territory and encompassing forty-three engagements,"[3] as the modern historian Howard N. Monnett describes it, before the much-depleted Confederate army—a small fraction of its peak strength—would finally limp back in early December to southwest Arkansas, where it spent the winter. As Price headed northeast in September, moving toward the Mississippi River and St. Louis, which he hoped to capture, he reported that he had had nearly 12,000 men—but some lacked horses and 4,000 had no rifles. The 15,000 ascribed to him by the 19th-century historian Wiley Britton is presumably an overestimate, but determining accurate numbers for the troops engaged in this loosely documented campaign and the casualties they suffered is still to some extent a matter of guesswork.[4] The shortage of arms is believable. Kirby Smith had not done enough to supply Price, but the real problem for the Confederacy was that it was running out of resources. Price hoped to capture those vital missing supplies from federal stores in Missouri and in this, at least, he was largely successful. Overall, however, he was not, although he won some engagements as he moved with no great rapidity through Missouri.

The fight at Pilot Knob on September 27 was no Confederate victory, although they took the place. Union resistance delayed Price's army and cost it 1,500 casualties.[5] Rosecrans had time to reinforce St. Louis, in the eastern part of the state, and the capital Jefferson City in the center, which persuaded Price not to make serious attempts to capture either place. When he bypassed St. Louis and turned west it turned the offensive into a strategic irrelevance from the perspective of Washington DC, except to the extent that it used up military resources needed elsewhere. Price was no longer threatening the wider Midwest, or control of the Mississippi River, but in effect was conducting a very large and intermittently very active raid. Bypassing Jefferson City put an end to the Confederate plan to have Thomas Reynolds, their gubernatorial pretender, sworn in there.

Price was not recruiting and conscripting[6] as many soldiers as he had hoped, but some did come in to compensate for losses, including about 1,500 at Boonville where the Confederate army stopped for several days in mid-October. On October 15, the Confederates won a victory at Glasgow along with a cache of federal weapons. As they fought their way west through Jackson County (where Montgomery had once lived), they were now all mounted and armed, and mostly battle-hardened. Price, encouraged by Shelby, his most capable subordinate, hoped to capture Kansas City and beyond it Fort Leavenworth, the regional U.S. Army base with its storehouse of supplies. Would he encounter stalwart and effective resistance from a sufficient number of Kansas troops? The political divisions in that state, and the "large number of untried volunteers" in Curtis' army, led the Confederates to believe the answer would be no.[7] But Price was pushing his luck too far.

Montgomery had arrived in August 1864 at his rural home near Mound City, and when he resigned his commission Price was not threatening Kansas. That situation would change, a fact which Montgomery likely appreciated earlier than Carney and his militia major general, George Deitzler.

Curtis had appreciated it by September 17, when he warned Carney that the militia might be needed, repeating on September 20 his request that the governor call out the state troops. Carney declined to do so, even when Curtis repeated the request more urgently on and around October 5, when Price was plainly headed west on the south side of the Missouri River, in the direction of Kansas.

The reason for inaction was internal party politics:

> The Kansas governor was so embroiled in a factional fight for power within the Kansas Republican party that he had time for little else. The Carney and Lane factions were slugging it out in a bitter election campaign that bid fair to become a war within a war. Democrats and Radical Democrats were merely present as the two Republican groups fought for the United States Senate seat as well as political control of the state.
>
> By the end of the first week of October General Curtis was almost frantic in his efforts to arouse the governor.

Major General James Blunt, who as a lieutenant colonel served under Montgomery in 1861, and over him at the battle of Westport in 1864. (Library of Congress)

But Carney "could not be convinced that Kansas was in danger," seeing the general as an ally of Lane, whose Senate re-election prospects would depend on who got elected to the Kansas legislature. Carney thought Curtis was raising the alarm as "just a device to get the militia mobilized and thus keep these Kansas citizen-soldiers away from the polls on election day."[8]

Carney was elected in 1862 as an ally of Lane, but unsurprisingly they fell out. The governor also had a bad relationship with Blunt.[9]

Carney finally called out the militia on October 9, although this would not mark the end of the politicization of state troops. Curtis declared martial law the next day, directing that:

> all men, white or black, between the ages of eighteen and sixty will arm and attach themselves to some of the organizations of troops for temporary military service. … our object is Price and his followers. His forces are now reported

> as retreating from Jefferson City in this direction. My advance to meet him is already moving. Let troops of every organization press forward to join in his repulse and pursuit.

Curtis' declaration, from Carney's perspective, might seriously disrupt the election by preventing most of the potential voters from participating. The general's version of calling out the militia turned out to mean conscripting most of the electorate, with no provision for absentee ballots. Carney had been confident of defeating Lane's faction at the polls, but now everything was in doubt. In his mind, the threat of political defeat was much more real than anything Price's Confederate army might do.

The governor's obstructive politicking was, however, helpful to Montgomery, in two ways. It gave him time to recover his health, and indirectly caused him to be promoted to lead the 6th Kansas Militia Infantry Regiment, which drew recruits from Linn and northern Bourbon counties and was headquartered in Mound City.

Montgomery said in his December 10 letter to Stearns: "I had just got able to eat my breakfast at the table, when Price's Raid brought everybody, in Kansas, into the field."[10] This meant he had hardly been able to arise from bed or chair until early October, which may be an exaggeration, since in the same letter he writes about doing some farm work before the militia was called up. It is also possible that he was directing his sons and others rather than physically doing most of the work himself. At any rate, he now rallied enough to actively participate in two to three weeks of strenuous campaigning. Possibly this was not good for his long-term health, although any deleterious effects do not appear to have set in by the time he wrote the letter.

When the call came conscripting all able-bodied men into the militia, Montgomery ignored concerns about his still recovering health and reported for duty. He had spent much of 1862 trying to get back into the war, then succeeded in doing so and fought far from home for most of the next two years. Now, when he thought he had resigned from participation in it, the war was coming back for him.

The muster roll of the 6th Kansas State Militia Regiment still exists, and lists about 768 men signing up between October 9 and October 13, including Evan Montgomery and John Montgomery.[11] No James

Montgomery, however, is listed. Since there is ample and incontrovertible evidence (including multiple references by generals and others in the *Official Records*) that James Montgomery did enlist in the 6th Militia and soon commanded the regiment, an explanation is called for.

Holman states that the John Montgomery in the regiment was James' son, but this is unlikely since he was only 13 years old. Montgomery's first-born son, from his first marriage, was James the younger, who was still on duty in the Department of the South. As James the elder told Stearns in the December 10 letter noted above, the 6th Militia "performed our share of service, particularly in the battle of Westport. In that battle my second son showed great steadiness of nerve, and skill as a marksman." (Typically, Montgomery shows no braggadocio about his own superb performance as colonel.) His "second son"—and Clarinda's first—was Evan, who signed up as a private with Company C under Captain Theodore Wilson on October 11. This is two days later than most of the regiment—and may reflect a family dispute. Evan was only 17, so a year younger than those legally required to serve, and one or both of his parents may at first have tried to prevent or dissuade him from doing so. John Montgomery was the second son of his mother, but the third of his father.

The purported "John Montgomery" enrolled even later, on October 13, with the "irregular Colored Militia attached Sixth." James Montgomery said in his letter to Stearns that the regiment had "thirteen companies of white, and two of black militia." The likely explanation for the mix-up is that James Montgomery spent four days helping raise two primarily African-American companies, one of which he signed up with as a private, with his name being transcribed in error as John. Unlike most of the regiment, that company is listed as serving until October 30, which accords with other indications that Montgomery was one of the few militia soldiers to stay in Blunt's army until the effective end of the pursuit of Price. Evan likely was sent home on October 26 with the rest of his unit, with his father's blessing and to his mother's relief. (It is also possible that John Montgomery was unrelated, and James Montgomery failed to be formally enrolled in the regiment that he would soon be leading—which would be his only recorded failure in the upcoming campaign.)

While James Montgomery's name does not appear on the muster roll, the first one listed on it was the regiment's first commander. This man, Lt. Col. James Snoddy, was appointed by Carney and, as subsequent events would shortly demonstrate, took his side in the political dispute with the Lane faction, which was very likely not the same side as Montgomery. While the latter had no political or military ambition at this point, and was prepared to serve in a humble capacity to defeat Price, it may also be the case that Snoddy—for political reasons—did not want him taking on any leadership role such as being an officer.

To further muddy the picture, it is not even clear whether the 6th Kansas was a cavalry or infantry regiment. Perhaps mounted infantry is the best description. Several of its companies are listed as cavalry on the muster roll, but most, including those in which Evan and John Montgomery are listed, were not so classified. The regiment is sometimes cited as infantry, or just militia without specifying cavalry or infantry. But a 2016 Army historian, Charles D. Collins, lists it as a cavalry regiment serving in both the Paola District Brigade of Deitzler's militia division of Curtis' Army of the Border, where it was commanded by Brigadier General William Fishback, and in Blunt's Provisional Cavalry Division, in the Third Brigade of Col. Charles W. Blair.[12] It was Blair who had effective command of the 6th Kansas, and some other militia regiments, but the confusion would prove dangerous.

The Third Brigade was Blunt's only one with most regiments not specifically designated as cavalry, but it did include cavalry regiments, too, including Blair's 14th Kansas. While the 6th Kansas would fight on foot at Westport, its soldiers would have ridden on (or possibly been carted in wagons by) horses when necessary behind the lines, as the regiment was shifted back and forth during the campaign.[13] Montgomery no doubt rode his own horse.

Thus, the regiment was able to move quickly north, following the orders of Curtis and Blunt, whom Curtis had told on October 13 to concentrate at Hickman Mills, south of Kansas City, Missouri. Some senior Kansas militia officers were opposed to taking their men outside Kansas—though Snoddy initially obeyed orders to do so.

The political disputation now seriously complicated and threatened the Union military chain of command. While the Third Brigade's militia regiments were, according to Blunt and Curtis, under the command of Blair—they were also regarded by Kansas authorities as under the command of Fishback. The latter outranked Blair and did not fancy taking his orders, which he thought should come from Deitzler, the gubernatorial appointee who commanded Curtis' other division.

Curtis reported that soon after his declaration of martial law on October 10:

> The Governor and Major-General Deitzler called on me to ascertain my purpose as to taking the militia out of the State, expressing apprehensions of difficulty on that point if such was my purpose. They also informed me that expressions of some of my officers had led them to distrust the whole matter of the militia movement, supposing it might be a political scheme gotten up by some around me [to prevent militia soldiers from voting in the upcoming November election].

Those "around" Curtis would have included two of his newly appointed staff officers, Lane and Colonel Samuel Crawford, the latter of whom was running for governor with Lane's support against Solon Thacher. Carney was not seeking re-election as governor because he hoped the new state legislature would put him in the U.S. Senate to replace Lane.[14] (Also on General Curtis' staff was Pomeroy, Lane's colleague in the Senate.)

Curtis patched things up for the moment, but it was hardly reassuring that Deitzler would be commanding a key part of his army in the coming campaign and asserting additional authority over the militia troops in Blunt's division including the 6th Kansas. Many militia soldiers complained at being sent even a few miles out of state into Missouri, despite the westward advance of Price. Some Kansas newspapers were denouncing Curtis' actions, still refusing to credit the reports of Price representing a threat to their state.[15]

In this charged atmosphere, on October 16:

> Without General Blunt's or Colonel Blair's knowledge, General Fishback commanded Colonel J. S. Snoddy to take his 6th Kansas Militia back to Kansas to assist in that state's protection.

Major General Samuel Curtis, commander of Kansas troops in the Westport campaign. (Brady's National Photographic Portrait Galleries, Library of Congress)

They started off in that direction, but when Blunt found out:

> [his] violent temper exploded. Ordering the 15th Kansas Cavalry in pursuit of the defecting column, General Blunt raced ahead and, in person, stopped the regiment. ... He placed General Fishback and Colonel Snoddy under arrest, sent them to Paola under guard, and marched the regiment back to Hickman Mills himself. The men of the 6th Kansas Militia returned willingly, cheering General Blunt as they marched along. On their return to camp they promptly elected as their colonel James Montgomery.[16]

Fishback later claimed he sent Snoddy back because of the threat from Confederate guerrillas.[17]

The men of the 6th Kansas had probably been of varying opinions regarding the original Republican factional dispute between Carney and Lane, but they could see it made no sense to move away from potential battle in the hour of need. After Blunt's intervention, as Blair wrote to

Curtis the next day, "… as the head of the column was turned, and the object of the change became generally known, a shout went up such as would cheer the heart of every patriot in the State if it could have been heard across the line." Blair wrote sympathetically of Fishback, which likely helped persuade Curtis to release him, but said "Colonel Snoddy is better as he is. Difficulties are bred about him wherever he goes, and he lives in an atmosphere of perpetual strife and animosity." He praised Montgomery, and said the regiment now seemed "united and harmonious."[18]

Some of these men had seen active service but most had probably not, either being relatively old for battle, like Montgomery, or young for it like his son Evan. These mostly green troops needed now, in the middle of an active campaign, to be quickly molded into a unified and effective fighting force. Montgomery was exactly the right man for the job, albeit it was not one he had expected. He had ample experience of quickly training men to be soldiers and had learned, through experience, the necessity of military discipline and cooperation with other officers and units.

The mutual, reciprocated confidence between Montgomery and his new command was soon proven justified. As Blunt would report, the 6th Kansas selected "the veteran soldier, Col. James Montgomery, under whose leadership the regiment did gallant service."[19]

Snoddy, as Blair had recommended, remained incarcerated until after Westport. Fishback, released by Curtis to appease Carney and Deitzler, would find his way back to the front. (In 1868, Montgomery was engaged in friendly correspondence about state and other politics with John T. Snoddy, who wrote from Lawrence.[20] It seems likely that he was a relative of James Snoddy.)

On October 18, 1864, as Price continued to approach, Blair's brigade was ordered to the Big Blue River, where they gathered in needed supplies including "subsistence, arms, blankets, and tents"[21] and entrenched on the west bank. The Big Blue flows north into the Missouri River, between Kansas City to the west and Independence to the east. Still Carney, Deitzler and their newspaper supporters continued to scoff at the notion that Price was an approaching threat, or that martial law was necessary, and as a result many militia troops deserted[22]—not, however, in Montgomery's regiment or elsewhere in Blair's brigade.

The 6th Kansas was among the militia regiments which had taken the field without enough guns for all the soldiers, a situation which was now remedied from Army depots in the Kansas City area. The regiment's defensive position also gave Montgomery a little time to train men in use of the new weapons, and bind them into a fighting force. As in Florida in early 1863, he found himself training and arming raw recruits immediately before they went into action. Their success in the upcoming campaign reflects well on all concerned.

Blunt, meanwhile, went east with cavalry to fight delaying actions against Price in Lexington on October 19, and at the Little Blue River and Independence on October 21. The Confederates continued to advance westward, and Blair's brigade with the 6th Kansas held to their defensive position on the Big Blue.

Monnett says: "North of the Kansas City–Independence road as it crossed the main ford was [positioned] the 6th Kansas State Militia under Colonel James Montgomery, together with six hundred colored volunteers, well-mounted and trained. Immediately behind Colonel Montgomery's cavalry ..."[23] Curtis expected the rebel attack at the main ford. The exact unit of these "colored militia" (as Curtis quoted Blair calling them[24]) is unclear, though they must have been in Blair's brigade and at least some may have been part of Montgomery's regiment.

Shelby's Confederates engaged Curtis' and Blunt's line in the vicinity of the main ford on the morning of October 22, in minor skirmishing which may have involved the 6th Kansas. But it was more of a feint than an assault, a diversion and holding action.

The main rebel effort came several miles upstream to the south at Byram's Ford, brushing aside Jennison's brigade and inflicting heavy casualties on militia[25] (not including Montgomery's men). Deitzler's laggardly failure to follow orders to vigorously reinforce the position contributed to the Union loss, although Fishback did good service on the retreat.[26] Blair's brigade had to march quickly back toward Kansas City in the late afternoon, their horses having been sent back previously without them. The rest of the Army of the Border was also forced back.

Regiments got mixed up in confusion that night before the battle of Westport, which took place a little south of a hamlet of that name, itself a couple of miles south of what was then Kansas City. (All of the battlefield is now within the pleasant Country Club District, including The Plaza, of that metropolis. This is in sharp contrast to the battle site of Olustee, Florida, which remains in the middle of nowhere.) Only Blunt's division was in place on the battlefield that early morning to face Shelby's Confederate division, and Blunt was lacking Blair's brigade.

Blair that night of October 22/23 was trying to find and organize all his troops. After a conference of war, Blunt ordered Blair's brigade down from Kansas City at 3am, and Curtis ordered most of his army down at the same hour—but few of their departures were timely. Blair, however, reported that "Montgomery got his regiment off promptly at the hour indicated," while the rest of Blair's command was sorting through logistical problems—mainly lack of horse transport.[27] Montgomery had retrieved his soldiers' horses, which they would use to get to Westport, while fighting the battle on foot. The longtime colonel's experience was paying off. He knew the importance of organization and sorting out supply issues to achieving military success. His diligence enabled the 6th Kansas to be present on the battlefield that morning earlier than the rest of Blair's brigade, and far ahead of Deitzler's division of militia regiments. The 6th Kansas was quickly put into action.

"Blunt decided not to wait for the Union Army to concentrate. Instead, he opted for a spoiling attack to buy time for the Kansas troops to get into position."[28] In Blunt's own report, he said he was planning on attacking at dawn, "and soon after sunrise the First, Second and Fourth Brigades were deployed into line of battle on the south side of the timber skirting Brush Creek, where Shelby's division, of Price's army, was advancing upon my line. Skirmishers were thrown forward …"[29] and battle commenced.

Blunt was strongly in favor of the whole Army of the Border making its stand at Westport, as he had made clear to his more cautious commander, Curtis, who, like Blair, was not yet come down from Kansas City.[30] Blunt's early attack—if it did not end in disaster—was also a way of making sure that Curtis would follow through on his commitment to fight on this battlefield. That made the attack, in which Montgomery led the only militia regiment and the only detachment of Blair's brigade, a crucial part of the battle. Shelby realized that he had to defeat Curtis now, before he could combine with Pleasonton. So, Shelby, too, given his head by Price, was planning to attack. The two front-line division commanders from the opposite armies, Blunt and Shelby, were well matched. Both were experienced, aggressive, capable generals who would perform well that day.

According to the report of Major Thomas I. McKenny, a staff officer to Curtis whose job, unlike some of his colleagues', was more military than political:

> Another fractional regiment, commanded by Colonel Montgomery, and a number of colored soldiers, which I placed under command of Colonel Montgomery, I formed on the left of McLain's battery, and in a dense wood far in the advance, and it is with pleasure I state they behaved gallantly under a hot fire. The enemy being pressed on all sides gradually fell back.[31]

That last sentence considerably smooths over and truncates the back-and-forth reality of the rest of the morning's fighting.

The "colored soldiers" referred to by McKenny may be the same militia troops who had fought next to Montgomery the day before at Big Blue River, sent down by Blair with Montgomery's regiment. It is also possible McKenny was unaware that the 6th Kansas, unlike the vast majority of regiments, contained both White and Black soldiers, so that he did not realize Montgomery's "fractional regiment" actually included African-American troops. (Although Curtis' call-up order, quoted above, had specified "all men, white or black," the U.S. military was not legally desegregated until after World War II by Harry Truman. That president had been raised in Independence a generation after it was fought over in the Westport campaign, and had many older relatives who were supporters of the Confederacy.[32]) Blair's report quoted above did not indicate anyone was missing in the early hours of that morning when "Montgomery got his regiment off promptly," which means Montgomery had his Black companies with him along with the White. He may have brought other Black troops with him from Blair's brigade and may have had additional Black troops placed under him by McKenny. All the senior officers on the Kansas side, including Blair, Blunt, and Curtis (and probably including more junior officers like McKenny), were aware of Montgomery's solid record commanding Black troops in the South. That may well have inclined them at Big Blue River and Westport to place additional Black soldiers under his command.

That morning of Sunday, October 23, Blunt was trying to advance southward, across Brush Creek and then uphill against Shelby's division coming north. (The creek flows eastward into the Big Blue River.) Both armies were on the offensive, and as the morning went on were sometimes attacking, sometimes defending. (Meanwhile at Byram's Ford on the Big Blue, Pleasonton was attacking against Marmaduke's Confederate cavalry.) Montgomery and his Black and White soldiers were fighting before the rest of Blair's brigade and all of Deitzler's division had arrived, in the center and forefront of Blunt's line of attack.

The precise timing of events, as often in the history of battles, is hard to determine. McKenny indicated his placement of Montgomery's regiment happened after 9am, but Blunt's first attack was under way well before then. The account by the 21st century historian Kyle Sinisi goes a considerable way toward explaining the apparent discrepancy. Blunt's initial advance across Brush Creek and up the wooded hill into farm fields beyond, through the early morning mist, did not meet Confederate resistance.

Then:

> Near 8am, the main line … finally ran into Shelby's skirmishers and artillery. About thirty minutes later, McLain's battery wheeled into position just beyond the belt of trees covering Brush Creek. McLain then divided his artillery, sending one section of two guns under Lieutenant George Eayre forward up Wornall Road to a place on the hill overlooking both Brush Creek and the prairie to the south. Eayre engaged Richard Collins's battery of Confederate artillery, while also lobbing a number of shells into the rear of the advancing Confederate cavalry. … Despite the effectiveness of Eayre's opening salvos, his section remained on station for only a short time before having to withdraw and replenish its ammunition. McLain then ordered Lieutenant Caleb Burdsal's second section to take the place of Eayre in the cannonade. … For the most part, the Unionists got the better of this part of the engagement. Eayre's section eventually rearmed and joined Burdsal's section, and together they emptied a galling fire into Collins, who was forced to displace not once but three times.[33]

They destroyed one of Collins' guns, and continued to shell the rebel cavalry, causing significant casualties as attested by Confederate Brigadier General M. Jeff Thompson, who commanded Price's best unit, the Iron Brigade. Almost as important, as it turned out, McLain's and Montgomery's men forced the Confederates to keep shooting at them. Shelby's front line (including the Iron Brigade) was running low on ammunition, and the general held up his advance for an hour or more while he sent up new supplies.

Montgomery's infantry was protecting Captain William McLain's Colorado Battery. Both units were then pulled back as Blunt retreated to Brush Creek.

According to Captain Richard J. Hinton of the Second Kansas Colored Infantry Regiment, McLain's battery was at first "in position at the edge of the timber, half a mile to the rear," but became closer to the front line as the rebels counter-attacked and its sections advanced. The Confederates were "receiving large reinforcements, and advancing with spirit and vigor. Their long lines pressed forward steadily." Then McLain responded: "Two guns, under Lieutenant Eayre, were ordered forward, taking position on the hill and overlooking the open prairie across which the enemy was advancing. The guns did excellent work, were double shotted with canister, while the range being short and the firing rapid, every shot told. The enemy's guns replied with vigor."[34] Then, as described by Sinisi above, McLain also sent Burdsal's section forward.

So, Montgomery's regiment and possibly associated Black militia had left Kansas City at 3am for the front line at Westport, while the rest of Blair's brigade followed at dawn. As a result, Montgomery arrived in time to be part of Blunt's first attack (although not in its first wave) while the rest of the brigade did not. McLain's battery wheeled into line about 8:30, according to Sinisi, but maybe a little later in reality, and McKenny then placed Montgomery's troops into position near it. They soon found themselves far in the Union advance as the gunners and infantry were sent forward while the Confederates counter-attacked, and other Union units were pushed back. McLain's guns were protected by Montgomery's rifles and played a major role in stalling the rebel advance, stabilizing the front. Then they were all part of the general retreat ordered by Blunt.

This retreat, though, was no disaster. Rather, Blunt had achieved his goal of holding off the Confederates from advancing beyond Brush Creek, while giving time for the rest of his division and Curtis' army to arrive. The morning's first attack and counter-attack had not significantly altered the armies' positions on the battlefield south of Brush Creek. But as a result of that first engagement the Confederates had already lost their best chance of victory, and Montgomery played a significant part in stopping them. His ability to obey orders and arrive ahead of the rest of his brigade at the battlefield, was almost as important as his decision at Olustee to march his reserve brigade without orders toward the sound of the guns. In each case, at the beginning of Westport and toward the end of Olustee, what he and his men did mattered. His and their promptness, courage and effectiveness had a positive impact on the course of both battles.

Blair came down from Kansas City to the right flank of the battlefield, near the state line but still in Missouri. Then the 6th Kansas, which had been in the center-left with McLain, moved quickly right to join Blair and participate in the flank attack which he was about to lead.

Command arrangements remained ambiguous. Fishback was again on the scene, and his report makes it sound as if he was in command of Blair's militia regiments, although it is highly doubtful that Montgomery regarded him as such. Certainly Blair, Blunt and Curtis did not think so, and Fishback did not press the point, no longer disputing or interfering with Blair's orders. To Montgomery's credit, he was able to coordinate positively with both Blair and Fishback, who both praised him in their reports. Fishback named three regiments and their commanders, including Montgomery, as having "behaved with splendid gallantry."[35] These commanders did indeed accompany their men advancing repeatedly toward the guns of the enemy.

The militia infantry regiments in Blair's brigade, including Montgomery's contingent, "moved into line like seasoned veterans."[36] Believing Shelby was about to flank him, Blair without waiting for orders decided to preempt the anticipated rebel attack, taking the 6th and two other regiments with him. Curtis approved Blair's move and sent reinforcements. They went through heavy timber and brush to an open field.

Blair reported: "A heavy fire was here opened on us from a corn-field which stretched out from our right front, and which seemed filled with skirmishers, and from a large brick house in an orchard just beyond, in which a party of sharpshooters was stationed. In a few minutes several of our men had fallen, and the fire was incessant and close. I immediately ordered the right of the brigade forward and drove the enemy from the corn-field and house, while the left of the line kept straight forward through a stubble-field on their flank. About half a mile to the front the cavalry and artillery came out the road on our left and we joined the line, relieving Jennison's cavalry from its position in support of McLain's battery. We then commenced driving the enemy steadily before us …"[37]

Like McKenny's report quoted above and other official accounts of the battle (it is rather a feature of such reports), Blair's last sentence jumps ahead to oversimplify the more confused and precarious reality of military conditions. In fact, it is unclear whether the events described in Blair's

Montgomery is buried in Mound City National Cemetery, Kansas, near the Union soldiers' monument. (Historic American Landscapes Survey, Library of Congress)

report describe his first flank movement or a considerably later attack, which Collins maintains.[38]

Jennison's report, on the other hand, as quoted by Curtis, says the army was forced back once again after Blair reinforced him at McLain's battery, before a general advance was ordered.[39] This was the same battery which Montgomery's regiment had fought beside earlier in the day, before Blunt had to pull the Union line back the first time. McLain's battery would continue to play a crucial role in the battle and campaign, so Montgomery's role in protecting it earlier that morning was important beyond its contribution to stopping the first and most promising (or dangerously threatening, from the Union perspective) Confederate attack. But his day was far from over. Like McLain and his gunners, Montgomery and his infantry continued to be engaged in the battle.

The flanking advance which Blair had led, then reinforced by Curtis along the line, made progress "up the heights", but before it "could reach the crest, the dashing General Shelby had reinforced his line and beaten the attackers back. Once more the Army of the Border retreated to Brush Creek. There General Curtis regrouped his forces and advanced up the heights again."[40]

Curtis also personally led an artillery battery on another right flanking maneuver which considerably bolstered the Union position. Blunt, meanwhile, was bringing up more artillery to outgun the Confederates, along with infantry and cavalry. McLain's battery continued to be very effective and was saved by Jennison's horsemen from a Confederate counter-attack. Blair's Third Brigade on the right, including Montgomery's regiment, continued to lead the Union advance.[41]

Gradually the Army of the Border, now including Deitzler's division, forced its way forward, until in the middle of the day Pleasonton broke through Marmaduke's Confederate defenses behind Byram's Ford and erupted on Shelby's right flank. This resulted in a precipitate rebel retreat followed by rearguard actions. Shelby would long survive the war, but he and other Confederate dead would be buried at Forest Hill Cemetery. That is the site of the "last stand" behind a stone wall where they held off, until dark,[42] the oncoming Union army, before continuing the retreat south.

The battle of Westport was over, the Union had won a decisive victory, and Price's great raid was no longer in any sense an offensive operation. It had quickly become a mere scramble to escape south with the fat wagon train of supplies which the Confederates had captured across the state of Missouri, and without taking too many more casualties.

As for the casualties of Westport itself, it is difficult to come up with precise figures. It was the largest battle Montgomery fought in, with over 30,000 troops engaged[43], the Union side outnumbering the rebels. But it was far from the "Gettysburg of the West" which some have hyperbolically called it. The fighting was not as intense and bloody as in greater conflicts like Shiloh and Spotsylvania—and, obviously, Gettysburg. Union losses were higher at the smaller southern battle of Olustee, where Montgomery's brigade had staved off disaster. And while some at that earlier battle had looked down on his looser, western style of command, here at Westport it was not out of place. Curtis' troops were not lining up to be mowed down in rigid, strictly controlled formations, and neither were their Confederate foes. Yet the Kansans were disciplined enough—with support from Pleasonton's Missouri cavalry—to win a complete victory.

Curtis estimated he suffered a total of 500 killed and wounded, but that did not include Pleasonton's losses. Shelby lost "eight hundred of his best men"[44], which does not include Marmaduke's losses. According to Monnett, "... the majority of units involved in the action did not report their casualties. 1,500 killed or severely wounded on both sides in the action of October 23 would be a conservative figure and for the three days of action, October 21, 22, 23, 3,500 would be as near a correct estimate as is possible."[45] Sinisi estimates lower numbers.

Blair's report gave more praise to Montgomery than any other regimental commander, listing him first on the list of those "I desire to make special mention of."[46] The "Honor Roll" listed by Curtis also named Montgomery.[47] Blunt's report, as noted above, also praised Montgomery, and mentioned him again positively in a closing section, along with the other two militia colonels in Blair's brigade, combined with a pointed dig against their unnamed superiors (*i.e.* Fishback, Deitzler and Carney). Of the three colonels and their men, Blunt said, "... their conduct was uniformly that of the true soldier and patriot, and worthy of emulation by their commander-in-chief and other superiors in the militia organization."[48]

Blair's report also indicates that he had lost touch with his subordinate commanders when he moved to Curtis' staff later in the campaign, and had no casualty figures from them. He also probably did not include those less than "severely" wounded in his estimate. "From the best information I can gather," he said, "the entire losses of the brigade killed, wounded, and prisoners, will not exceed 100, of which twenty-five were taken from Colonel McCain's regiment at one time [at Big Blue River]."[49] While Blair's estimate sounds low, the exact casualties of the Third Brigade and the 6th Kansas Militia Regiment are not recorded. The 6th Kansas was obviously in the thick of the fighting at Westport, more so than the great majority of militia regiments, which may have meant it suffered more than most. But its losses do not appear to have been very high. Montgomery's style of combat was not one to unnecessarily sacrifice the lives of his men. And by Westport his cautiously courageous and experienced leadership was at its most effective.

Despite having eaten little or nothing for days, the behavior of the 6th Kansas in the pursuit south on October 24 continued to be exemplary. They were partly motivated by concern for their homes and kin, because Price had swerved into Kansas and was approaching Linn County. This was the burned-over southern border land between Missouri and Kansas, which had been the scene of conflict over slavery for a decade, often targeting civilians, and would now be fought over one last time. Given the increasingly brutal nature of the Missouri guerrilla war, Montgomery's soldiers had reason to be very worried about what the Confederates would do. Most militia regiments, at the request of Carney and Deitzler and by agreement of Curtis, had been released from service immediately after—on the same day as—the battle of Westport. But three regiments of militia soldiers from southeastern Kansas, where Price was headed, remained for the moment in the Army of the Border.

Pleasonton's cavalry, now in the lead of the Union army, camped on the night of October 24 at the Marais des Cygnes River, in Linn County. Blair reported that:

> my brigade brought up the rear of the column, and receiving no orders, stood by our horses' heads in the rain all night, or until the roar of artillery announced that the battle was begun. Most of my militia had fallen out in the terrible march of the day before from fatigue and want of food, leaving me only my batteries, the Sixth Regiment, Colonel Montgomery, and Eves' Battalion, and being satisfied that there would be some heavy fighting at the front, before my brigade could cross the river, I hurried forward to see if my individual services could be of any avail.[50]

Thus Blair slipped away from the remnants of a brigade which had mostly ceased to exist, having dropped out on the way down from Westport—but not Montgomery and his regiment. They were still there. Now, however, they were left in the rear without their brigade commander and behind Pleasonton's cavalry, which, under Curtis' overall command, engaged in three attacks on October 25. The second of them, Mine Creek, was a real battle and an overwhelming Union victory—and the one closest to Montgomery's home. It was fortunate for Clarinda and the children that Pleasonton pressed so hard on the Confederate army that day, because more than a few of Price's men would have heard about Fort Montgomery and might well have been inclined to attack it, had they been given leisure and opportunity to do so.

Pleasonton's most effective brigade commander was a 30-year-old lieutenant colonel, Frederick Benteen, who played the key role in attacking and routing a much larger force of Confederates across the rolling prairie of Mine Creek. After the war he would serve as a captain in the 7th Cavalry, and in 1876 fought hard defensively at the battle of the Little Bighorn, saving the regiment from annihilation.

Most—perhaps all—of the remaining Kansas militia soldiers, including Evan Montgomery, were sent home on October 26, the day after Mine Creek and the two other cavalry engagements. This was authorized by a Curtis order on that date.

Fishback said that following Curtis' order:

> I ordered all the militia at Fort Scott from my district to march to the vicinity of their homes and hold themselves in readiness to repel raids subject to the commander in chief, among whom was the gallant Col. James Montgomery, commanding Sixth Regiment Kansas State Militia, who of my brigade was last to quit the chase.[51]

It is not clear whether James Montgomery actually went home on October 26. As noted above, the "irregular Colored Militia attached Sixth" on the regimental muster roll are listed as serving until October 30, and the "John Montgomery" listed as part of this unit is very likely a clerical error for James Montgomery. Probably all militia soldiers were given the option of going home on October 26. But Montgomery may well have communicated directly with Blunt or Curtis, and at their request kept serving in the Army of the Border with other volunteers until October 30, two days after the battle of Newtonia. Union command disputes continued, as they had throughout the campaign, to hamper the efficiency of the pursuit of Price. But Montgomery, who had engaged in plenty of disputes with senior officers in previous campaigns, was no longer inclined to do so.

Other Montgomerys saw the aftermath of battle. As the colonel wrote to Stearns on December 10:

> The enemy were hurried through Kansas so rapidly that they had little time for mischief; and our little town escaped without injury; though a battle was fought close by it, and in sight of my place. When this last named battle was over, my wife and daughters, with other female friends hurried to the field, in search of friends, each hoping for the best, but fearing the worst. Their anxiety was soon relieved by hearing that those they sought were still safe, and pursuing the enemy: They were, however, in time to be of use in relieving the wants of the wounded.[52]

It is unclear whether the battle referred to was Mine Creek, which took place within Linn County but not literally "in sight of" Fort Montgomery, or lesser but uncomfortably closer military encounters. Because Price's retreating army actually did have some "time for mischief", including in the direction of Montgomery's home. It made two unsuccessful attempts to capture Mound City on October 25, and Kansas militia soldiers—though probably not Montgomery's regiment—helped repel the second one. Blunt had reinforced a small garrison there with Col. Thomas Moonlight's cavalry brigade, which fought off the first attack, but then Moonlight and most of his men set off south to protect Fort Scott. To replace them in Mound City, Blunt sent in some militia from Paola, over 30 miles north, which had been ordered south at midnight by Curtis. The militia helped fight off the second attack, which may have been made by guerrillas.[53]

Whether or not it fought before Mound City, Montgomery's regiment was in the rear of the general Union advance. This seems to have resulted in it not being actively engaged in the three cavalry combats on October 25, at Marais des Cygnes and Mine Creek, Kansas, and Charlot's Farm, Missouri, on the Marmaton River. Nor did it fight as a unit at the battle of Newtonia, Missouri, three days later, which marked the last significant action of the campaign as Price continued to retreat south. He veered west into Indian Territory in November, with his much-reduced army re-emerging the next month into southwestern Arkansas, where they spent the winter.

The rebel soldiers had crossed into Kansas the previous day, October 24, and murdered some settlers near Trading Post.[54] According to a 21st-century historian quoting from a participant, the Confederates also:

> looted supplies from the nearby homesteads. Shelby's adjutant stated, "Haystacks, houses, barns, produce, crops, and farming implements were consumed before the march of his squadrons and what the flames spared, the bullet finished," and that the Rebels soothed, "the wounds of Missouri by stabbing the breast of Kansas." Union soldiers then "hung some of the prisoners in retaliation for the wanton destruction of Kansas farms and alleged violations against the female residents of Trading Post."[55]

The wounds would not be soothed by more killing, and there is no indication that during this campaign Montgomery was involved in any of it outside battle—no act of retaliation, no execution of a prisoner or deserter. In Missouri, as in many other states where slavery was legal until the Civil War, banditry, revenge, and political murders would continue after the surrenders, as some former Confederates refused to accept defeat. But Clarinda Montgomery and her daughters and stepdaughter did help tend the actual wounded, as peace finally came to the Kansas side of the border. The Army set up a hospital in Mound City on October 26.[56]

In Kansas, at least and at last, the peace and freedom which the Montgomerys had fought for so long, finally prevailed—although continued waves of western settlement would bring their own challenges to law and order. With Price driven out and Lincoln re-elected soon after, most

Kansans were anxious to move on from recent perils and focus on their peacetime livelihood. In their haste, they often left important historical details, like the casualties of the Westport campaign, undocumented. But some of the Union soldiers killed at Mine Creek and Marais des Cygnes were buried in Mound City, in what became a little national cemetery adjacent to the town burying ground. Montgomery's bones would ultimately be laid there with them.

The aftermath of the campaign includes one dark cloud from 450 miles away in Colorado, yet falling over the reputation of Curtis. His harsh orders that summer encouraged Colonel John Chivington to perpetrate the Sand Creek Massacre on November 29, 1864, killing more than 100 Indian women and children. Captain Silas Soule ordered his men not to participate and testified against Chivington in the official inquiry, which forced his superior to resign from the Army. Nor did Curtis defend the colonel's conduct, but the damage was done.

Soule had been a young ally of Montgomery's in prewar Kansas. In early 1860, they went on a dangerous two-man undercover mission to Charles Town, Virginia, to scout out the possible rescue of John Brown's companions. He then moved to Colorado, joining the U.S. Army when Civil War came. Soule fought in the 1862 battle of Glorieta Pass, which defeated the Confederate invasion of New Mexico.

Blunt had his reputation damaged in postwar financial dealings with Indians. Like Lane, he was also suspected of profiting from wartime contracts, and would suffer from poor mental health in his later years.[57]

Crawford, after almost two terms as governor, resigned in November 1868 to go back briefly into the Army, commanding a Kansas regiment serving with George Armstrong Custer against the Indians.

Lane was re-elected to his Senate seat the next year as a result of his Republican faction beating Carney's in the 1864 legislative elections, but (as we shall see) it did him little good.

The public legacies of Curtis, Blunt, and Lane—maybe Crawford, too—like that of Montgomery and most notable human beings, were to some extent morally ambiguous. Exceptions might include Soule and Tubman, two close allies of Montgomery.

General Hood's offensive in Tennessee, the Confederacy's main campaign toward the end of 1864 to which Price's great raid was a sort of supplemental prequel, was crushed at the battles of Franklin and Nashville, in late November and mid-December. Thomas' victorious army at Nashville included reinforcements under Maj. Gen. A. J. Smith, which Rosecrans had sent from Missouri once Price was defeated.

Sherman's march to the sea was not an assured success until he captured Savannah, Georgia, on December 21.

But the thorough defeat of Price's raid was accomplished in October, well before Election Day on November 8, and had electoral ramifications far beyond Kansas. Like Sheridan's Shenandoah Valley campaign in Virginia which preceded it, the military campaign in Missouri and Kansas, especially the battle of Westport, was another sign of federal success, and so contributed to Lincoln's re-election. Most Northern voters perceived that under current policies, the end of the war was in sight—although relatively few of them would have been familiar with the details of the campaign in Missouri and Kansas. Still, if the Union victory there was not greatly noticed in faraway population centers, an equivalent defeat would have been, and would have had a negative electoral effect. And the non-military event which the voters themselves brought about, the election victories of Republicans including and especially Lincoln, amounted to the Confederacy's most crushing defeat. The election results made Union victory in the Civil War, along with emancipation of all slaves, a virtual certainty.

While Montgomery's role in these matters—his Last Hurrah as a soldier—was not as prominent as the generals', it was significant and admirable.

CHAPTER 7

Back to the Land and the Lord

The Lost Cause school of Southern historians, begun by former Confederate generals such as Jubal Early, and becoming highly influential for many years with mainstream American historians, tended to downplay the role of slavery in causing the Civil War. Instead, its adherents stressed factors such as the tariffs sought by Northern industrial manufacturers and opposed by the rural South.

Montgomery, though, was as much an agrarian as any southerner, and was happy to resume farming now that the war was winding down. The happiness of the reunion with his wife Clarinda and family was enhanced by the birth of their last child, a daughter, Nellie, on September 8, 1865. His health had suffered in the war, limiting his ability to do as much vigorous physical work as in his youth. But Clarinda, 12 years younger, was used to operating the farm, and most of their children were now old enough to help.

Montgomery was also as religious as any Christian Confederate, and resumed his preaching in these postwar years. He "returned to his farm in Linn County and also returned to his earlier profession as a preacher. He led the First Day Adventist church congregation in Linn County until his death." Another source says he "abandoned the 'Campbellite' faith, became a First-Day Adventist, and preached that doctrine at various places in Kansas."[1]

But it is also likely that his view of Reconstruction differed greatly from that of most White southerners. He would have been glad to see ratification of the 13th, 14th and 15th amendments to the Constitution in the years after the war ended, and would have shared Northern outrage at attacks on the former slaves who tried to use these new laws to assert their political rights.

On the other hand, not all Montgomery's former allies shared the same views on Reconstruction. Jim Lane had been re-elected U.S. senator from Kansas, but then angered some of his radical Republican friends by siding with President Andrew Johnson, who was increasingly opposed to Black civil rights. Lane was probably partly motivated by a desire to retain presidential patronage in Kansas. Still, his political problems can hardly explain his suicide in 1866. Lane and Montgomery hit a low point in their careers in the ruthless 1861 Missouri campaign, but they each played a role in the Union victory. Whereas Montgomery returned to family, farm, and faith after the war, Lane could not escape personal demons amid the turmoil of public life. His successor as senator was another Republican Union veteran, Edmund G. Ross, who ironically became a more famous ally of Johnson's when his was the swing vote in the Senate in 1868 which saved the president from impeachment. Ross went on to lose re-election in 1870, but persevered, and in 1885 (long after Lane and Montgomery were dead) was appointed territorial governor of New Mexico by Grover Cleveland, the first Democratic president since Buchanan.

The year before Lane's death, in April 1865, with the Civil War not yet ended, U.S. Army Captain Silas Soule had married in Colorado. Then, three weeks later, he was killed while on duty in Denver suppressing a disturbance. His killer was never brought to justice, and it was never determined if the incident was connected to Soule's testimony about Chivington's Sand Creek massacre. But his death must have been a painful reminder to Montgomery that not all the world's evils were connected to slavery and its abolition—the latter a cause which had been supported by both Chivington and Soule, along with Lane, Blunt, and most of Montgomery's associates.

According to Kansas census records, Montgomery's eldest son, James, served out the war with the 34th U.S. Colored Infantry in the South. Evan Montgomery, after fighting at Westport with the Kansas militia, went on to serve in Virginia with the 1st Massachusetts Heavy Artillery. Both of the elder sons, like their father, had turned out to be good soldiers.

Montgomery, as he told Stearns, was willing to continue to recruit for the Civil War army even after he himself was no longer serving it—but not solely for idealistic reasons.

> There are a number of young men here who wish to enter the service. In view of the fact that our state gives no "Counties," [*sic.* Probable mis-transcription for Bounties] while we are far ahead of our quota, I have advised them to enlist in Massachusetts, or some other state which pays large bounties. They have not the means to travel on, but I will forward them, if by so doing, I can benefit myself as well as them. Now, I wish you to inform me what bounty your state pays, on enlistment, and what aid to the families of enlisted men. If I find I can save myself, and something more, by the Operation, I will bring you a few recruits, this winter.[2]

Kansas did not need to pay bounties to recruit soldiers because it had a very high proportion of volunteers, but Montgomery apparently felt that Massachusetts and the prosperous Stearns, between them, might pay enough to make it worthwhile for both him as facilitator and the volunteers if the latter enlisted from there. It is not certain whether anything came of this scheme, or whether Stearns approved of it, but one indication that it did go ahead is Evan Montgomery's enlistment in a Massachusetts regiment. Montgomery's materialistic approach perhaps foreshadows a significant strain in the spirit of postwar America, a time which at its most plutocratic and corrupt levels in the corridors of power and finance, became known as the Gilded Age. Montgomery, however, was never tainted by financial scandal, and never enriched himself.[3]

Nor was he exploiting Stearns, as just a parasite on that rich benefactor. Nor had he ever been. Back when he was commanding a brigade besieging Fort Wagner, he wrote in a September 4, 1863, letter to Clarinda: "In addition to the amount of money which I now send you, I have just sent Fifty-two Dollars to George I. Stearns, of Boston, being money with interest which I borrowed of him in Washington last winter."[4] There is no real doubt that he and his family members, including the two sons who volunteered for the Army and fought in the war, had worthy motives for their involvement in public affairs. Those ranged from philanthropy to patriotism, and always included a determination to accomplish the abolition of slavery.

The Gilded Age was hardly a factor in Linn County, and there are much more positive ways of viewing the new preoccupations of most Americans, plunging back into regular life. Montgomery was interested in making money to support his family, which for the past decade had often had to survive in his absence the dangers and droughts of life along the border country of southern Kansas and Missouri. But the drought was over now, and although that brought different problems for farmers, as he told Stearns, his focus now was on making a living through agriculture, not dubious recruitment schemes. Farming not fighting was now his priority. And prospects were promising:

> We have had a very wet fall; and the winter, so far, continues wet. I had sowed twenty acres of wheat, and plowed seventy acres more, which I intended to sow, when I was interrupted by Price's Raid. The weather, while we were in the service, was the best of the season; but the very day I got home it commenced raining; and has kept the ground so wet, ever since, that I could do nothing with it. Our labor, however, will not be lost, as the land, plowed this fall, will be in good condition for oats and Hungarian grass, with only the labor of harrowing. The quantity of corn raised on my place this season, is about one hundred acres: averaging thirty-three bushels to the acre, and selling, in the field, at $1.50 per bushel: the purchaser hauling it himself. I have sold some at that price, and could sell the product of a thousand acres at that if I had it, wheat is $2.00, oats the same as corn. Prairie hay $.10 in the stack. Cattle, Hogs, Mules, and Horses, in proportion to everything else. At these prices, farming pays better than fighting. I have been thus particular in writing about my private affairs on account of the interest which I know you take in my welfare. My oldest son is still with the Regiment in Florida. I am now exercising my skill, as a carpenter, in the way of adding conveniences to my dwelling.[5]

As he and his family continued to work on the farm in the years after the war, Montgomery likely heard about Reconstruction's progress in the Beaufort area of South Carolina, where Black citizens shared in growing prosperity as they exercised new political and civil rights. He had contributed to the Port Royal Experiment there during the war, which laid the groundwork for the area's future success. He would have known and worked with Robert Smalls, the former slave and Union sailor and soldier from Beaufort, who was elected after the war to the

South Carolina legislature, and, after Montgomery's death, to the U.S. Congress.

Much closer to home, he would have noted in 1867 the murder of Joseph Bailey, sheriff of Vernon County, Missouri—which is adjacent to the southern end of Linn County, Kansas—by pig-stealing former Confederate bushwhackers. Bailey, like Montgomery himself but with less controversy, had served with distinction as a Union colonel on obscure fronts of the Civil War.

Montgomery's friend and comrade Harriet Tubman was farming and doing other work on her property near Auburn, NY, where many years later she would build an infirmary and a home for the aged, leaving everything at her death to the African Methodist Episcopal Zion Church. In 1869, she married a younger man (though he would predecease her) named Nelson Davis. He was a veteran of the 8th U.S. Colored Troops Infantry Regiment, whose Civil War service, like Montgomery's, included the battle of Olustee.

Montgomery probably shared the radicals' frustration with the policies of President Johnson who they thought was not doing enough to protect the rights of African-Americans. He likely backed the more assertive policies of Johnson's successor, President Grant, to suppress White terrorism such as that perpetrated by the Ku Klux Klan. While Montgomery's relatively early death was a loss to himself and his family, at least he was spared knowing about the coming collapse of Reconstruction and the establishment of the Jim Crow order through most of the South, where many of the gains made by Black Americans were reversed until the rise of the civil rights movement in the mid-20th century.

But these were fights Montgomery had to leave to others. He had been away from his wife and family for much of the past decade, especially during the most recent war years, while they, often at considerable risk to themselves, had supported his decisions and the abolitionist cause. They were not rich people. Now, aged 50 with a large family to support including a newborn daughter, it was his turn to cultivate the land and help work it to provide for them all. He spent considerable time with the Kansas historian, Holloway, and paid ordinary, more-or-less casual attention to current politics. Except for explicitly religious events, he left the public stage.

The war had shaken the faith (or confirmed the disbelief) of many young surviving soldiers, such as the future U.S. Supreme Court justice Oliver Wendell Holmes Jr. and the writer Ambrose "Bitter" Bierce. According to a modern historian of Civil War attitudes to death, "As they faced horrors that forced them to question their ability to cope, their commitment to the war, even their faith in a righteous God, soldiers, and civilians alike struggled to retain their most cherished beliefs, to make them work in the dramatically altered world that war had introduced." Older abolitionists like Montgomery and Tubman, whose political faith had grown out of their religious one, were less likely to find either threatened by events.

> In face of the profound upheaval and chaos that civil war brought to their society and to their own individual lives, Americans North and South held tenaciously to deeply rooted beliefs that would enable them to make sense of a slaughter that was almost unbearable. Their Victorian and Christian culture offered them the resources with which to salve these deep spiritual wounds.[6]

But, in Montgomery's case, his religious practice might be subject to changes in form to deal with newly salient issues.

Up to the Civil War, the 19th century in America had seen a large-scale revival of Protestant evangelical religion, in which Montgomery had participated throughout his life, along with a steady growth in Roman Catholic, Jewish, and other religious practice. But there were countervailing trends, including a rise in skepticism among intellectuals, especially those influenced by Charles Darwin's writings about evolution. And the fast-rising "spiritualist" movement seems to have had materialist roots, in the movement of tables and other devices to supposedly communicate with the dead. The terrible losses of the war made many doubt the existence of a benign, all-powerful deity. But at the same time, they moved the longtime skeptic Lincoln to a profound religious analysis of the war in his Second Inaugural Address.

As for Montgomery, despite having an eye for the main chance in brokering enlistments, unsuccessful postwar efforts to secure a military pension, and determination to make a profit from the farm, it was by no means just materialist concerns that occupied his mind. But he had also moved beyond his prior denominational loyalties, in both more ecumenical and sectarian directions.

Montgomery had been raised as a Congregationalist and became a preacher in the new Campbellite or Christian Church as a young man. According to an 1883 *History of the State of Kansas:*

> ... after the war he became an Adventist, belonging to the "First-Day Adventists," not to the "Seventh-Day Adventists." He was known as a "Soul Sleeper," because he believed in and advocated the doctrine that from death to the Judgment Day the soul is unconscious or "sleeps." He spent much time in thought upon religious subjects, and held discussions and preached in Mound City, Fort Scott and elsewhere from the close of the war to the time of his death.[7]

Mound City's Catholic Church was not built until 1941, but there was a Catholic mission to the Indians on Sugar Creek in the 1840s, near what would become Fort Montgomery. The future canonized Saint Rose Philippine Duchesne lived there for a while, and the mission moved north in 1847 to St. Marys, Kansas. In Montgomery's time, Linn County had various Protestant churches at some of which he preached, not confining himself to the relatively few fellow practitioners of First-Day Adventism.

The Adventist movement is part of the tradition of American Protestantism derived from the Dutch Reformation theologian Jacobus Arminius, who embraced free will, as opposed to the strict Calvinist doctrine of predestination. More directly, it can be traced to a Baptist from upstate New York and Vermont named William Miller, who preached the imminent second coming of Christ in 1844. When this failed to happen in the "Great Disappointment", Adventists splintered into various factions, the most successful of which turned into the Seventh-Day Adventists, who recognize Saturday as the sabbath.

The First-Day Adventists retained the traditional Sunday sabbath, as well as Bible-based trinitarian beliefs. They became the Advent Christian Church, whose key leader, Joshua V. Himes, favored abolition, temperance, and women's rights, and inclined toward pacifism. The church's modern website teaches that on judgment day, when souls awake, the righteous will receive everlasting life in a heaven on earth "forever free from sin and death", while the lives of wicked will suffer "complete extinction of being"—as opposed to the eternal torture of the damned which was preached by some other denominations.

The modern church also states:

> We believe that war is contrary to the spirit and teaching of our Lord and Master, Jesus Christ; that it is contrary to the spirit of true brotherhood; and that our influence should be used against it. We believe the Bible also teaches that properly constituted government is ordained of God and is a divine instrument for man's welfare and protection. When an Advent Christian decides on the basis of Scripture and conscience, either to bear arms or to submit to penalties imposed for his refusal to do so, local Advent Christian congregations should extend continued fellowship and nurture.

Such teachings might not at first glance seem like a good fit for Montgomery the Old Testament style warrior, who was willing to defy the federal government in armed conflict in prewar Kansas and had to learn to be merciful. But on further consideration, one can see why he might have been receptive to them.

His last sermon was described 30 years later by Theodosius Botkin, a young Union veteran who would become a judge and state legislator:

> On the Sunday before his death, in December, 1871, Montgomery preached a sermon at Trading Post, the scene of the Hamelton [sic] or Marais des Cygnes massacre. It was my privilege to hear his discourse. I sat near the front, with Austin Hall and Amos Hall on the one hand and Mr. and Mrs. Harvey Smith upon the other. The Halls were of the number of Hamelton's victims who fell at the first on that tragic morn in May, 1858.

Amos Hall had been wounded, and Austin Hall feigned death. Also present at the service, Botkin said, were "a score of more" of Montgomery's comrades at that desperate time, and the preacher began by getting everyone to sing *The Battle Hymn of the Republic.* "Be not deceived," he said then. "God is not mocked; for whatsoever a man soweth, that shall he also reap."

Botkin does not say this, but the "theme" of the sermon he describes sounds similar to that of Lincoln's Second Inaugural. It dealt with:

> the accountability of communities, institutions and nations to the same laws of God that govern the individual. The discourse was logical, powerful and impressive. Before us stood the tall and slender form of that greatest man, if history were

> written true, in all the sanguinary struggles that preceded the civil war. His shaggy shock of long, black hair and his shaggier black whiskers united to entirely enclose in a circle the forehead, the eyes and nose, but left enough exposed to reveal the deep and sincere earnestness and enthusiasm of their possessor. He seemed to fairly vibrate with the importance of the great truths that filled his bosom.

Botkin quotes Montgomery quoting himself in 1858, calling on Austin Hall "to remember … when I prophesied that the remaining years of slavery could be numbered upon the fingers of one hand, and that in that period I would lead a host of negro soldiers, dressed in the national uniform, in the redemption of our country and the negro race from the curse of slavery."[8]

While Botkin's account is definitely worth having, his focus on Montgomery being the "greatest man" in the "sanguinary" prewar history of Kansas, with the Civil War itself reduced to a self-aggrandizing prophecy, falls a little flat for this last public occasion. It is natural enough that Montgomery should have focused on such matters so near the site of the Marais des Cygnes massacre, in the presence of its wounded victims and family members of the slain, and of men who fought with him against those who committed such historic crimes. It is true enough that he regarded his and his comrades' work to abolish slavery, beginning in prewar Linn County, Kansas, with justified pride, and that all of them were very likely to have been supporters of the Grant administration's vigorous ongoing efforts to suppress the Klan and affirm Black civil rights. That involved men with guns, U.S. marshals and soldiers, arresting and prosecuting civilians on suspicion of racial terrorism.

But Montgomery grew and learned a lot—including from his own grave errors of judgment—for a long time after 1858, and his greatest accomplishments came as a soldier six years later. It is likely that he continued to learn and grow after the war, and that he, like other Americans, struggled to deal with its trauma and meaning, and with what he had done and experienced. He may have repented some of his actions, wishing he had been more merciful. With his fellow First-Day Adventists, he was likely considering how the church could be true to core Christian principles in modern America, helping its people to rise above the evils of both war and appeasement, violence and injustice. It is often the case that commenters on Montgomery's life focus excessively on prewar Kansas, just as many see Tubman mostly in the context of prewar Maryland. The real achievements of these two friends and comrades can only be appreciated in true perspective on a much broader canvas.

Montgomery's religiosity, his often-unkempt appearance (with no military spit and polish), were regarded as fanatical, even tending toward insanity, by unsympathetic contemporaries and some historians who followed in their footsteps. But most accounts of those who knew him are much more generous. Even men from very different backgrounds, such as his fellow abolitionists and Union colonels Shaw and Higginson, who strongly disagreed with some of the things that he did, also recognized his finer qualities. Montgomery drew people with him to risk their lives, in or out of the army, in the cause of ending slavery.

The war's aftermath, as the 21st-century historian Drew Gilpin Faust says, seemed to open up:

> a new and different moral universe, one in which unimaginable destruction had become daily experience. Where did God belong in such a world? How could a benevolent deity countenance such cruelty and such suffering? Doubt threatened to overpower faith—faith in the Christian narrative of a compassionate divinity and a hope of life beyond the grave, faith in the intelligibility and purpose of life on Earth.[9]

Montgomery resisted negative or cynical answers to such questions, rather adapting his lifelong Christian faith to affirm the inherent dignity of every human life. If, at the end of his own life, that put him at odds with the intellectual tendency of the age, the same might be said of the decreasingly skeptical Lincoln.

Botkin does not say Montgomery seemed in bad health, although his underlying constitution had been damaged in wartime service, limiting his ability to do physical farm work in his last years. His death appears to have been sudden and unexpected, perhaps a heart attack or stroke.[10] They buried him near where his youngest children had been born, at Fort Montgomery. Once the literal bulwark of anti-slavery resistance in southern Kansas, it was now just the center of the Montgomery family universe. But they moved away not very long after, and on Decoration Day in 1885 James Montgomery's body was moved (no doubt with

Clarinda's permission) to the small national cemetery section of the Mound City burial ground, now known as Woodland Cemetery. Fort Montgomery no longer stands at its original site, but it, too, or rather a replica, has been moved to (*i.e.* reconstructed at) Mound City Historical Park for public display.

Montgomery's body was buried in the little military section of the cemetery, with other Civil War soldiers, some killed in the nearby battles of 1864. The names of three of those buried near him are unknown, listed only as "U.S. soldier." Like the others, he has a standard white U.S. military grave marker, but his, unlike most of theirs, does not list his service in Kansas or Missouri. (Nor, of course, does it say anything about his paramilitary prewar activities.) Rather, the gravestone says he was colonel of the Second South Carolina Colored.

Montgomery raised and organized that regiment and was in command in its initial campaign in Florida in early 1863, and later in South Carolina at Combahee Ferry. Those men were not in his brigade at the battle of Olustee in Florida the next year. But they were serving under him—now designated the 34th U.S. Colored Troops—for the last months of his time in the South. They were with him when he lost brigade command, and when he was restored to it, fighting at Johns Island on July 9, 1864. He was with that regiment at the beginning and end of his service in the Department of the South, where he made his most significant military contribution. That was also the place he was working with other abolitionists, Black and White, male and female, both to win the war and make a success of the peace. To a great extent they succeeded in that Port Royal-Beaufort area of South Carolina.

Montgomery's service in Kansas and Missouri is also important, especially his final role in repelling Price's raid. By then, he had long since outgrown the undisciplined and sometimes indefensible conduct of his jayhawking days, proving himself to his old comrades to be an effective and courageous combat officer.

Most of Montgomery's nine children were adults or close to it when he died, able to help his widow Clarinda run the farm—but also when the time came to move away from it, as she did by 1876. In that year she sold the Linn County property, except for the small family cemetery whose graves included those of her husband and mother.[11] She moved with the younger children to the home of her married daughter Mary Jane Dunbar in Richland, Kansas, southeast of Topeka. Census records in 1880 show her continuing to reside there.

By 1900, the 73-year-old Clarinda was living in Cowlitz County, Washington, in the southwestern part of that state, not far from the Pacific Ocean. In the same vicinity were her married children Mary Jane, Hugh, John, and Lewis. They and their families were part of Cowlitz County's population of 7,877. It was timber and farming country, and Hugh, like his father, worked in both trades. Lewis was a "timber cruiser" and logger, then worked in real estate. Hugh and Lewis moved to Oregon, where the latter's son Lewis Jr. became a successful logger. These Montgomerys, like their ancestors, had kept on moving west while sticking together. Clarinda died in 1902.

Other children also went west. The ex-soldier Evan ended up in Colorado, where his widow applied for a Civil War pension in 1904.

The youngest child, Nellie, born at Fort Montgomery not long after the Civil War ended, went to live in Oklahoma and then California, where she died on October 22, 1957. Two of her five children predeceased her, one of these being Samuel Firebaugh, who served in World War I and then became a railroad fireman in Michigan. He had seven children of his own, but two of them died with him in a boating accident on the Huron River near Detroit in 1937.[12] Still Nellie lived on into the civil rights era of Martin Luther King and Rosa Parks, and her youngest child, Montgomery's granddaughter, lived until 1996.

One branch of Lewis' descendants includes great-grandchildren who in 2021 were living in California, Nevada, and Minnesota. His father's family line has scattered and embedded itself through the restless nation which the Civil War patriarch did his part to save.

James Montgomery's name has not quite faded away and is as likely to be scorned as celebrated. While some of that criticism is unfair, it is true that he, like many others on both sides of the massive conflict over slavery, did things which are impossible, at least in retrospect, to defend. But he also took part in something redemptive, from before the Civil War and through it, from the geographic center of America to the

Atlantic Sea Islands, the South Carolina heart of the Confederacy, south to Florida and back to Kansas-Missouri.

Most often alongside Black soldiers and civilians, he staked his life with theirs in a national crusade to raise four million African-Americans and their many more descendants into freedom, against ruthless and effective Confederate resistance. In a civil war embittered by the racist stain of slavery, they fought together to overcome.

Bibliography

Apthorp, William Lee. *Montgomery's Raids in Florida, Georgia, and South Carolina.* 1864 manuscript. Edited by Daniel L. Schafer, Professor of History, University of North Florida. unf.edu/floridahistoryonline.

Ash, Stephen V. *Firebrand of Liberty: The Story of Two Black Regiments that Changed the Course of the Civil War.* New York: W. W. Norton & Co., 2008.

Badger, Joseph. *A Memoir of Rev. Joseph Badger.* Hudson, Ohio: Sawyer, Ingersoll & Co., 1851.

Benedict, Bryce. *Jayhawkers: The Civil War Brigade of James Henry Lane.* Norman: University of Oklahoma Press, 2009.

Botkin, Theodosius. *Among the Sovereign Squats.* Kansas Historical Society Collections, Vol. 7, 1901–02.

Bradford, Sarah H. *Harriet Tubman: The Moses of Her People.* 1869, 1886. New York: Citadel Press, 1994.

Broadwater, Robert P. *The Battle of Olustee, 1864: The Final Union Attempt to Seize Florida.* Jefferson, North Carolina: McFarland & Co., 2006.

Brown, William Wells. *The Negro in the American Rebellion: His Heroism and His Fidelity.* Boston: Lee & Shepard, 1867.

Burchard, Robert. *One Gallant Rush: Robert Gould Shaw and His Brave Black Regiment.* New York: St. Martin's Press, 1965.

Castel, Albert. *Civil War Kansas: Reaping the Whirlwind.* Lawrence, Kansas: University Press of Kansas, 1958, 1997.

Castel, Albert. *General Sterling Price and the Civil War in the West.* Baton Rouge: Louisiana State University Press, 1993.

Castel, Albert. *Kansas Jayhawking Raids into Western Missouri in 1861.* Missouri Historical Review, October 1959.

Clinton, Catherine. 2004. *Harriet Tubman: The Road to Freedom.* New York: Little, Brown and Co.

Collins, Charles D., Jr. *Battlefield Atlas of Price's Missouri Expedition of 1864.* Fort Leavenworth, Kansas: Combat Studies Institute, US Army Combined Arms Center, 2016.

Collins, Robert. *General James G. Blunt: Tarnished Glory*. Gretna, Louisiana: Pelican Publishing Company, 2005.

Collins, Robert. *Jim Lane: Scoundrel, Statesman, Kansan*. Gretna, Louisiana: Pelican, 2007.

Commager, Henry Steele, ed. *The Blue and the Gray*. Indianapolis, Bobbs-Merrill: Fairfax Press. 1950, 1982. Vol. 1.

Conner, Robert C. *General Gordon Granger: The Savior of Chickamauga and the Man Behind "Juneteenth."* Philadelphia, Pennsylvania: Casemate, 2013.

Cornish, Dudley Taylor. *The Sable Arm: Black Troops in the Union Army, 1861–1865*. University Press of Kansas, 1956, 1987.

Cutler, William G. *History of the State of Kansas*. Chicago: A. T. Andreas, 1883.

Dictionary of American Biography, Volume 13. New York: Scribner's, 1943.

Dirck, Brian R. "James Montgomery and Redemptive Violence." *Kansas History: A Journal of the Central Plains* 27 (Spring–Summer 2004), 100–15.

Dougherty, Kevin. *Strangling the Confederacy: Coastal Operations of the American Civil War*. Philadelphia: Casemate, 2010.

Du Bois, W. E. B. *John Brown*. 1909. Oxford, UK: Oxford University Press, 2007.

Earnest, Ola May. "A Tribute to James Montgomery." *Linn County News* (October 1989).

Earnest, Ola May. "Col. Montgomery's Family Cemetery Found." *Osawatomie Graphic* (June 22, 1989).

Egerton, Douglas R. *Thunder at the Gates: The Black Civil War Regiments that Redeemed America*. New York: Basic Books, 2016.

Emilio, Luis F. *A Brave Black Regiment: The History of the Fifty-Fourth Regiment of Massachusetts Volunteer Infantry 1863–1865*. Boston, 1891, 1894. New York: Da Capo Press, 1995.

Etcheson, Nicole. *Bleeding Kansas: Contested Liberty in the Civil War Era*. Lawrence, Kansas: University Press of Kansas, 2004.

Etcheson, Nicole. "James Lane's Revenge." *New York Times Disunion* blog (October 26, 2011).

Faust, Drew Gilpin. *This Republic of Suffering: Death and the American Civil War*. New York: Alfred A. Knopf, 2008.

Fox, Simeon M. "The Story of the Seventh Kansas." *Transactions of the Kansas State Historical Society* (1903–1904. Vol. VIII), 13–49. Topeka: George A. Clark, State Printer, 1904.

Gilmore, Donald. *Civil War on the Missouri–Kansas Border*. Gretna, Louisiana: Pelican Publishing, 2005.

Goodrich, Thomas. *War to the Knife: Bleeding Kansas, 1854–1861*. Mechanicsburg, Pennsylvania: Stackpole Books, 1998.

Goodwin, Doris Kearns. *Team of Rivals: The Political Genius of Abraham Lincoln*. New York: Simon & Schuster, 2005.

Goodrich, Thomas. *Black Flag: Guerrilla Warfare on the Western Border, 1861–1865.* Indiana University Press, 1995, 1999.

Grigg, Jeff W. *The Combahee River Raid: Harriet Tubman & Lowcountry Liberation.* Charleston, South Carolina: The History Press, 2014.

Hamilton, Nigel. *Monty: The Making of a General.* London: Hamish Hamilton, 1981.

Higginson, Thomas Wentworth. *Army Life in a Black Regiment.* 1870. Boston: Beacon Press, 1962.

Higginson, Thomas Wentworth, ed. Christopher Looby. *The Complete Civil War Journal and Selected Letters.* University of Chicago Press, 2000.

Holloway, J. N. *History of Kansas.* Lafayette, Indiana: James, Emmons & Co., 1868.

Holman, Tom L., *James Montgomery, 1813–1871.* Unpublished 1973 doctoral thesis for Oklahoma State University, available online at shareok.org.

Horstman, Jonathan William. *The African-American's Civil War: A History of the 1st North Carolina Colored Volunteers. 1998.* 1st NC Colored Volunteers—Chapter 2, Part 1 (ncgenweb.us)

Journal of the Senate of Missouri. ... Appendix to the Journals of the Twenty-First General Assembly of Missouri. Documents in Relation to Border Difficulties Accompanying the Governor's Message. Jefferson City: W. G. Cheeney, Public Printer. 1861.

Kirkman, Paul. *The Battle of Westport: Missouri's Great Confederate Raid.* Charleston, South Carolina: The History Press, 2011.

Larson, Kate Clifford. *Bound for the Promised Land: Harriet Tubman, Portrait of an American Hero.* New York: Ballantine Books, 2004.

Mitchell, William Ansel. *Linn County, Kansas: A History.* Kansas City: Campbell-Gates press/Charno Bindery, 1928.

Montgomery, James. Montgomery papers, Kansas Historical Society.

Monaghan, Jay. *Civil War on the Western Border, 1854–1865.* Lincoln, London: University of Nebraska Press, 1955, 1984.

Monnett, Howard N. *Action Before Westport 1864.* University Press of Colorado, revised edition 1995.

National Archives. Freeman, Elsie, Wynell Burroughs Schamel, and Jean West. "The Fight for Equal Rights: A Recruiting Poster for Black Soldiers in the Civil War." *Social Education* 56, 2 (February 1992), 118–120. [Revised and updated in 1999 by Budge Weidman.]

Oates, Stephen B. *To Purge This Land With Blood: A Biography of John Brown.* Amherst: University of Massachusetts Press, 1970, 1984.

Official Records (Abbreviated in endnotes as *OR*) *The War of the Rebellion: A Compilation of the Official Records of the Union and Confederate Armies.* Washington, 1902.

The Ohio Gazetteer, 11th edition. Columbus, Scott and Wright, 1833.

Phillips, Christopher. "Montgomery, James." *Civil War on the Western Border: The Missouri-Kansas Conflict, 1854–1865.* https://civilwaronthewesternborder.org/encyclopedia/montgomery-james.

Moore, Frank, ed., *The Rebellion Record: A Diary of American Events, with Documents, Narratives, Illustrative Incidents, Poetry, Etc.* (New York: G. P. Putnam, 1863), VI: 578–579. "The Retaliatory Act, Confederate Congress, May 1, 1863." House Divided: The Civil War Research Engine at Dickinson College.

Rafiner, Tom A. *Caught Between Three Fires: Cass County, Mo., Chaos, and Order No. 11, 1860–1865*. Xlibris, 2010.

Renehan, Edward J., *The Secret Six: The True Tale of the Men Who Conspired with John Brown*. Crown Publishing, University of South Carolina Press, 1995, 1996–97.

Rose, Philip F. *John Brown's Virginia Raid*. Trafford Publishing, 2013.

Rose, Willie Lee. *Rehearsal for Reconstruction: The Port Royal Experiment*. Oxford, UK: Oxford University Press, 1964, 1976.

Reynolds, David S. *John Brown, Abolitionist*. New York: Alfred A. Knopf, 2005.

Rybczynski, Witold. *A Clearing in the Distance: Frederick Law Olmsted and America in the 19th Century*. New York: Touchstone, Simon & Schuster, 1999.

Schafer, Daniel L. *Thunder on the River: The Civil War in Northeast Florida*. Gainesville, Florida: University of Florida Press, 2010.

Shaw, Robert G., Duncan, Russell, ed. *Blue-Eyed Child of Fortune: The Civil War Letters of Colonel Robert Gould Shaw*. Athens, Ga.: University of Georgia Press, 1992, 1999.

Sinisi, Kyle S. *The Last Hurrah: Sterling Price's Missouri Expedition of 1864*. Lanham, Maryland: Rowman & Littlefield, 2015.

Soldiers of the United States Colored Troops with Connection to Hilton Head, Hilton Head, South Carolina: Heritage Library. Soldiers of the United States Colored Troops Formed on Hilton Head—Heritage Library Foundation (accessed at https://heritagelib.org/soldiers-of-the-united-states-colored-troops-formed-on-hilton-head on November 22, 2021).

Spencer, Platt R. *History of Ashtabula County, Ohio*. Williams Brothers, 1878.

Spurgeon, Ian Michael. *Soldiers in the Army of Freedom: The 1st Kansas Colored, the Civil War's First African American Combat Unit*. Norman, Oklahoma: University of Oklahoma Press, 1976.

Stanley, David S. *An American General: The Memoirs of David Sloan Stanley*. Santa Barbara, California: The Narrative Press, 2003.

Stephens, George E. (ed. Donald Yacavone). *A Voice of Thunder: The Civil War Letters of George E. Stephens*. Urbana: University of Illinois Press, 1997.

Stowe, Harriet Beecher. *Uncle Tom's Cabin*. Boston: John P. Jewett & Co., 1852.

Sutton, Robert K. *Stark Mad Abolitionists: Lawrence, Kansas, and the Battle over Slavery in the Civil War Era*. New York: Skyhorse Publishing, 2017.

Titterington, Dick. *Sterling Price Returns: The Southern Counteroffensive to Retake Missouri in 1861*. Overland Park, Kansas: Trans-Mississippi Musings Press, 2014.

Titterington, Dick, *Self-Guided Tour to the Battle of Westport near Loose Park*. 2015–16, http://www.transmississippimusings.com/media/docs/tour-guides/tour-westport-walking-long-20150407.pdf.

Trego, Joseph H. Unpublished diary, 1861–63. Topeka: Kansas Historical Society Archives.

Tuttle, Charles R. *A New Centennial History of the State of Kansas*. Madison, Wisconsin: Inter-State Book Co., 1876.

Warren, Robert Penn. *John Brown: The Making of a Martyr*. Payson & Clarke, 1929; Southern Classics Series, 1993.

Welch, G. Murlin. *Border Warfare in Southeastern Kansas, 1856–1859*. Pleasanton, Kansas: Linn County Historical Society, 1938, 1977, 2004.

Wesley, Charles H., and Romero, Patricia W. *Afro-Americans in the Civil War: From Slavery to Citizenship*. Cornwells Heights, Pennsylvania: The Association for the Study of Afro-American Life and History, 1967, 1969.

Willis, Deborah. *The Black Civil War Soldier: A Visual History of Conflict and Citizenship*. New York: NYU Press, 2021.

Endnotes

Introduction: From Guerrilla Outlaw to American Soldier

1 Dudley Taylor Cornish, *The Sable Arm: Black Troops in the Union Army, 1861–1865* (University Press of Kansas, 1956, 1987), xvi.

Chapter 1: Westward Bound

1 William G. Cutler, *History of the State of Kansas*. Chicago: A. T. Andreas, 1883. See also J. N. Holloway, *History of Kansas* (Lafayette, Ind.: James, Emmons & Co., 1868); William Ansel Mitchell, *Linn County, Kansas: A History* (Kansas City, 1928); the *Dictionary of American Biography* (New York: Scribner's, 1943); and other sources. Some say the younger Montgomery was a nephew or great-nephew of the general, but this does not appear to be accurate. I have not been able to trace the precise relationship, but the widespread assertion that there was a blood connection may be true.

2 Hamilton, Nigel. *Monty: The Making of a General* (London: Hamish Hamilton, 1981), 12–14.

3 *Dictionary of American Biography, Volume 13* (New York: Scribner's, 1943).

4 Information from message to author via ancestry.com from Elizabeth Jeffords, a descendant of the emigrant Montgomerys.

5 Much of the genealogical information comes from web sites such as RootsWeb, Ancestry.com and findagrave.com, and from *A Montgomery Family Genealogy* by W. J. Montgomery, and from the Delaware County NY Genealogy and History Site.

6 *Ashtabula Sentinel* (May 19, 1880).

7 Platt R. Spencer, *History of Ashtabula County, Ohio* (Williams Brothers, 1878).

8 *Geneva Times*, Ashtabula County, Ohio.

9 Tom L. Holman, unpublished 1973 doctoral thesis for Oklahoma State University, available online at shareok.org; 5.

10 *Ibid.*

11 While most sources say 1814, Holman, *op. cit.*, says 1813.
12 *The Ohio Gazetteer, 11th edition* (Columbus, Scott and Wright, 1833), 81.
13 *Ibid.*, 233.
14 Holman, *op. cit.*, 7.
15 *Ibid.*, 7–8.
16 *A Memoir of Rev. Joseph Badger* (Hudson, Ohio: Sawyer, Ingersoll & Co., 1851).
17 *Dictionary of American Biography*, *op. cit.*
18 Holman, *op. cit.*, p. 8.
19 Holloway, *op. cit.*, Cutler, *op. cit.*
20 *Dictionary of American Biography*, *op. cit.*
21 Cutler, *op. cit.* See also Christopher Phillips, "Montgomery, James," *Civil War on the Western Border: The Missouri-Kansas Conflict, 1854–1865.* https://civilwaronthewesternborder.org/encyclopedia/montgomery-james.
22 Rybczynski, Witold. *A Clearing in the Distance: Frederick Law Olmsted and America in the 19th Century* (New York: Touchstone, Simon & Schuster, 1999), 31.
23 Holman, *op. cit.*, 8.
24 Dirck, Brian R. "James Montgomery and Redemptive Violence," *Kansas History: A Journal of the Central Plains* (27, Spring–Summer 2004), 105.
25 Robert K. Sutton, *Stark Mad Abolitionists: Lawrence, Kansas, and the Battle over Slavery in the Civil War Era* (New York: Skyhorse Publishing, 2017), 144.
26 Mitchell, William Ansel. *Linn County, Kansas: A History* (Kansas City: Campbell-Gates press/Charno Bindery, 1928) 14–15.
27 Robert G. Shaw, Russell Duncan, ed., *Blue-Eyed Child of Fortune: The Civil War Letters of Colonel Robert Gould Shaw* (Athens, Georgia.: University of Georgia Press, 1992, 1999), 363–4.
28 Holman, *op. cit.*;p. 9.
29 Harriet Beecher Stowe, *Uncle Tom's Cabin* (Boston: John P. Jewett & Co., 1852).
30 Holman, *op. cit.*, 10.
31 Dirck, *op. cit.*, 105.

Chapter 2: Bleeding Kansas and John Brown

1 Nicole Etcheson, *Bleeding Kansas: Contested Liberty in the Civil War Era* (Lawrence, Kansas: University Press of Kansas, 2004).
2 *Dictionary of American Biography*, *op. cit.*
3 *Holman*, *op. cit.*, 14–16; and Holloway, *op. cit.*, 496.
4 Carl von Clausewitz, *On War*, 1832.
5 Bob Dole, Foreword to Sutton, Robert K., *op. cit.*
6 Paul Kirkman, *The Battle of Westport: Missouri's Great Confederate Raid* (Charleston, South Carolina: The History Press, 2011), 42.
7 Cutler, *op. cit.*, chapter on Linn County, Early Political Troubles.

8 Jay Monaghan, *Civil War on the Western Border, 1854–1865* (Lincoln, London. University of Nebraska Press, 1955, 1984), 81. Sutton, *op. cit.*, estimates Clarke's numbers at 400.
9 Holman, *op. cit.*, 30.
10 Ola May Earnest, president of Linn County Historical Society. "A Tribute to James Montgomery," *Linn County News* (1989).
11 Holloway, *op. cit.*, 495–7.
12 Charles R. Tuttle, *A New Centennial History of the State of Kansas* (Madison, Wisconsin: Inter-State Book Co., 1876), 419–20.
13 *Ibid.* 421.
14 Holloway, *op. cit.*, 502–3.
15 Sutton, *op. cit.*, 63–4.
16 Quoted in Bryce Benedict, *Jayhawkers: The Civil War Brigade of James Henry Lane* (Norman: University of Oklahoma Press, 2009), 21.
17 Tuttle, *op. cit.*, 422.
18 Holloway, *op. cit.*, says Montgomery's men took $250 on one of these raids.
19 Benedict, *op. cit.*, 21.
20 Tuttle, *op. cit.*, 422–3.
21 Holman, 32, via Holloway, *op. cit.*
22 Holloway, *op. cit.*, 505.
23 Holman, *op. cit.*, 38–9.
24 Holloway, *op. cit.*, 507–8.
25 Holman, *op. cit.*, 42–5.
26 Kansas Historical Society, through territorialkansasonline.ku.edu.
27 Sutton, *op. cit.*, 55–6.
28 Robert Collins, *Jim Lane: Scoundrel, Statesman, Kansan* (Gretna, Louisiana.: Pelican, 2007), 141.
29 Theodosius Botkin, "Among the Sovereign Squats," (Kansas Historical Society Collections, Vol. 7, 1901–02), 438–9.
30 Dirck, *op. cit.* 109.
31 Botkin, *op. cit.*, 440–1.
32 Joseph H. Trego letter to wife Alice, through territorialkansasonline.ku.edu.
33 Feb. 17, 1858, letter from J. G. Anderson to brother, through territorialkansasonline.ku.edu.
34 Holloway, *op. cit.*, 513.
35 G. Murlin Welch, 1938, 1977, 2004. *Border Warfare in Southeastern Kansas, 1856–1859* (Pleasanton, Kansas: Linn County Historical Society), 49.
36 *Ibid.*, 51.
37 David S. Stanley, *An American General: The Memoirs of David Sloan Stanley* (Santa Barbara, California: The Narrative Press, 2003), 93.
38 *OR*, Vol. 41, Part 1, 493.
39 Montgomery papers, *Civil War on the Western Border*, Kansas Historical Society.

40 Welch, *op. cit.*, 95.
41 David S. Reynolds, *John Brown, Abolitionist* (New York: Alfred A. Knopf, 2005), 269.
42 Holman, *op. cit.*, 74.
43 Robert Penn Warren, *John Brown: The Making of a Martyr* (Payson & Clarke, 1929; Southern Classics Series, 1993), 290.
44 Welch, *op. cit.*, 99–102.
45 *Ibid.*, 113; Tuttle, *op. cit.*, 430; Holloway, *op. cit.*, 540.
46 Dirck, *op. cit.*, 106. See also Earnest, *op. cit.*
47 Holloway, *op. cit.*, 541.
48 Welch, *op. cit.*, 114.
49 Oates, Stephen B. *To Purge This Land With Blood: A Biography of John Brown* (Amherst: University of Massachusetts Press, 1970, 1984), 261; and Warren, *op. cit.*, 298; Holman, *op. cit.*, 84.
50 Holloway, *op. cit.*, 544.
51 Welch, *op. cit.*, 122.
52 Holman, *op. cit.*, 85–6.
53 Welch, *op. cit.*, 123.
54 Warren, *op. cit.*, 300.
55 Holman, *op. cit.*, 91–4.
56 *Ibid.* 94–9; and Benedict, *op. cit.*, 23.
57 Holman, *op. cit.*, 104.
58 Edward J. Renehan, *The Secret Six: The True Tale of the Men Who Conspired with John Brown* (Crown Publishing, University of South Carolina Press, 1995, 1996–97), 254.
59 *Ibid.*, 255; and Holman, *op. cit.*, 113.
60 Monaghan, *op. cit.*, 117.
61 Holman, *op. cit.*, 120, 204–5.
62 Kansas Historical Society.
63 Earnest, *op. cit.*
64 Etcheson, *op. cit.*, 221, says this hanging was the work of Montgomery. But Holman, *op. cit.*, 123–4, ascribes it to Jennison, with Montgomery approving the action.
65 Holman, *op. cit.*, 123–5, 128–9.
66 Monaghan, *op. cit.*, 121.
67 Sutton, *op. cit.*, 146.
68 Albert Castel, *Civil War Kansas: Reaping the Whirlwind* (Lawrence, Kansas: University Press of Kansas, 1958, 1997), 43. See also Botkin, *op. cit.*, 433. Botkin respected both Montgomery's and Jennison's opposition to slavery, but along with other contemporary historians regarded Montgomery as much the superior character.
69 Dirck, *op. cit.*, 107–8, 112.
70 *Journal of the Senate of Missouri. … Appendix to the Journals of the Twenty-First General Assembly of Missouri. Documents in Relation to Border Difficulties Accompanying the Governor's Message.* (Jefferson City: W. G. Cheeney, Public Printer, 1861).

71 Etcheson, *op. cit.*, 221.
72 *Ibid.*, 222.
73 Phillips, *op. cit.*
74 Holman, *op. cit.*, 131–2.

Chapter 3: Civil War

1 Mitchell, *op. cit.*, 15.
2 Holman, *op. cit*, 136–7. Also see May 8, 1861, letter to George Stearns, James Montgomery Papers, Kansas Historical Society.
3 Simeon M. Fox, "The Story of the Seventh Kansas," *Transactions of the Kansas State Historical Society* (1903–1904. Vol. VIII), 13–49. Topeka: George A. Clark, (State Printer, 1904), 14.
4 Castel, *op. cit.*, 44.
5 James Montgomery Papers, Kansas Historical Society.
6 Ola May Earnest, Linn County Historical Society, *Linn County News* (March 26, 1998).
7 Holman, *op. cit.*, 152–3; and Benedict, *op. cit.*, 59.
8 James Montgomery Papers, Kansas Historical Society.
9 Holman, *op. cit.*, 140–41.
10 Castel, *op. cit.*, 45.
11 Benedict, *op. cit.*, 5–9; and Holman, *op. cit.*, 152–3.
12 Dick Titterington, *Sterling Price Returns: The Southern Counteroffensive to Retake Missouri in 1861* (Overland Park, Kansas; Trans-Mississippi Musings Press, 2014), 172.
13 Holman, *op. cit.*, 154–5.
14 *The War of the Rebellion: A Compilation of the Official Records of the Union and Confederate Armies (OR)*. Series I, Vol. 3 (Washington, 1902), 163.
15 *OR*, Vol. 50, 436.
16 Titterington, *op. cit.*, 194–5.
17 *Harper's Weekly*. Abraham Lincoln and Previous Proclamations. https://kpgmuh390.omeka.net/items/show/14.
18 Monaghan, *op. cit.*, 195.
19 Joseph H. Trego, Unpublished diary, 1861–63. Topeka: Kansas Historical Society Archives.
20 Trego, *ibid.*, an anti-slavery ally of Montgomery from prewar days, is probably the best source. A lieutenant in the 5th Kansas Cavalry, he says "we were trying the prisoners," following which five of them "were taken out and shot." While he does not say who authorized the so-called trial and executions, Montgomery was in command of the expedition and most likely the responsible party. See also Titterington, *op. cit.*, 197–8; Tom A. Rafiner, *Caught Between Three Fires: Cass County, Mo., Chaos, and order No. 11, 1860–1865* (Xlibris, 2010), 87; Donald

Gilmore, *Civil War on the Missouri-Kansas Border*, (Gretna, Louisiana: Pelican Publishing, 2005), 136; Thomas Goodrich, *Black Flag: Guerrilla Warfare on the Western Border, 1861–1865* (Indiana University Press, 1995, 1999), 19–20; and Howard Mann, *True Tales of the Tenth Kansas Infantry. The Joys of Jayhawking: Words from the Perpetrator's [sic] Mouths* (Civil War Round Table of Kansas City. https://cwrtkc.org/man_true_tales_1). Primary sources in addition to Trego include another Union soldier, Henry Palmer, who does not directly implicate Montgomery. The diary of Captain William Creitz (Kansas Historical Society), who was in Trego's regiment, does not mention executions. Some sources appear to mix up these killings with what happened a few days later at Osceola. The history is further confused by soldiers under Jennison being engaged at Morristown in 1861, both before and after this skirmish.

21 Benedict, *op. cit.*, 89–90.

22 William Monks, *A History of Southern Missouri and Northern Arkansas*, quoted in Henry Steele Commager, ed., *The Blue and the Gray* (Indianapolis, Bobbs-Merrill: Fairfax Press. 1950, 1982), Vol. 1, 381–4.

23 Robert C. Conner, *General Gordon Granger: The Savior of Chickamauga and the Man Behind "Juneteenth"* (Philadelphia: Casemate, 2013), 56, 62.

24 Drew Gilpin Faust, *This Republic of Suffering: Death and the American Civil War* (New York: Alfred A. Knopf, 2008), 46.

25 *OR*, Series I, Vol. III, *op. cit.*, 196.

26 *Ibid.*

27 Titterington, *op. cit.*, 247–51.

28 Holman, *op. cit.*, 160.

29 Monaghan, *op. cit.*, 196.

30 Fox, *op. cit.*, 15.

31 *OR*, Vol. 53, 743.

32 Albert Castel, "Kansas Jayhawking Raids into Western Missouri in 1861," *Missouri Historical Review* (October 1959).

33 Monaghan, *op. cit.*, 197.

34 Titterington, *op. cit.*, 287–8.

35 Holman, *op. cit.*, 163.

36 Monaghan, *op. cit.*, 207.

37 Sutton, *op. cit.*, 151–2.

38 James Montgomery Correspondence, Kansas Historical Society.

39 *OR*, *op. cit.*, (Series I, Volume 8), 415.

40 *Ibid.*, 702.

41 Albert Castel, *General Sterling Price and the Civil War in the West* (Baton Rouge, Louisiana: Louisiana State University Press, 1993), 62–5.

42 *Daily Conservative*, Leavenworth, Kansas (Dec, 21, 1861), Linn County Museum.

43 Holman, *op. cit.*, 164–6.

44 *Ibid.*, 168–9.

45 Robert Collins, *General James G. Blunt: Tarnished Glory* (Gretna, Louisiana: Pelican Publishing Company, 2005), 46.
46 Sutton, *op. cit.*, 151–2; and Cornish, *op. cit.*, 77.
47 Holman, *op. cit.*, 170–1; and Cornish, *op. cit.*, 72–3; and Ian Michael Spurgeon, *Soldiers in the Army of Freedom: The 1st Kansas Colored, the Civil War's First African American Combat Unit* (Norman, Oklahoma: University of Oklahoma Press, 1976), 58–9.
48 Cornish, *op. cit.*, 74.
49 Kirkman, *op. cit.*, 50, 64.
50 Cornish, *op. cit.*, 103–5.

Chapter 4: With Tubman in the South

1 Quoted in Henry Steele Commager, ed., *The Blue and the Gray* (Indianapolis, Bobbs-Merrill: Fairfax Press. 1950, 1982), Vol. 1, 6–7.
2 Deborah Willis, *The Black Civil War Soldier: A Visual History of Conflict and Citizenship* (New York: NYU Press, 2021), 62.
3 Holman, *op. cit.*, 180–2; and Cornish, *op. cit.*, 138.
4 Kevin Dougherty, *Strangling the Confederacy: Coastal Operations of the American Civil War* (Philadelphia, Pennsylvania: Casemate, 2010), 52–4.
5 Catherine Clinton, *Harriet Tubman: The Road to Freedom* (New York: Little, Brown and Co., 2004).
6 *Ibid.*, 91.
7 Charles H. Wesley, and Patricia W. Romero, *Afro-Americans in the Civil War: From Slavery to Citizenship* (Cornwells Heights, Pennsylvania: The Association for the Study of Afro-American Life and History, 1967, 1969). p. 107.
8 Sarah H. Bradford, *Harriet Tubman: The Moses of Her People* (1869, 1886. New York: Citadel Press, 1994), 93–4.
9 Willis, *op. cit.*, 9.
10 Clinton, *op. cit.*, 164.
11 Cornish, *op cit.*, 138.
12 Bradford, *op. cit.*, 99.
13 *Ibid.*, 138.
14 Cornish *op. cit.* 138.
15 Stephen V. Ash, *Firebrand of Liberty: The Story of Two Black Regiments that Changed the Course of the Civil War* (New York. W. W. Norton & Co., 2008), 103.
16 Thomas Wentworth Higginson, *Army Life in a Black Regiment* (1870. Boston: Beacon Press, 1962), 104–5.
17 Quoted in Daniel L. Schafer, *Thunder on the River: The Civil War in Northeast Florida* (Gainesville: University of Florida Press, 2010), 144.
18 *Ibid.* 144–5.
19 Ash, *op. cit.*, 113–14.

20 *Ibid.*, 154.
21 Higginson, *op. cit.*, 114–15.
22 Schafer, *op. cit.*, 153.
23 Kate Clifford Larson, *Bound for the Promised Land: Harriet Tubman, Portrait of an American Hero* (New York: Ballantine Books, 2004), 211.
24 Schafer, *op. cit.*, 153.
25 *Ibid.*, 154.
26 Cornish, *op. cit.*, 140.
27 Thomas Wentworth Higginson; Christopher Looby, ed., *The Complete Civil War Journal and Selected Letters* (University of Chicago Press, 2000), 116–22; and Ash, *op. cit.*, 168.
28 *OR*, Vol. 14, Chap. 26, 233; and Ash, *op. cit.*, 152–3.
29 Higginson, *Journal*, *op. cit.*, 117, 122; and Ash, *op. cit.*, 161, 189–90.
30 Ash, *op. cit.*, 167–70.
31 Schafer, *op. cit.*, 157.
32 Ash, *op. cit.*, 211–12.
33 *Ibid.*, 177–8, 198–9.
34 Higginson, *Journal*, *op. cit.*, 146, 154, 158.
35 Holman, *op. cit.*, 203.
36 Bradford, *op. cit.*, 99.
37 Willie Lee Rose, *Rehearsal for Reconstruction: The Port Royal Experiment* (Oxford, UK; Oxford University Press, 1964, 1976), 244.
38 Jeff W. Grigg, *The Combahee River Raid: Harriet Tubman & Lowcountry Liberation* (Charleston, South Carolina: The History Press, 2014), 71.
39 Bradford, *op. cit.*, 102; see also Larson, *op. cit.*, 210; and *The Commonwealth* newspaper of Boston, July 10, 1863, quoted by Earl Conrad at HarrietTubman.com.
40 Frank Moore, ed., *The Rebellion Record: A Diary of American Events, with Documents, Narratives, Illustrative Incidents, Poetry, Etc* (New York: G. P. Putnam, 1863), VI: 578–579 "The Retaliatory Act, Confederate Congress, May 1, 1863," House Divided: The Civil War Research Engine at Dickinson College.
41 National Archives. Elsie Freeman, Wynell Burroughs Schamel, and Jean West. "The Fight for Equal Rights: A Recruiting Poster for Black Soldiers in the Civil War." *Social Education* (56, 2 February 1992), 118–120. [Revised and updated in 1999 by Budge Weidman.]
42 *OR*, Vol. 14, Chap. 26, 462.
43 Grigg, *op. cit.*;71–2.
44 Douglas R. Egerton, *Thunder at the Gates: The Black Civil War Regiments that Redeemed America* (New York: Basic Books, 2016), 101; and Ash, *op. cit.*, 171.
45 *OR*, Vol. 14, Chap. 26, 298–306.
46 The Harriet Tubman museum in Auburn, New York, for example, refers to the destruction of Confederate "ammunition houses," "weapons" and "stockpiles of ammunition." But Grigg casts doubt on such claims.

47 Larson, *op. cit.*, 212–13.
48 *Ibid.*, 213. See also William Lee Apthorp, *Montgomery's Raids in Florida, Georgia, and South Carolina*. 1864 manuscript. Edited by Daniel L. Schafer, Professor of History, University of North Florida. unf.edu/floridahistoryonline.
49 Apthorp, *op. cit.*
50 Bradford, *op. cit.*, 99–100.
51 Wesley, *op. cit.* 108.
52 Quoted in Holman, *op. cit.*, 208, 210.
53 Bradford, *op. cit.*, 101–2.
54 Larson, *op. cit.*, 216.
55 Quoted in Larson, *op. cit.*, 217.
56 *Ibid.*, 223. However, Gillmore's Feb. 4, 1864, order to Seymour setting the Florida expedition in motion, including Montgomery's brigade, said "You will see that no females accompany your command ..."
57 Quoted in Rose, *op. cit.*, 247.
58 Holman, *op. cit.*, 207.
59 Rose, *op. cit.*, 251.
60 Luis F. Emilio, *A Brave Black Regiment: The History of the Fifty-Fourth Regiment of Massachusetts Volunteer Infantry 1863–1865* (Boston, 1891, 1894. New York: Da Capo Press, 1995), 40.
61 *Ibid.* See also Robert Burchard, *One Gallant Rush: Robert Gould Shaw and His Brave Black Regiment* (New York: St. Martin's Press, 1965), 104.
62 *OR*, Vol. 14, Chap. 26, 466–7.
63 Cornish, *op. cit.*, 182; and Ash, *op. cit.*, 83.
64 Rose, *op. cit.*, 252.
65 Emilio, *op. cit.*
66 *Ibid.*, 41.
67 Apthorp, *op. cit.*
68 *OR*, Vol. 14, Chap. 26, 318.
69 Emilio, *op. cit.*, *41*.
70 Burchard, *op. cit.*, 108.
71 Quoted in Emilio, *op. cit.*, 42.
72 Burchard, *op. cit.* 109.
73 Emilio, *op. cit.*, 44.
74 Shaw, *op. cit.*, 364.
75 Cornish, *op. cit.*, 150.
76 Egerton, *op. cit.*, 105.
77 *OR*, Vol. 14, Chap. 26, 318–19.
78 Dirck, *op. cit.*, 103.
79 Apparently based on an 1859 book, *Kansas in Eighteen Fifty-Eight*, by William P. Tomlinson.
80 Burchard, *op. cit.*, 52, 104.

81 Shaw, *op. cit.*, 364; and Holman, *op. cit.*, 9.
82 Willis, *op. cit.*, 79.
83 Ash, *op. cit.*, 92–3; and Feb. 7 order from Hunter (via Assistant Adjutant General Charles Halpine) to Colonel Morgan at Key West, Kansas Historical Society Montgomery correspondence.
84 *Soldiers of the United States Colored Troops with Connection to Hilton Head*, Hilton Head, South Carolina: Heritage Library. Soldiers of the United States Colored Troops Formed on Hilton Head—Heritage Library Foundation.
85 Shaw, *op. cit.*, 378–9.
86 *OR*, Volume 28, Part 2, 11–13.
87 *Ibid.*, 5.
88 Egerton, *op. cit.*, 106.
89 *OR*, Vol. 28, Part 2, 15–16.
90 *OR*, Vol. 28, Pt. 1, 8.
91 *OR*, Vol. 28, Part 1, 584–5; Part 2, 31.
92 Burchard, *op. cit.*, 127–8.
93 *Ibid.*, Part 1, 755.
94 *Ibid.*, 201.
95 *OR*, Series 3, Vol. 3, 424.
96 Shaw, *op. cit.* 374.
97 *OR*, Vol. 28, Pt. 1, 210. No doubt many of the captured did not survive the war. Holman (*op. cit.*, 227), says only nine enlisted men of the 54th were killed with another 158 wounded, but modern estimates of the dead are much higher. Part of the difficulty in being precise, in addition to the deaths in captivity, is that a substantial number were buried in mass graves.
98 Larson, *op. cit.*, 221.
99 *OR*, Vol. 28, Pt. 2, 62, 123.
100 Cornish, *op. cit.*, 246.
101 Kansas Historical Society, Kansas Memory, James Montgomery correspondence.
102 *Ibid.*
103 *OR*, Vol. 28, Pt. 1, 209.
104 *Ibid.*, 210. Emilio (*op. cit.*) gives figures of four dead and four wounded from the 54th.
105 National Archives. Elsie Freeman, Wynell Burroughs Schamel, and Jean West, "The Fight for Equal Rights: A Recruiting Poster for Black Soldiers in the Civil War." *Social Education* (56, 2, February 1992), 118–120. [Revised and updated in 1999 by Budge Weidman.]
106 Ash, *op. cit.*, 208. See also *The Color of Bravery*, American Battlefield Trust, https://www.battlefields.org/learn/articles/color-bravery.
107 Cornish, *op. cit.*, 194–5.
108 Larson, *op. cit.*, 225.
109 Holman, *op. cit.*, 199.

110 Egerton, *op. cit.*, 232–5.
111 *OR*, Series 3, Vol. 4, Section 1, 2267.
112 Cornish, *op. cit.*, 191.
113 *OR*, Vol. 28, Pt. 2, 123.
114 Egerton, *op. cit.*, 210.

Chapter 5: Olustee and After

1 Robert P. Broadwater, *The Battle of Olustee, 1864: The Final Union Attempt to Seize Florida* (Jefferson, North Carolina: McFarland & Co., 2006), 1–2.
2 *Ibid.*, 24, 34, 116. See also *OR*, Vol. 35, Pt. 1, 473.
3 *OR*, Vol. 35, Pt. 1, 474. See also Holman, *op. cit.*, 233–4.
4 Schafer, *op. cit.*, 178–84.
5 Broadwater, *op. cit.*, 50.
6 *Ibid.*, 72.
7 *Ibid.*, 117.
8 *Ibid.*, 117–20.
9 *OR*, Vol. 35, Pt. 1, 315.
10 Broadwater, *op. cit.*, 122.
11 *Ibid.* 123.
12 *Ibid.*, 124. Also see Emilio, *op. cit.*
13 *Ibid.*, 125.
14 Jonathan William Horstman, *The African-American's Civil War: A History of the 1st North Carolina Colored Volunteers*. 1998, 1st NC Colored Volunteers—Chapter 2, Part 1 (ncgenweb.us).
15 Broadwater, *op. cit.*
16 Compiled Military Service Records of Volunteer Union Soldiers Who Served with the United States Colored Troops: Infantry Organization, 31–35th, The National Archives, *Civil War Era NC*, https://cwnc.omeka.chass.ncsu.edu/items/show/2753.
17 Broadwater, *op. cit.*, 126–32; and Egerton, *op. cit.*, 224.
18 William Wells Brown, *The Negro in the American Rebellion: His Heroism and His Fidelity* (Boston: Lee & Shepard, 1867), 221.
19 *OR*, Vol. 35, Part 1, 289–90.
20 *OR*, Vol. 50, p. 24.
21 Conner, *op. cit.*, 84–112.
22 Broadwater, *op. cit.*, 157–9; and Schafer, *op. cit.*, 188–9, Holman, *op. cit.*, 240.
23 *Ibid.*, 3.
24 *Ibid.*, 78, 141–6 (See also Schafer, *op. cit.*)
25 *OR*, Series 2, Vol. 7, 876.
26 *Reminiscences of William Frederick Penniman*, Southern Historical Collection of the Manuscripts Department, University of North Carolina Library, Chapel Hill. Battleofolustee.org.

27 *OR*, Vol. 35, Part 1, 298.
28 Broadwater, *op. cit.*, 186.
29 Quoted in Doris Kearns Goodwin, *Team of Rivals: The Political Genius of Abraham Lincoln* (New York: Simon & Schuster, 2005), 651.
30 Broadwater, *op. cit.*, 164–5; and *OR*, Vol. 35, Pt.1, 35–6.
31 *OR*, Vol. 35, Pt. 1, 371; and *OR*, Vol. 53, p. 103; *OR*, Vol. 35, Pt. 2, 54.
32 *OR*, Vol. 35, Pt. 2, 78.
33 Holman, *op. cit.*, 251.
34 *OR*, Vol. 35, Pt. 2, 95.
35 *Ibid.*, 100.
36 Holman, *op. cit.*, 247.
37 *Soldiers of the United States Colored Troops with Connection to Hilton Head, op. cit.*
38 Congressional Medal of Honor Society.
39 OR, Vol. 35, Pt. 1, 8ff, 400. Also see Holman, *op. cit.*, 248–50, and Emilio, *op. cit.*
40 *OR*, Vol. 35, Pt. 2, 112–14.
41 *OR*, Vol. 35, Pt. 1, 409.
42 *OR*, Vol. 35, Pt. 1, 84–6.
43 *Ibid.*, 16.
44 *Soldiers of the United States Colored Troops with Connection to Hilton Head, op. cit.*
45 Larson, *op. cit.*, 226–7.
46 Montgomery papers, *Civil War on the Western Border*, Kansas Historical Society.
47 Holman, *op. cit.*, 252, 258.
48 Faust, *op. cit.*, 4.
49 Montgomery papers, *Civil War on the Western Border*, Kansas Historical Society.
50 Earnest, *op. cit.*

Chapter 6: The Westport Campaign

1 Castel, *op. cit.*, 228–9.
2 *OR*, Vol. 41, Part 1, 309.
3 Howard N. Monnett, *Action Before Westport 1864* (University Press of Colorado, revised edition 1995), vii, 21.
4 Quoted in Commager, *op. cit.*, 401.
5 Kirkman, *op. cit.*, 74.
6 Commager/Britton, *op. cit.*, 402.
7 *Ibid.*, 102.
8 *Ibid.*, 36–7.
9 Robert Collins, *op. cit.*, 111, 180–2.
10 Montgomery papers, *Civil War on the Western Border*, Kansas Historical Society.
11 Kansas Historical Society.

12 Charles D. Collins, Jr. *Battlefield Atlas of Price's Missouri Expedition of 1864* (Fort Leavenworth, Kansas: Combat Studies Institute, US Army Combined Arms Center, 2016), 202–5.
13 Author interview in June 2017 with Daniel L. Smith, chairman of the Monnett Battle of Westport Fund and former president of the Civil War Round Table of Kansas City. See also Monnett, *op. cit.*, 71.
14 Robert Collins, *op. cit.*, 126, 188.
15 *OR*, Vol. 41, Part 1, 471–3.
16 Monnett, *op. cit.*, 45.
17 *OR*, Vol. 41, Part 1, 620.
18 *OR*, Vol. 41, Part 4, 57–8.
19 *OR*, Vol. 41, Part 1, 572.
20 Kansas Historical Society.
21 *OR*, Vol. 41, Part 1, 482.
22 Albert Castel, *Civil War Kansas: Reaping the Whirlwind* (Lawrence, Kansas: University Press of Kansas, 1958, 1997), 190–1.
23 Monnett, *op. cit.*, 71.
24 *OR*, Vol. 41, Part 1, 482.
25 Albert Castel, *Civil War Kansas: Reaping the Whirlwind* (Lawrence, Kansas: University Press of Kansas, 1958, 1997), 193.
26 *OR*, Vol. 41, Part 1, 537.
27 *Ibid.*, 485, 598.
28 Charles Collins, *op. cit.*, 95.
29 *OR*, Vol. 41, Pt. 1, 575.
30 Kirkman, *op. cit.*, 102.
31 *OR*, Vol. 41, Part 1, 538.
32 Kirkman, *op. cit.*, 132.
33 Kyle S. Sinisi, *The Last Hurrah: Sterling Price's Missouri Expedition of 1864* (Lanham, Maryland: Rowman & Littlefield, 2015), 219–22.
34 Quoted in Dick Titterington, *Self-Guided Tour to the Battle of Westport near Loose Park*, (2015–16), 12. http://www.transmississippimusings.com/media/docs/tour-guides/tour-westport-walking-long-20150407.pdf.
35 *OR*, Vol. 41, Part 1, 621.
36 Monnett, *op. cit.*, 102; and Kirkman, *op. cit.*, 108.
37 *OR*, Vol. 41., Pt. 1, 599.
38 Charles Collins, *op. cit.*, 107.
39 *OR*, Vol. 41., 488.
40 Monnett, *op. cit.*, 103.
41 *Ibid.*, 108.
42 Monaghan, *op. cit.*, 336.
43 Kirkman, *op. cit.*, 13.
44 Monaghan, *op. cit.*, 336.

45 Monnett, *op. cit.*;123–4.
46 *OR*, vol. 41, Pt. 1, 597–600.
47 *Ibid.*, 519.
48 *Ibid.*, 578.
49 *Ibid.*, 600.
50 *Ibid*, 599.
51 *Ibid.*, 622.
52 Kansas Historical Society.
53 Charles Collins, *op. cit.*, 137; and Curtis, *OR*, Vol. 41, Pt. 1, 493.
54 Castel, *op. cit.*, 196. Also author interview in June 2017 with Ola May Earnest, president of Linn County Historical Society.
55 Charles Collins, *op. cit.*, 121, 131.
56 *OR*, Vol. 41, Pt. 1, 552.
57 Robert Collins, *op. cit.*, Chapters 14 and 15, "Fade Away" and "Tarnished Glory."

Chapter 7: Back to the Land and the Lord

1 Sutton, *op. cit.*, 231–2; and *Dictionary of American Biography***,** Volume 13 (New York: Scribner's, 1943).
2 The Dec. 10 letter to Stearns, much quoted in this and the previous chapter, is at the Kansas Historical Society.
3 Cutler, *op. cit.*, 303.
4 Kansas Historical Society.
5 *Ibid.*
6 Faust, *op. cit.*, xviii, 31.
7 Cutler, *op. cit.*, 302–3.
8 Botkin, *op. cit.*, 432–3.
9 Faust, *op. cit.*, 267.
10 Phillips, *op. cit.*
11 Ola May Earnest, *Osawatomie Graphic* (June 22, 1989), Linn County Museum.
12 *Lima News* (Ohio, August 6, 1937).

Index

Note: *italicised* page numbers indicate illustrations